THE
MERCHANT PRINCES

Guide to the Management Gurus
Managing with the Gurus
ICI: the Company that Changed our Lives
Mayfair: a Social History
Harewood: the Life and Times of an English Country House
The Entrepreneurs

THE
MERCHANT
PRINCES

Family, Fortune and Philanthropy:
Cadbury, Sainsbury and John Lewis

Carol Kennedy

HUTCHINSON
LONDON

First published in the United Kingdom in 2000 by Hutchinson

The Random House Group Limited
20 Vauxhall Bridge Road, London SW1V 2SA

Random House Australia (Pty) Limited
20 Alfred Street, Milsons Point, Sydney,
New South Wales 2061, Australia

Random House New Zealand Limited
18 Poland Road, Glenfield
Auckland 10, New Zealand

Random House South Africa (Pty) Limited
Endulini, 5A Jubilee Road, Parktown 2193, South Africa

Random House Group Limited Reg. No. 954009
www.randomhouse.co.uk

A CIP catalogue record for this book
is available from the British Library

Papers used by Random House are natural, recyclable
products made from wood grown in sustainable forests.
The manufacturing processes conform to the environmental
regulations of the country of origin.

ISBN 0 09 178447 6

Typeset in Garamond by MATS, Southend-on-Sea, Essex
Printed and bound in Great Britain by
Biddles Ltd, Guildford and King's Lynn

In loving memory of my mother, Grace Kennedy,
who saw the start of this book and was a never-failing source
of optimism, enthusiasm and encouragement.

CONTENTS

ACKNOWLEDGEMENTS

My grateful thanks are due to Sir Adrian Cadbury and his wife Susan, for the generous time and help they gave to my research, including access to papers relating to the family and the company, and the loan of many books and documents; also to Sir Dominic Cadbury, chairman of Cadbury Schweppes, and to John Crosfield CBE, author of the privately printed Cadbury family history, for his reminiscences.

I also owe many thanks to Sir Stuart Hampson, chairman of the John Lewis Partnership, for granting me access to the company archives at Stevenage, and to Judith Faraday, the Partnership's archivist, for guiding me through them, lending me rare books by John Spedan Lewis, and enabling me to visit the two country houses in Hampshire that Spedan Lewis left for the use of the Partnership. I am also grateful to her colleagues in the business information department, especially David Forrai, for much help and guidance, to Pauline Graham, for many years a senior member of the Partnership, and to Peter Lewis, the last family chairman.

In the Sainsbury section, I am indebted to Eric Clark for his thorough genealogical and other researches into the Sainsbury family and firm; to Nick Kochan for valuable contributions, and to my late cousin, the actress Hazel Bainbridge, for memories of the little-known Sainsbury stage connection in the 1920s.

Carol Kennedy, London, November 1999.

INTRODUCTION

BEING PART OF A family is a universal human experience, at once suffocating, infuriating, comforting and supportive. For some it is a prison to be escaped from as soon as possible, for others a fortress against the world; for most, perhaps, something in the middle, there when it's needed. Literature offers us extremes of the family experience, from the sentiment of *Little Women* to the utter bleakness of *King Lear*. The pre-war playwright Dodie Smith called it a 'dear octopus'. At the start of *The Forsyte Saga*, John Galsworthy writes of 'that mysterious concrete tenacity which renders a family so formidable a unit of society, so clear a reproduction of society in miniature'.

In turn, society creates icons in the family image, for good or ill. George Orwell famously described pre-war England as a family with the wrong members in control. The British royal family was effectively invented by Queen Victoria and Prince Albert and today's incumbents look upon themselves as 'The Firm', a glorified family business. The Sicilian and American Mafia are built on family models, and gangland families still exert power in certain parts of London, though they have lost the phosphorescent, rotten glamour that surrounded the Kray twins and their society hangers-on thirty years ago. We are fascinated by the way some privileged political or social dynasties appear touched by fate, like America's Kennedys,

India's Gandhis and Ireland's Guinnesses, with their untimely deaths in successive generations.

We also pick up likenesses to ourselves. It is surely more than coincidental that, as the nuclear family has fragmented in Anglo-American society over the past twenty years (lone parents now head about a quarter of all families with dependent children in the UK, three times the ratio thirty years ago), the Queen's family has grown more openly dysfunctional, seen to be just as prone to divorce, incompatibility, bad behaviour and inter-generational rows as the rest of us.

Nowhere are the dynamics of family, both positive and negative, exposed in the raw more than in the family business, because the family business is driven by money and ambition. Transpose the generational rows that occur in every family – the fierce sibling rivalries, the jealousy over an inheritance or just day-to-day quarrels about the housekeeping – into a business context and the potential for disaster is immediately plain, especially at a crisis point such as who is to get the chairmanship or how to deal with a hostile takeover bid. The tensions and struggles for dominance built into every family, the intimidating ambitions of parents for children who may not want or be able to fulfil them, gain a lethal edge where the wealth and future of a business is at stake.

Sometimes these internal wars burst into the open, as happened a few years back in two of the biggest privately owned companies in Britain – C.&J. Clark, the Somerset shoe manufacturers, and the Littlewoods pools and mail-order empire owned by the Moores of Liverpool. The Clarks were split bitterly between selling or keeping the company (the older generation won, and kept it). The Moores brothers, Peter and John, were fierce rivals for the chairmanship but in the end their father, Sir John Moores, sacked one and came back in his eighties to take control. Another public drama worthy of a soap opera on one of his own TV channels has been on show in Rupert Murdoch's media empire since his third marriage to a fiercely ambitious Chinese TV executive thirty years his junior. Will the children of his second wife Anna still come into their inheritance? It's an explosive brew.

Unlike Tolstoy's observation in *Anna Karenina* about happy and unhappy families, successful family businesses, like the ones in this book, do not necessarily resemble each other, whereas those that fail tend to fail in the same way, usually through poor succession management or one of the heirs proving incompetent to develop the enterprise. Sometimes the talent gene simply runs out: 'clogs to clogs in three generations' is an aphorism well grounded in fact. If the business does survive past the third generation, another deadly factor will be lurking to sabotage it: complacency and a built-in resistance to change. Once in a while, complacency combines with incompetence and loss of control at the top to destroy the most impregnable-seeming dynasty. That was the fate of the Barings and their grand 200-year-old bank, which numbered the Queen among its investment clients. It was brought down almost overnight in 1995 by the unsupervised gambles of a young derivatives trader in Singapore, Nick Leeson.

But family business is big business everywhere. Thirteen per cent of the FTSE's largest 100 companies in the UK and 35 per cent of the Fortune 500 list in the US are estimated to fall within the broad definition of a family business: one where the voting control is in the hands of a given family and where the family has the final say in the strategic direction of the firm and its succession. Family businesses generate 40 per cent of GDP in the US and employ 60 per cent of its workforce; in Germany the figures are 66 per cent and 75 per cent respectively (the famous 'Mittelstand' or medium-sized family firms); in the UK they account for 75 per cent of GDP and 50 per cent of employment. Asian Pacific economies are built on family conglomerates, many of them now global empires like Hutchison Whampoa, founded by Li Ka-shing of Hong Kong.

Many huge multinationals are still family controlled, including Mars, Toyota, Honda, Woolworth, Marriott, Estée Lauder, Levi Strauss, Sweden's mighty Wallenberg group, Michelin, L'Oreal, Fiat and Benetton, although professional managers run most of them. Famous drinks companies remain in the embrace of their founding families – Seagrams, Pernod Ricard, Remy Cointreau, France's leading champagne houses and the world's biggest brewing company, Anheuser-Busch. A handful of family firms have notched up astonishing longevity. The Hoshi hotel company of Japan claims to date from the year 718 and is now in the hands of the forty-sixth generation of the founding family. Italy's Beretta family are still making guns after 450 years; the Antinori family wine business goes back to 1351.

Yet between two-thirds and three-quarters of family businesses either collapse or are sold during the first generation, a fact that testifies to the genetic lottery and family frictions. Only one in ten makes it beyond the third generation and the succession problem keeps many founding entrepreneurs awake at night. Rarely is the founder's entrepreneurial drive and commitment matched by his heir, though what is generally required of the second generation is less an entrepreneur's flair than the ability to manage a developing business. The Victorians often solved this by having large enough families for at least one son in each generation to be a successful driver of the business and for others to provide family management in depth, on the old royal principle of 'heirs and spares'.

The three merchant businesses whose family sagas are traced in this book are very different but all have managed the hazardous transition from the nineteenth-century business world into that of the twenty-first, bending to change in their organisations and ownership but so far not breaking. All three retain some of the culture implanted by their founders, all are among the most respected employers in Britain, and until the spring of 1998 two of them still had a member of the founding family at their head. All the families behind them share something else, an impulse to invest their fortunes back into society: either into improving their employees' working life, or, like the Sainsburys, as late-flowering patrons of the arts and sciences. Philanthropy among the self-made rich has been common enough from Andrew Carnegie to Bill Gates, but it is curiously rare in benefiting a family company's own workers – there aren't many Bournvilles in industrial history, and even fewer John Lewis Partnerships.

Both the Sainsburys and the Cadburys in their early generations had enormous broods, which provided their businesses with a rich mix of ability. John James Sainsbury, founder of the original dairy business in 1869, fathered a round dozen, six sons and six daughters, of whom the eldest son, John Benjamin, took a dominant role well before his father's death (and made a convenient marriage into the Dutch Van den Bergh margarine family, another large, interlocked business dynasty and a founding member of Unilever). Six Sainsburys ran the firm until the line stopped in 1998. Perhaps, as one of its competitors thinks, it should have stopped in 1992 and a professional manager taken over before Sainsbury's lost its long-unchallenged market leadership. The family still, however, controls over a third of the shares, and will have a say in its future.

The Cadburys also bred large families, who all seemed to be genetically blessed with a powerful social conscience and a gift for management. George Cadbury, the third-generation Quaker visionary who created Bournville and a miniature welfare state for his employees, had five children by his first marriage and six by his second. One of his grandsons, Sir Dominic Cadbury, is still chairman of Cadbury Schweppes, now a £4bn global organisation. Since 1824, when John Cadbury first opened his tea and coffee house in Birmingham's Bull Street, four generations have poured a consistent stream of talent and commitment into the business.

Unlike the Sainsburys, some of whom rather resemble Galsworthy's Forsyte family – 'no branch of which had a liking for the other' – the Cadburys offer a striking model of family values, linked to but no longer dependent on their Quaker heritage. Here is a large, scattered yet cohesive group of siblings, cousins, uncles and aunts spanning generations, gathering on family occasions in a much-loved holiday home, keeping in touch with, as Dominic Cadbury says, a 'sense of belonging'. Only one branch of the vast clan was involved in the chocolate business that made the Cadbury fortune, and for most of those, the connection remains only through the trusts set up by their Victorian and Edwardian forebears at Bournville. The Cadbury family now owns only around 2 per cent of the shares.

The John Lewis family was different again, revolving essentially around only two generations. Its unique contribution to British business history hinged on the powerful character of the founder's son, who determined, against his intimidating father, to give his inheritance away. There is no other example in history of the heir to such a great business enterprise voluntarily making over all his assets to his employees – even the strongest social impulses of the Quaker Cadburys never approached that radicalism, and the upwardly striving Sainsburys would have thought it madness.

The partnership idea conceived by John Spedan Lewis before the First World War, which he expected to become widespread in British industry, is still almost unknown outside the John Lewis stores, with the exception of a handful of owner-managed companies in the north of England. Nearly ninety years after Spedan Lewis dreamed it up in a hospital bed, it fits all the fashionable ideas for a twenty-first century company with its employee shareholders and inclusive 'stakeholding'. Yet at the time of writing the unthinkable was happening: a host of employees or 'partners' were calling for Spedan's creation to be sold off or floated on the stockmarket and the proceeds distributed as six-figure windfalls. Late twentieth-century materialism was challenging a unique Utopian vision of fair shares and happiness at work.

In the event, the break-up debate fizzled out – this time. If the John Lewis Partnership were broken up, it would mean the end of more than its founder's high ideals. It would also be the end of the nearest thing in business to the extended family, where different generations and relationships form a self-supporting network – in this case, successive generations of partners since 1929. But perhaps this too reflects a society in which, in the Anglo-American culture at least, the extended family is on the way out.

Yet the family itself is wired into our survival genes, and so, for many families, is the impulse to create a business that will go on building wealth for its descendants. The family business will survive in all its rich variety, though not many will develop such remarkable corporate DNA as those founded by John Cadbury, John Lewis and John James Sainsbury.

PART ONE

THE CADBURYS:
QUAKER CONSCIENCE

CHAPTER 1:

PURE COCOA AND GOOD WORKS

THE A303, once known as the London to Exeter road, is a highway loaded with history and romance, arching like an arrow into the heart of the West Country through the farmlands of Hampshire, Wiltshire, Dorset, Somerset and Devon and flanked halfway by the misty megaliths of Stonehenge. Today the romantic journey west is truncated at its start by the M3 motorway, from which the A303 branches off near Basingstoke; by-passes have cut off some of the pretty towns and villages like Zeals and Ilminster, and Stonehenge is fenced off from its perpetual trudging circle of visitors, but the sudden sight of it, cresting a rise in the road, is still enough to lift the heart. Sometimes at harvest-time, farmers in the fields opposite construct a mini-Stonehenge out of corn stooks, a pleasing visual joke. (At the time of writing, it looks as though these pleasures will be lost when the road is plunged into a tunnel as part of a plan to relieve traffic congestion around the ancient stones.)

All three of the great merchant families in this book had their origins in the rich farming country off the A303. The Lewis family, originally Welsh, migrated like many of their fellow-countrymen across the Bristol Channel into Somerset and by the seventeenth century were settled in the cattle market town of Shepton Mallet where the John Lewis who was to found the department store business was born in 1836 to a cabinet-maker. A little closer to London, north of the present A303, lie Trowbridge and Melksham in Wiltshire, an area of pig-farming and meat-processing where the Sainsbury family were in the provisions business for two generations before John Sainsbury left to set up as a hatter in Lambeth, south London. His son, John James, born in 1844, was to become the master-grocer to Victorian London and found Britain's most successful food retailing business of the twentieth century.

Most deeply rooted in the West Country until the late eighteenth century were the Cadburys, every traceable branch of whose vast network of interlocking families originally came from Dorset, Somerset or Devon. They were established in these three counties as far back as the twelfth century and signs off the A303 near Yeovil still mark their origins with the villages of North and South Cadbury and the ruins of Cadbury Castle, an ancient Celtic fort epitomising the old English meaning of the Cadbury name, a fortified hill. Cadbury Castle is one of several places in England with a claim to having been the seat of King Arthur and the original of Camelot. Another Cadbury Castle, now just a dome-shaped hill, lies eight miles north of Exeter.

The largest concentration of Cadburys before 1650 was to be found in Devon and Somerset, each county showing Cadbury names on the rolls of thirteen or fourteen parishes. The chocolate dynasty and the Quaker connection both originated with John Cadbury, born in 1696, who followed the trade of a woolcomber in the village of Burlescombe, about four miles west of Exeter. Devon in the seventeenth century was a prosperous hub of the woollen industry, with Exeter and Tiverton as the main centres of production, and combing was the painstaking hand process of turning raw wool into the fibres from which worsted thread was spun.

In his late twenties, John Cadbury met another Exeter woolcomber, Richard Tapper, and fell in love with his daughter Hannah. Tapper was a Quaker who had joined the Society of Friends in 1683, some thirty-five years after its founding by George Fox, and Cadbury joined the Society shortly before he and Hannah were married in a Quaker ceremony in

Exeter on 26 June 1725. They set up home in Exeter but four of their five children died in infancy. The survivor, Joel, a serge-maker who later turned to accountancy, was widowed after only three years of marriage and also lost one of his two children in infancy.

Joel's second marriage was to Sarah Moon, the daughter of a Bristol tanner, and they were luckier in the terrible lottery of child mortality at that time; four of their six children survived into adulthood. One emigrated to the United States and became a farmer in Ohio, founding a whole dynasty of American Cadburys, while the youngest son, Richard Tapper, named for his grandfather, was destined to move the geographic centre of the family from Devon to Birmingham. As other branches of the family died out, he would become the ancestor of all the Cadburys still living in Britain in the late twentieth century.

Richard was born in Exeter on 6 November 1768. He was devoted to his mother Sarah, a stoic and cheerful woman who taught her son how to cope with adversity and affectionately inculcated, in his own words, 'the love of virtue and true piety, endeavouring to elevate the mind above everything that was grovelling, mean or low'. The day when he left home by stagecoach, aged fourteen, to be apprenticed to a draper in Stroud, in faraway Kent, was engraved on his mind, as he wrote years later to his son Benjamin, as a 'dark and dreary morning, and I thought my heart would break when I took leave of my dear mother'.

Richard's apprenticeship to William Chandler lasted only eighteen months before the firm went bankrupt: as the army was demobilised after the American War of Independence, many debts for uniforms were left unpaid. Richard moved to Gloucester to join another draper, James White, and worked for him until he was twenty-one. He then made the traditional move to London and spent the next four years working for a silk mercer and linen draper named Jasper Capper in Gracechurch Street in the City (the firm was to become the linen specialist Robinson and Cleaver of Regent Street).

In an age when children knew no carefree adolescence, their teenage years being filled with hard work and learning a trade, young Cadbury turned the social virtues taught by his mother into a practical way of life. At nineteen, so he recalled to his son Joel, he was earning £20 a year, 'out of which I respectably clothed myself, found my washing and pocket money, and always appeared so respectable as to be the invited guest among the first families of Gloucester'.

In London, earning £40 a year at Capper's, he 'not only maintained a respectable appearance but in many cases was enabled to be generous and purchased many books, amongst which is Rees Encyclopedia, now in the book case'. He did not, he told Joel, ask so much as a shilling of his father, and the Quaker self-discipline for which he and his descendants would become renowned was evident in his early twenties. In spending money, he said, 'I considered first if it was for unnecessary gratification, and if the thing I wanted was extravagant in price, in either case I resisted it scrupulously and conscientiously. This conduct has enabled me to give generously to those in need.'

Unlike many young men who gravitated to the capital to complete their business training and then hoped to start their own shop, Richard Cadbury seemed at first uncertain of his ambitions. He returned to Exeter for a while to help his father in his accountancy business and briefly toyed with the idea of following his elder brother Henry to America, but a Quaker friend dissuaded him, saying 'it is not paved with gold, nor is there more comfort there than here'. Instead, Richard and a London friend named Joseph Rutter who had visited Birmingham decided there was a better future for them as linen drapers in the Midlands manufacturing town, destined to become the hub of the Industrial Revolution and the 'city of a thousand trades'.

Birmingham, recorded in the Domesday Book in 1085–6 as being a small community 'worth 20 shillings', had since the sixteenth century been a prospering centre of cutlery manufacture and small metal products such as buttons, nails, horses' bits, bolts and screws. During the Civil War the town manufactured 15,000 sword-blades for Cromwell's Parliamentary forces but refused to supply the Royalists. By the time Joseph Rutter visited it in the early 1790s it was a boom town, with a population that had grown six times since 1720 to over 70,000.

Birmingham was also a great Quaker centre, and the two young men were assured of a network of contacts when they arrived there on a Saturday early in 1794 and put up at the White Hart inn. The following morning, Sunday, they attended the Bull Street Meeting and were introduced to, among others, Charles Lloyd, co-founder of Lloyds Bank, who escorted them on a tour of the town before taking them back to his fine house in Edgbaston.

One of the letters of introduction they had brought with them from London was to the engineer Matthew Boulton, partner of the Scots inventor James Watt. Boulton's works at Soho had been manufacturing Watt's steam engines since 1774 and had just begun to show a profit. James Phillips, writing to him on behalf of young Cadbury and Rutter, said: 'If I did not think them of more than common worth I should not venture on this step – I have, however, not the smallest doubt but they will do my recommendations credit, and that they will when well-known be esteemed an acquisition to your Town.'

Wherever Quakers formed a sizeable community they soon established an effective network of mutual business self-help. If a Friend should get into financial difficulties with his business, other Friends would rally round and act like modern management consultants, analysing the firm's finances and advising on the best course of action. Once a Quaker apprentice had qualified, funds would often be provided for him to set up in business. 'The apprentice system,' wrote an American business historian, 'became the primary source of young, well-trained, ethically sound people who were to sustain Quaker businesses from generation to generation.'

By the late eighteenth century those businesses, growing successful on the Quaker values of hard work, honesty, fair dealing, meticulous bookkeeping and social equality, spanned a huge section of British industry and commerce from brewing to banking, engineering to cotton, chemicals to china. Several of the famous banking families, such as the Barclays and the Gurneys, had started in textiles, but with their universal reputation for probity, the Quakers had a natural affinity for financial services. (Price Waterhouse, the giant accountancy business that is now merged with Coopers and Lybrand, had Quaker roots.) One of the unexplained anomalies of Quaker business was that many Friends, with their tradition of plain living and high thinking, tended to look askance at the new luxury trades such as coffee, tea or chocolate, yet the three greatest names in the chocolate industry – Cadbury, Fry and Rowntree – were all devout Quaker dynasties.

Whether or not the Quaker freemasonry in Birmingham produced financial backing for the young drapers from London, by the summer of 1794 they had acquired premises in a former inn at 92 Bull Street in the heart of Birmingham's shopping district. They set up in business as Cadbury and Rutter, living in the ample accommodation that the rest of the house provided. Many Quaker women came to them for linens, muslins and calicoes, among them the prison reformer Elizabeth Fry. The partnership lasted four years, after which Rutter went back to London, and the name R. T. Cadbury, Linen Draper and Silk Mercer, appeared alone on the firm's books.

By the time he was in sole charge of the business, Richard Cadbury had been married for two years, to a distant cousin by marriage called Elizabeth Head. She was to bear him seven children in the first seven years of their marriage, followed by three more; the beginning of a tradition of enormous Cadbury families. The business did well, helped by colourful window displays of fine silks draped over tall Oriental jars, and by 1816 Cadbury had a second shop nearby.

The Cadburys were devout Quakers and Richard began the family tradition, which continued well into the twentieth century, of reading Scripture to his staff at a weekly gathering before work. He was not as personally austere as his son John, founder of the chocolate business, and until John persuaded him to join the temperance movement some years later, he would invite customers to take a convivial glass of wine in a curtained-off part of the shop.

Richard Tapper Cadbury quickly became a figure to be reckoned with in early nineteenth-century Birmingham. He had a touch of the autocrat about him and with his tall, physically vigorous presence that lasted into extreme old age – he lived to ninety-one – he was known locally as 'King Richard'. As early as 1801, when he was thirty-two, he was elected a commissioner under the Birmingham Street Acts, which governed every aspect of the city (a post he would hold for fifty years) and an overseer of the poor, beginning the long Cadbury tradition of public service in Birmingham which continues to this day.

Overseers were leading businessmen in the community whose duties consisted of hearing petitions for relief and keeping an eye on institutions for the poor such as hospitals and workhouses. In practice, their weekly meetings mainly consisted of dining convivially together at public expense, followed by copious amounts of brandy. Richard Cadbury's son John, elected an overseer in his turn at the age of thirty-one, was outraged by the contrast between the lavish spread of food and drink and the hungry paupers waiting for parish relief. At the first dinner he attended, he spoke vehemently for abolishing the custom on the grounds of both legality and decency, and despite one old overseer who said unashamedly, 'I spakes for the dinners,' he succeeded in getting them abandoned.

Richard's civic service involved, as well as much charitable work with schools and hospitals, becoming a commissioner with responsibility for planning the first redevelopment of Birmingham in the 1850s. This saw the construction of Corporation Street – until the 1960s one of the grandest commercial thoroughfares in Europe – and incidentally swept away the Cadburys' original home and business premises in Bull Street. 'King Richard' was also a dedicated crusader against the slave trade, which despite William Wilberforce's success in getting it made illegal in 1807, was still being transacted in British ports off foreign ships.

John Cadbury, Richard's third son, was a strong personality and destined to become the driving force behind a new family business. He was born in 1801 over the shop in Bull Street, which had a garden behind it with flowers, currant bushes and a summerhouse where he and his brothers and sisters played in childhood. When he was fifteen, his father apprenticed him, not to another draper but to a Quaker acquaintance called John Cudworth, who dealt in tea in the Briggate district of Leeds. Six years later he went to London to complete his training with the bonded tea house of Sanderson, Fox and Company, and in 1824 returned to Birmingham. With a sum of money given to him by his father 'to sink or swim', he started his own tea-dealing and coffee-roasting business at 93 Bull Street, next door to the family draper's where Benjamin, the eldest brother, was now working and would take over when Richard Cadbury retired in 1828. Sarah, the first-born, had by this time married into the Barrows, another Birmingham Quaker family, and Joel, the second son, had followed his uncle Henry in emigrating to the United States, founding a separate Cadbury dynasty which is still prolific in Pennsylvania.

John Cadbury at twenty-three was a self-confident young man who advertised his wares in the *Birmingham Gazette*, among them 'Cocoa Nibs, prepared by himself, an article affording a most nutritious beverage for breakfast' – by which he probably meant simply roasting the beans (nibs) and pounding them in a mortar. At this time 'patent cocoa' and chocolate were sidelines to his main business of tea and coffee, and it was not until 1831 that he began to manufacture cocoa and chocolate in a factory in Crooked Lane, off Bull Street, the activity that marked the beginning of the Cadbury's chocolate company.

Chocolate, the Aztec delicacy that was appropriated by the Spaniards and later spread through the leisured classes of Europe in the mid seventeenth century, had reached England at almost the same time as coffee. The first coffee house opened in Cornhill, in the City of London, in 1652, and the first chocolate house in the capital was advertised five years later, in Queen Head Alley, Bishopsgate Street. The taste of the beverage was quite different from modern chocolate, more bitter than present-day bitter chocolate, and almost savoury – the Aztecs added chillies and other spices. It was also extremely rich to the point of indigestibility, since the process of separating the cocoa butter from the bean had not yet been perfected. (At Cadbury World, the historical 'experience' offered to tourists today in the Cadbury factory at Bournville, visitors can taste an approximation of seventeenth-century chocolate.)

When chocolate was first made into a drink it was popularly supposed to have medicinal, or at least beneficial qualities. Modern molecular research supports this to some extent: among the 1,200 different chemical components in chocolate – six times as many as there are in fruit flavours such as lemon or strawberry, which makes it impossible to synthesise chocolate in the laboratory – are mood-elevating substances such as phenylalanine, anandamide and phenylethylamine. The two latter chemicals are found naturally in the human brain and help to arouse emotions and heighten sensations. Anandamide, which was discovered in chocolate only in 1996, is similar to the active ingredient in marijuana known as THC (tetrahydrocannabinol), while phenyl-ethylamine is known to produce an emotional reaction similar to falling in love. These findings by American chemists, detailed in a book on the US chocolate giants Mars and Hershey (*The Chocolate Wars*, by Joel Glenn Brennan) suggest – but do not prove – that the powerful chemical cocktail in chocolate is what draws unhappy people to gorge on it and also encourages in some an addictive pattern of consumption.

Not surprisingly, chocolate was linked historically with aphrodisiac properties. Montezuma, the Aztec leader of the early sixteenth century, was said to have drunk up to fifty cups of the foaming brown liquid before visiting his harem. Casanova thought chocolate a more effective tool of seduction than champagne, and the French gourmet Brillat-Savarin also considered it a sexual stimulant. No modern chemical analysis, however, supports this theory any more than it does the idea that oysters or asparagus can arouse sexual desire.

Cadbury was not the first chocolate manufacturer in England: that honour goes to a family called Churchman in Bristol, whose business was taken over by the Quaker Joseph Fry in 1761, enabling Fry's – part of Cadbury's since 1919 – to claim to be the oldest chocolate firm in Britain. John Cadbury, however, knew the value of what we would now call brand promotion. His tea and coffee shop in Bull Street was among the first in Birmingham to boast plate-glass windows, and the proprietor could often be seen polishing them himself early in the morning. Legend has it that he employed a Chinese in full native dress to weigh and package his tea, but his descendant, Sir Adrian Cadbury, thinks it was more likely that he had a full-length figure of a Chinaman, in the fashion of a cigar-store wooden Indian, to advertise the products.

Cocoa powder, from which the drink could be made quickly and conveniently, was introduced to the market around 1830 and Cadbury saw an opportunity to expand his business by manufacturing it. He bought a warehouse in Lamb Yard, Crooked Lane, a winding back street which ran behind Bull Street, enabling the warehouse to be entered directly from the Cadbury shop. While all this expansion was going on,

Cadbury, still in his twenties, had already been widowed. His first wife, Priscilla Ann Dymond of Exeter, died two years after their marriage in 1826, leaving no children. The year after he started his manufacturing business John married Candia Barrow, the young sister of his brother-in-law John Barrow. Candia and Barrow were to become recurring first names among Cadbury generations from then on.

This second marriage produced a brood of eight children – one daughter, Maria, and seven sons, one of whom died at two days old. From the remaining brothers would emerge the two great visionaries of the Cadbury business and the founders of Bournville, Richard (1835–99) and George (1839–1922). The boys and their siblings had a comfortable country upbringing in a large house in Calthorpe Road, Edgbaston, then surrounded by fields and country lanes, but even by early Victorian standards it was a disciplined and restrictive childhood.

John Cadbury was personally spartan in his habits – he never sat on an upholstered chair until he was seventy and because the Quakers thought music frivolous he gave up the flute, which he had played as a young man, and would not permit a piano in the house, although two musical boxes were deemed acceptable. George's biographer, A. G. Gardiner, wrote that

> this stern martyrdom of the senses, physical and intellectual, left an abiding impress on George Cadbury's character. It drove all the energy of his nature into certain swift, deep channels, and left large spaces of life – the worlds of pleasure and aesthetic emotion – wholly unexplored. It was this concentration of purpose that was the source of his remarkable achievements.

The children were exhorted to run a mile each morning before breakfast, which they accomplished by circling the lawn twenty-one times with their hoops. The only books permitted, apart from the Bible and religious tracts, were Bunyan's *Pilgrim's Progress*, Foxe's *Book of Martyrs* and one or two early children's books with a moral, such as *Uncle Tom's Cabin* by Harriet Beecher Stowe and *The Wide, Wide World* by Elizabeth Wetherell. Although their parents did not run a carriage, Richard and George were allowed to have ponies, which they were expected to groom, muck out and saddle up themselves.

Yet the children did not seem to feel themselves deprived; quite the reverse. Maria, the daughter, wrote: 'Our home was one of sunshine . . . Home was the centre of attraction to us all, and simple home pleasures our greatest joy.' They all enjoyed cultivating the garden where peaches and nectarines grew on the walls, and which may have bred George's insistence on six fruit trees in every garden in Bournville. The family went on seaside holidays to what was then the village of Blackpool, staying in a cottage on the south shore where the children built sand castles and romped in the boisterous seas, or to a farm at Ingleborough in Yorkshire.

John Cadbury was as active and traditional a Quaker as his father, dressing in the flowing frock coat and broad-brimmed hat favoured by the Friends, and he was even more rigorous in teetotalism – which, indeed, he had succeeded in imposing on his parent. He lectured on the virtues of abstinence, demonstrating that someone who refrained from alcohol could afford a joint of roast beef and a quartern loaf while an habitual drinker on the same wage could only buy a herring and a penny's worth of bread. When he was frequently challenged as to what would happen to the barley crops if they were not used for brewing, he had barley puddings prepared to his wife's recipe, which he would hand round, steaming, for the audience to see how nutritious they were – a stunt that led to him being nicknamed 'Barley-pudding Cadbury'.

Like his father, he was busily involved in Birmingham's civic administration. He also served as an overseer of the poor and a street commissioner, was a governor of Birmingham General Hospital and sat on a committee to bring moral and religious education to infants' schools. He set out to encourage saving by working men, and when a director of one of the local savings banks was proved to have embezzled depositors' money for his own business, he campaigned for the transfer of savings accounts to the Post Office. A government inquiry followed and eventually the Post Office Savings Bank was set up in 1861. (His great-grandson, Sir Adrian Cadbury, heads a Birmingham charity campaigning for low-cost banking in deprived areas where the clearing banks don't think it worth operating.)

John Cadbury was also involved in wider social campaigns, including the establishment of an 'Animals' Friend Society', which sought to protect animals in the Midlands from the cruelty of cock-fighting and the abuse of stage-coach horses, which were often driven until they dropped of exhaustion. It became the forerunner of the RSPCA. His other great campaign, in which the novelists Charles Kingsley and Charles Dickens were instrumental in changing society's attitudes, was to abolish the barbaric practice of master sweeps using young boys to clear soot-filled chimneys. Cadbury paid for a number of sweeps to be given mechanical brushes and mounted a demonstration at a local stately home, Hagley Hall in Warwickshire, to show how quickly and scientifically chimneys could be cleaned with the equipment. But it would take thirty-five years and two Acts of Parliament before the exploitation of child sweeps was finally stamped out.

Soot and smoke were an obsession with Cadbury in other ways. Among the many civic committees he chaired was the Steam Engine Committee, set up to mitigate the growing problem of industrial smoke pollution. Birmingham in the full roar of industrialisation, with furnaces, foundries and mills turning out nails, screws and other metal essentials, was clouded by black smoke day and night, and Cadbury's own premises at Crooked Lane were the subject of a complaint about smoke. To solve it, he acquired a new process called Beddington's patent, which burned up the smoke before it was emitted, and urged its adoption by other manufacturers. In 1852, by which time Crooked Lane had been demolished to make way for the new railway and Cadbury's had set up in a brick-built factory in Bridge Street, *Chambers' Edinburgh Journal*, a noted periodical of the time, ran an article about the chocolate firm, commenting on the remarkable lack of smoke from its new engine-chimney. John Cadbury, who personally showed the journalist, Walter White, round his plant, explained proudly how the Beddington's apparatus controlled smoke emission and stated: 'there is no need that any chimney in Birmingham should smoke more than that'.

By the time the new factory was built in 1847, John had been joined by his brother Benjamin, who had given up running the family drapery business the year before and been replaced by old John Cadbury's nephew Richard Barrow. The brothers – the firm was henceforth known as Cadbury Brothers – took a thirty-five-year lease at £150 a year, from Michaelmas 1847, on the flat-roofed two-storey brick building. There was a courtyard behind for carts and wagons, which entered through an archway from the street, and the factory was backed by a tall chimney. It was all still standing in 1931 when the centenary history of Cadbury Brothers was published, but the site later became a cinema car park, as Adrian Cadbury remembers from his childhood.

The manufacture of cocoa, heavily advertised with medical testimonials as 'Homeopathic Cocoa', was now Cadbury Brothers' chief activity along with 'French Fancy Chocolates', but their product list also included a variety of household staples such as patent fire lighters, washing powder made by Hudson's, the soap suppliers to Queen Victoria, linen and cotton twine and the 'servant's friend' – blacklead for shining coal-fire grates. The building also acted as a warehouse for tea and coffee, which continued to be sold by the firm until the early 1870s.

The *Chambers' Edinburgh Journal* article, 'Visit to a Chocolate Manu-factory', described in detail how the twenty-horsepower steam engine powered four ovens, which over a ten-hour day roasted two tons of cocoa 'nibs' or beans. The nuts were then broken up in the 'kibbling-mill' and the husks separated out. The discarded material, reported *Chambers'*, was repacked into the empty sacks and shipped to Ireland 'where it is sold at a low price to the humbler classes, who extract from it a beverage which has all the flavour of cocoa, if not all its virtues'. The mass of cracked nut was then processed, by heat and pressure, so as to squeeze out the rich oil or butter, and the resulting thick liquid, resembling 'half-frozen treacle', was poured into a pan to be ground between millstones.

The *Chambers'* reporter also took note of the Cadbury Brothers' enlightened employment practices, which were rare in 1852 and already foreshadowing the firm's reputation for looking after the moral and physical welfare of its workforce and for providing educational facilities. Cadbury's was the first company to introduce a weekly half-holiday – in Victorian industry the six-day week was normal – and organised excursions to the country on Saturday afternoons. Female workers were selected for their 'good moral character' (nothing was stipulated about the morals required of men) and earned from five to nine shillings a week for working from 9 a.m. to 7 p.m. daily. An hour was allowed for a midday meal and tea was provided. Twice a week the women were allowed to leave work an hour early to attend evening school.

The firm was now expanding geographically as well as in its volume of sales. At the beginning of 1854, when the Cadbury brothers were granted a royal warrant to supply cocoa to Queen Victoria, they opened their first London office at the quaint address of 148½ Fenchurch Street in the City. By 1860 Cadbury's had warehouses at several other locations and in September 1862 the main offices moved to 79 Basinghall Street, moving in 1871 to 134 Upper Thames Street.

Then suddenly everything began to go wrong. In 1855 John Cadbury's wife Candia died of consumption, and soon afterwards he suffered a serious bout of rheumatic fever. The lingering effects of the disease, which even today has the habit of recurring and leading to chronic debilitation, coupled with his profound grief over Candia's loss, affected his management of the business. Benjamin, who never seems to have made much impact on any of the family businesses, could not fill the gap left by his brother's ill health. By 1859 the workforce had dwindled to about half and wages were cut to a meagre four shillings and sixpence a week. Benjamin retired in 1860 and a year later John Cadbury decided to hand over the business to his second and third sons, Richard and George, then aged twenty-five and twenty-one, who had already worked in the factory for eleven and five years respectively.

George was to become the most influential and innovative of all the Cadburys and a pioneer of industrial relations, but when he and Richard took over, the firm was dying on its feet. Over fifty years later, George recalled: 'It would have been far easier to start a new business than to pull up a decayed one which had a bad name. The prospect seemed a hopeless one, but we were young and full of energy.'

They were also extremely self-disciplined, thanks to their upbringing. Each brother had inherited £5,000 from their mother and now each put £4,000 into the business, which was losing money heavily. Richard, who married Elizabeth Adlington of Mansfield two months after taking over joint control, found his investment dwindling rapidly. By 1863 the business had swallowed all but £150 of his capital. His bachelor brother George fared better, having managed to save £1,500 by living on a shoestring – one year he spent only £25 on everything, including clothes, travel and charities. 'It was the money I saved by living so sparely that carried us over the crisis,' he said years later.

George carried Quaker frugality to extremes. In the first years of the partnership, he gave up tea and coffee and his morning newspaper to save money (and time) that could be devoted to business. Each day was meticulously planned out in his diary. In winter he rose at 6 a.m., arrived at work by 7 a.m. and walked home to midday dinner at his father's house in Edgbaston. He had a 'tea' of bread and water at the factory and often worked until 9 p.m. In summer his regime was to get up at 5.15 a.m. and work until 6 p.m. Early photographs show a good-looking young man, of middle height, with a large, handsome head and a determined expression.

George's spartan life was not without its pleasures, though some were of a rigorous kind. He and Richard both loved to skate before dawn on winter mornings and watch the sun rise before going in to work. The brothers also organised a works cricket team and played hockey and football. On Sunday mornings, George rose at 5.30 a.m. and rode for ninety minutes into Birmingham to teach at the first adult school, a practice he began at twenty years of age and continued for over half a century.

Before the coming of the Education Act of 1870, these adult schools were the only way in which working-class men who had received scant, if any, schooling, could learn how to read and write. George's class consisted of 300 youths, who grew to maturity with their teacher and formed a close companionship with him and each other. Reading, writing and Bible study were the staples of learning, but George had the ambition that the schools should be centres of good citizenship as well. Nearly 140 years on, that idea is again being mooted as part of the state school curriculum.

After five years of the partnership, with Richard's inheritance nearly all gone and the business still ailing, both brothers were seriously thinking about new careers. George had originally wanted to become a doctor, but had spent time working in the Rowntree grocery business at York and now considered becoming a tea-planter in the Himalayas. Richard was thinking about becoming a surveyor. Then, in the mid 1860s, growing political concern about the adulteration of food, and pressure for legislation, triggered a catalyst in Cadbury Brothers' fortunes.

In those days every cocoa manufacturer, including the big three Quaker firms – Cadbury's, Fry's (the oldest established chocolate and cocoa makers who had begun in Bristol in 1748) and Rowntree's, which had entered the field by acquisition of Tuke's cocoa, chocolate and chicory business in York in 1862 – routinely added other substances to the raw cocoa, usually sugar, sago, potato starch, flour or arrowroot, in order to cut the over-rich natural product and make it digestible. None of the firms regarded this as 'adulteration', arguing that the added substances were all wholesome and nutritious, but the groundswell of public opinion was moving against the practice. Only about one-fifth of Cadbury's own cocoa consisted of the natural ground-up bean, the rest being made up of potato starch, sago flour and treacle. It was not a product of which the firm was proud.

George Cadbury told his biographer, A. G. Gardiner, how around this time he heard of a machine in Holland, invented in 1828 by C. J. van Houten, which could squeeze out the excess cocoa butter, thus removing the need for starchy additives and producing a purer drink. 'I went off to Holland without knowing a word of Dutch, saw the manufacturer, with whom I had to talk entirely by signs and a dictionary, and bought the machine. It was by prompt action such as this that my brother and I made our business.'

Cadbury's production of the first 'pure cocoa essence' in 1866 did indeed make their business, but they had to work hard to promote it, and they did so with a single-minded intensity that eventually resulted in competitors complaining that Cadbury's were trying to run them out of business. They began by deluging doctors with sample packets and were rewarded with favourable articles in the *Lancet* and the *British*

Medical Journal as well as in the grocery trade papers. The cocoa essence was also advertised on the side of London omnibuses. Fry's of Bristol took another two years to bring out its own unadulterated cocoa, by which time Cadbury's had secured a market lead that was to last thirty years. Rowntree's, which could not afford the sophisticated Dutch machinery, nearly went out of business in 1879 and was only saved by adopting a French invention called crystallised gum pastilles, the forerunner of Rowntree's Fruit Gums.

In 1872 and 1875 two Acts of Parliament were passed outlawing the adulteration of all foodstuffs, which gave Cadbury's immense free publicity for their 'pure' cocoa, since George gave evidence to the committee appointed to look into the working of the 1872 Act. He soon took advantage of this heaven-sent opportunity in an aggressive way.

In 1873 George Cadbury publicly claimed in a letter to the Royal Society for the Promotion of the Arts, Manufactures and Commerce, now known as the RSA, that all cocoa which had anything added to it was 'adulterated' and should be labelled chocolate or chocolate powder. This looked to his competitors like a shameless attempt to stop the public buying their products. Cadbury's letter was challenged by a man called John Holm who read a paper to the RSA later that year asserting that the words cocoa, cacao and chocolate in fact all described the same product, though chocolate in powder form was a finer preparation than cocoa. He also challenged Cadbury's use of the pejorative word 'adulteration' applied to any of the products made by his own firm, Dunn and Hewitt.

Grocers were confused by the row and several court cases ensued over the sale of so-called 'adulterated cocoa'. Joseph Storrs Fry II, who would take over from his uncle Francis as chairman of the family firm in 1878, engaged in an open war of words with George Cadbury in the *Grocer* magazine, arguing with justification that the Adulteration Act was never intended to apply to cocoa with admixtures of wholesome ingredients such as sugar, sago or treacle. 'The real question is whether the purchaser gets what is sound and wholesome, and that which he expects to get,' wrote Fry. As every magistrate trying the current crop of cases had found, that was only 'common sense and justice', he argued.

Dunn and Hewitt joined in by accusing the Cadburys of a misleading statement in order to push their own new product. The statement in question was: 'Caution: when cocoa thickens in the cup it proves the addition of starch.' The Cadburys made this statement, said Dunn and Hewitt, knowing that in the public mind the word 'starch' meant only the starch used in laundry work. The row dragged on for years, with various unsuccessful prosecutions, brought by health inspectors, over low grades of cocoa. Eventually, changing public tastes and more disposable income in people's pockets forced the cheaper grades out of the market.

Fancy chocolates, the other main product line for the cocoa companies, were much less controversial. Fry's introduced their famous Chocolate Cream, which was to endure as a leading brand long after the firm was merged with Cadbury in 1919 and taken over in 1935. Chocolates were made with a great variety of fillings and became the favourite romantic gift, especially when the boxes grew more decorative. In the late 1860s, Richard Cadbury, who was a talented amateur painter, had experimented with printing some of his designs and using them to decorate the box-lids. The first chocolate box painting, which was to give its name to a whole genre of sentimental pictorial art, was of a small girl in a muslin frock with a kitten on her lap and a red flower in her hair. It was first used on boxes of Cadbury's 'chocolate-crèmes' in the New Year gift season of 1869. Sadly for Richard, his wife Elizabeth died that New Year's Eve, leaving him with four small children, among them Barrow and William Adlington, who were to become leading members of the family firm.

In 1873, two years after Richard married his second wife, Emma Wilson and while the advertising war over 'adulteration' was at its height, George Cadbury broke his bachelor status at the age of thirty-four. His bride was Mary Tylor from a London Quaker family, and in the fourteen years of their marriage they had five children, including Edward (1873–1948), who was to enshrine the Cadbury philosophy of industrial relations in a classic of early business literature, *Experiments in Industrial Organization*, published in 1912. After Mary's death in 1887 – the first wives of this generation of Cadburys had a high mortality rate

– George married Elizabeth Mary Taylor, known as Elsie, and had another six children. One of this second family was Laurence Cadbury (1889–1982), who became the father of Adrian and Dominic Cadbury, consecutively the last family chairmen of the modern Cadbury Schweppes.

A third Cadbury brother, Henry, born in 1845, joined Richard and George in 1869, taking over the firm's commercial travelling in the West Country, but the association lasted only six years before Henry died of typhoid, that great Victorian killer, leaving a widow and infant daughter. The other three brothers to Richard and George all died prematurely: Joseph, born in 1841, lived only two days; Edward died at twenty-three and John, who emigrated to Australia, died in Brisbane aged thirty-two. Natural selection, it seemed, was ensuring that the two most dynamic and innovative brothers survived to carry the business forward.

In the 1870s the firm of Cadbury Brothers began to expand in a serious way outside England, beginning with Ireland – then still part of the British Isles – and establishing agents in Chile and Canada and a shop in Paris in the fashionable Faubourg St Honoré. This was taking coals to Newcastle with a vengeance, since French chocolates were regarded as the acme of the chocolate-maker's art. At Bridge Street, the paternalist regime established by John Cadbury continued, with Richard and George giving morning readings from the Bible to the assembled employees. These gatherings had been reinstated by popular demand after the brothers discontinued them, and went on well into the 1900s, when the timing was changed to three times a week. In winter, if business was slack, the employees would be given a half-day off for skating, and George Cadbury bought a boneshaker bicycle for the young men to learn the art of cycling in their meal breaks: successful learners were allowed to take the bike home in turns. As well as granting Saturday afternoons off, the firm was a pioneer of the newly introduced bank holidays.

Working hours were from 8 a.m. to 7.30 p.m. in winter and 6 a.m. to 2.30 p.m. in summer, with half an hour allowed for breakfast (coffee provided) and twenty minutes for lunch. The Cadburys believed in early starts and early nights as moral virtues – among other things the practice avoided the temptations of Birmingham in late evening – and the employees were all young and trainable (also, one might assume, cheap). Women were obliged to leave once they married (the Cadburys had strict views about the role of wives and mothers, despite George's own second wife, Elsie, becoming a power in public life) and men when they turned twenty-one.

The girl workers were provided with material to make their own white, washable dresses to present a clean, hygienic appearance. There was unusual informality for the time among employers and employees, with everyone calling each other by their first names. If someone didn't like his given name, the partners would amiably rechristen him – one called Zacharia unaccountably became Fred – and usually the new name stuck. The partners also often played cricket and football with the men and at one cricket match took all eleven wickets between them.

As the 1870s progressed, Bridge Street was becoming too small for the expanding business and the brothers began to think seriously about the advantages of having a food factory in the clean air and healthy surroundings of the country. In June 1878 they bought fourteen-and-a-half acres between the villages of Stirchley, King's Norton and Selly Oak, about four miles from Birmingham. The site consisted mostly of sloping meadowland flanked to the north by a trout stream called the Bourn and well placed for access by the railway and the Worcester and Birmingham Canal, which ran parallel to each other to the east.

The Cadburys wanted to ensure room for the foreseeable development of the firm and the community they planned around it, and in the 1920s the family bought up more of the hilly land around Bournville to protect it from Birmingham's encroachment. Even in the late 1990s, the village has a countrified air about it, with quiet, almost rural roads cutting through the surrounding woodlands. Birmingham with its roaring ring roads and spaghetti tangle of motorways has been held at bay without the countryside in between being covered with grid-like housing estates.

George Cadbury drew up rough plans for the new factory, which were worked up by a local architectural firm, George H. Gadd, with the assistance of George's eldest son Barrow. The site was named Bournville after the little stream, and because it sounded vaguely French, which was thought to be a good association for a chocolate business. Adrian and Dominic Cadbury still pronounce the name with the accent on the second syllable, perhaps a legacy of the French connection. The first brick was laid in January 1879, a good quarter-century before Milton Hershey, America's premier chocolate maker, laid out his own factory town at Hershey, Pennsylvania, with roads named Chocolate Avenue and Cocoa Avenue.

The Cadburys directed the construction work themselves, hiring their own workmen rather than contracting out. The first modest plan for housing involved just sixteen semi-detached dwellings for the foremen, built on the road to the south of the works. Each had a garden front and back and was rented for the modest sum of five shillings a week. At the back of the houses was an orchard planted with apple, plum, pear and cherry trees so that the workers could enjoy fresh fruit in season, and an open-air swimming pool was built.

Birmingham's business community thought the scheme quite mad, and confidently predicted it would end in disaster; as, indeed, they predicted that closing on Saturday afternoons would be Cadbury's ruin. The Industrial Revolution was still only half a century old, and it was considered the natural order of things for business and manufacturing to be conducted in the smoky cities. Furthermore, the Midlands businessmen told each other over their substantial club dinners and post-prandial port and brandy, fresh air and green fields could hardly compensate for removing one's business from the city's pool of labour and all the conveniences of urban life, which included living near one's place of employment.

Undaunted, the brothers made a deal with the railway company – then the Birmingham West Suburban Railway, later absorbed into the London Midland and Scottish (LMS) – to provide cheap weekly tickets for those employees who still had to live in Birmingham. Construction of the factory proceeded at a brisk pace, with everything finished and ready to move into by October 1879. During construction old John

Cadbury, now in his seventies, came to inspect the site at frequent intervals, and continued to do so when the new factory was in full working order.

One such visit revealed how the Cadbury generations had become progressively more ascetic: Richard Tapper Cadbury had enjoyed drinking wine but had been persuaded by his son John to take the pledge; John with his hard chairs and plain living was austere enough, but Richard and George, his sons, continued to live so frugally at Bournville that their father was moved to rebuke them for dining off little more than meat bones. Each week their diet consisted of the same basic fare: a leg of mutton which was cut into two. The first, larger half was roasted on Monday, served cold on Tuesday and hashed or minced on Wednesday. The smaller half was boiled on Thursday and the bones and scraps served up in some form on Friday.

Their father happened to call unexpectedly one Friday when a young clerk, Edward Thackray, was having lunch with the brothers, and John Cadbury was shocked to find the trio with little more than bones on their plates. His concern was less for his sons, who were after all responsible for their own welfare, than for the employee: he was 'a growing youth', said John Cadbury, and he needed a more substantial meal. Thackray was evidently not daunted by the experience, because he went on to become a senior member of the firm by the First World War, in charge of buying the raw cocoa at London auctions and of the advertising department. He used to recall being invited by George Cadbury to kneel in prayer in his office before some weighty decision had to be made.

The new factory was built to a rectangular one-storey design, lit by skylights and without windows on its southern side, because the heat of the sun could affect the chocolate production. There was a kitchen and, later, a gas grill for employees to cook themselves a hot meal, and dressing rooms where both men and women could dry their coats and boots if the weather was wet, and change into their work clothes. Adjoining the factory was a field in which the male employees were encouraged to play football or cricket, while the women were provided with a garden area with swings and seats. In the 1880s, the Bournville cricket team produced a noted England wicket-keeper, Arthur Lilley.

These were working conditions such as no other company in the Midlands provided, but it was only the beginning of a far-reaching vision in George Cadbury's mind.

CHAPTER 2:

'CHRISTMAS ALL YEAR ROUND'

GEORGE CADBURY WAS ONE of the most remarkable industrialists of an age rich in talented and visionary businessmen. His long life – he was to outlive his brother Richard by twenty-five years, surviving into the 1920s, which must have seemed like another planet to this Victorian Quaker – enabled him to develop the Bournville experiment and build it into a lasting corporate culture. It also gave him the opportunity to become a newspaper baron in the Liberal cause and to pursue his social visions on a wider scale – campaigning for the old-age state pension among other reforms.

He married twice and fathered eleven children in all, five by his first wife Mary, who died in 1887, and six by the second, Elizabeth, always known as Elsie, who became a leading public figure in her own right and was made a Dame of the British Empire in 1934. Elsie had something of the formidable yet compassionate presence of Eleanor Roosevelt and outlived her husband by nearly thirty years, dying full of honours in 1951 at the age of ninety-three. The sons of George's two families and their descendants made Cadbury's into the modern business that joined Schweppes in 1969. Mary's sons Edward, George Jr. and Henry ran the firm in its formative years up to the Second World War, with Laurence and Egbert, sons of the second marriage, contributing new thinking in the inter-war years and Laurence leading it after the war. For the last third of the twentieth century Laurence's sons Adrian and Dominic have managed the company, negotiating the merger with Schweppes and running the multinational Cadbury Schweppes, but there are now only two Cadburys apart from Sir Dominic working in the one-time family business.

George and Richard had run the business as a sort of dual patriarchy, much respected and even loved by their employees. Their qualities complemented each other as in all the best business partnerships – George the original thinker and daring spirit, fuelled by intense convictions; Richard the steadying, balancing influence. Despite their sometimes daunting habits of austerity, such as the boiled bones for lunch, both exuded a warmth and unforced goodwill that led people to say of each, 'it was Christmas with him all the year round'.

For Richard, however, Christmas came to a premature end in 1899 when he was on a holiday visit with his family to Egypt and Palestine. For both George and Richard, foreign holidays seem to have been the one luxury in their quotidian pattern of plain living, high thinking and hard work at Bournville. The family albums are full of pictures of grand hotels in Italy, Switzerland and the South of France where they took suites of apartments to accommodate parents and children and kept diaries of days spent 'basking in the sun' and going for long walks.

In his sixties Richard had developed a keen interest in Egyptology and with Emma and their four younger daughters had spent some weeks there at the beginning of 1897, visiting Cairo, Gizeh, the Great Pyramid and the Sphinx, Karnak on the Nile and countless tombs and temples of the pharoahs. From Egypt they took a ship for Jaffa and visited Jerusalem, Hebron, Bethlehem, Jericho, the Dead Sea and Jordan. This part of the holiday was strenuous, riding by day for eight hours at a stretch with a rest at noon, and camping by night in an elaborate arrangement of tents; some with folding beds for sleeping, another for dining and one to house the kitchen. They saw Nazareth, the Sea of Galilee, Cana and the site of the Sermon on the Mount, returning via Damascus to Beirut and thence home.

In February 1899 they journeyed again to Egypt and Palestine, this time taking their eldest daughter Edith and her husband and the three youngest daughters. Richard, who like his brother taught adult school classes, busied himself making notes for lectures, sketching historic sites and taking rubbings and photographs. On 12 March, after a visit to the American hospital in Assiut where they noticed a fearful smell from some drains, Richard Cadbury complained of a sore throat. It grew worse as they reached Cairo, but a doctor advised it was merely 'Nile throat' and that the fresher air of Palestine would improve it. By the time they arrived in Jerusalem on 18 March, Richard could barely speak and even milk was intensely painful to swallow. His illness was finally diagnosed as diphtheria and three days later he was dead.

Richard's sudden death at sixty-four devastated George, for their relationship had been very close. It also brought about a rapid change in the business. Only a few weeks before, the brothers had signed an agreement that if either should die, the survivor and the executors should convert the privately owned family business into a limited liability company. This duly took place on 13 June 1899, and Cadbury Brothers Ltd. came into being with £950,000 capital, divided equally between ordinary shares and 6 per cent preference shares. George Cadbury was chairman and the other executive directors consisted of Richard's sons Barrow and William and George's sons Edward and George Cadbury Jr. These four were to work together as a team for more than thirty years, but almost from the beginning, power began to shift to the younger generation.

All four had worked their passage in the firm and contributed differently to its development. Barrow had assisted in drawing up the plans for the original Bournville factory while on vacation from Owens College, Manchester in 1879, and in 1882 had joined the firm as personal assistant to his father and uncle. He would in due course head the cashiers' department and become chairman of the British Cocoa and Chocolate Company, the holding company created for the merger with J. S. Fry in 1919. William Adlington Cadbury, whose signature still forms the Cadbury's logo on every wrapper, took an engineering apprenticeship and spent some months working in the German chocolate firm of Stollwerck in Cologne. On joining the family business, he assumed responsibility for the buildings and machinery at Bournville. His eventual career would make him chairman of Cadbury Brothers and Lord Mayor of Birmingham.

Edward, George's eldest son, joined the firm when he was twenty, in 1893, and worked through a number of departments to learn the business, as would later generations of young Cadburys. When the company changed its status in 1899, he was given two main areas of responsibility: to develop the export business, which had begun in 1881 with an office in Melbourne, Australia, and had since expanded to India, South Africa, Canada and France; and to organise the women who formed the bulk of the Bournville workforce. It was the latter task that brought out Edward's progressive thinking on industrial relations and gave rise in 1912 to his still-remarkable book, *Experiments in Industrial Organization*. Edward's nephew Adrian Cadbury was to use it as an inspiration when he came to chair the firm in the 1960s and to recommend it in turn to his younger brother Dominic.

George Jr., five years younger than Edward, might well have pursued a career outside the firm but was given no choice. In 1897 he was at University College, London, in his first year of reading for a science degree when, to his acute disappointment, his father insisted that he was needed in the business and recalled him to Bournville. He too was despatched to Stollwerck's factories in Germany and Hungary to learn about advanced chocolate manufacturing techniques. When the limited liability company was formed, he assumed responsibility for the technical and scientific side of the business: he standardised the chocolate recipes and brought in new automatic machinery, including an automatic moulding machine which had the effect of doubling output.

The move to Bournville in 1879 had unleashed two decades of fast growth under the dual partnership of the Cadbury brothers. The original factory soon proved too small; by 1889 its area had almost doubled, and by 1899 it had trebled. In 1884 a spur from the Midland Railway was run into the factory for unloading the raw cocoa and loading the finished products. Men still working at Bournville in the late

1990s remember starting their Cadbury careers as 'trolley boys', pushing the heavy iron trolleys laden with cartons of chocolate into the sidings – Adrian Cadbury had his spell on them too.

The railway company stipulated that a charge was to be paid by Cadbury Brothers for the siding until the value of the traffic using it reached £10,000 a year, but this was easily exceeded in the first year and the charge was never levied. In 1895 the brothers bought the land immediately to the north, west and south of the works, an estate belonging to a mansion called Bournbrook Hall. This enabled them not only to provide for future expansion but also to improve recreational facilities for the workers, including a fully equipped sports ground and county-class cricket pitch covering twelve acres.

George Cadbury was also beginning to acquire the land he would use for his great community housing experiment known as Bournville Village. From the moment that the brothers conceived their vision of 'a factory in a garden', it was their intention to build a community around it, so that the workers could live in pleasant surroundings nearby, but Bournville was never intended solely for the employees of Cadbury Brothers. George Cadbury saw the dangers of private developers cashing in on the economic magnet created by the Cadbury factory, of land values soaring and of houses being crammed together to provide maximum return, eventually resulting in conditions not much better than the Birmingham slums from where the chocolate workers had come.

Determined to control development of the land, he bought 120 acres around the works, gradually adding to it until the area covered 842 acres in all. He wanted to create a balanced community, not a company village but a true cross-section of occupations and income levels such as would be found in a village that had grown organically over time. In 1895 the garden city idea was in its infancy; a few visionaries such as Patrick Geddes and Ebenezer Howard were beginning to write and speak about town planning, but Howard's book *Tomorrow*, which laid the groundwork for Letchworth and Welwyn garden cities, was still three years in the future. In its social sweep and mix, Bournville was quite different from previous integrated works communities such as Sir Titus

Salt's Saltaire near Bradford, built in the 1850s to house his wool workers, and soap tycoon William Lever's Port Sunlight, set up in the 1880s as a 'tied' village outside Liverpool. (Lever saw his enterprise as a form of profit-sharing: he would rather put the money into housing and recreation, he said, than see it go down his workers' throats as whisky or 'fat geese for Christmas'.)

George Cadbury planned every detail of Bournville Village to an extraordinary degree. He worked out the size of each house and garden, with no more than seven houses to the acre. Each house would have a garden at least three times its own floor area and be planted with six fruit trees. He calculated that a sixth of an acre was roughly all that a man who had worked all day in a factory could be expected to cultivate in his leisure hours, and that 'from one-eighth of an acre, vegetables and fruit worth at least half a crown a week could be grown'. In 1901, explaining how his vision had taken root and that the main object of providing this wholesome leisure activity with its home-grown diet was to 'improve the physique of the nation', he said: 'The question that came to me was "What have you to offer working men in the evening except the public house?" and this was the answer I arrived at, "The most legitimate occupation is for them to come back to the land". . .'

He laid down the proportions of the roads – forty-two feet wide and lined with trees, the houses to be set back at least twenty feet from the pavements. The houses were to be all of different elevations, with a deep garden at the back. The gardens were pre-planted, each with six fruit trees, and the company encouraged the gardening habit with hand-books, plants, bulbs and evening classes, even offering mowing machines for hire. Initially 142 houses were built, most with three bed-rooms, a sitting room, kitchen and scullery where, until separate bathrooms were introduced, the bath was concealed under a tabletop or hinged so that it could be folded back into a cupboard.

Some of the houses were sold at cost (£250) on 999-year leases with a nominal ground rent of fifty-five shillings, the company advancing half the cost at 2½ per cent interest and providing loans for the remaining 50 per cent at 3 per cent interest. After twelve years the house was paid for. The leasehold system was chosen to enable the ground landlord to maintain the village character and appearance. But some individuals sold on their leases at a huge profit, so the policy was changed to weekly tenancies until the late 1920s, when Cadbury's responded to requests to buy. Today, there are 2,431 Bournville Village Trust tenants, paying rents ranging between £40 and £75 a week; 2,042 freeholders and 1,735 leaseholders, along with a number of outside tenants. House prices vary widely, from £80,000 to £400,000 for the largest and newest.

The original sixteen houses built for Cadbury's foremen became 300 houses by the end of 1900, at which time George Cadbury handed over the entire estate, then consisting of 370 houses on 500 acres and valued at around £170,000, to a charitable trust. At the time he stated that his gift represented the bulk of his fortune outside the business, and added:

> 'I have seriously considered how far a man is justified in giving away the heritage of his children, and have come to the conclusion that my children will be all the better for being deprived of this money. Great wealth is not to be desired, and in my experience of life it is generally more of a curse than a blessing to the families of those who possess it. I have ten children. Six of them are of an age to understand how my action affects them, and they all entirely approve.'

The Bournville Village Trust has endured for nearly a century and still governs everything from the colour of a painted front door to the ban – unsuccessfully challenged in 1998 by a local trader – on the sale of alcoholic liquor. Originally administered by George Cadbury, his wife Elsie and his two eldest children, Edward and George Jr., the trust's composition was soon expanded by George Cadbury's wish to include appointees from the Birmingham City Council and the Society of Friends. Today there are twelve trustees, three-quarters of them appointed by family members from the descendants of George Cadbury or the sons of his brother Richard. The other three trustees are appointed by Birmingham Council, the Society of Friends and Birmingham University.

The trust's constitution laid down that the income from rents and sales was to be primarily used for repairs and maintenance and secondarily for extending the estate. By 1922 when George Cadbury died there were 1,100 houses in an area of 1,800 acres, and a population of about 5,500. Today there are over 7,500 houses, but no record is kept of how many are occupied by Cadbury employees.

A distinguished architect of the Arts and Crafts period, W. Alexander Harvey, was brought in by George Cadbury to design a small group of public buildings for the village including two schools, the Friends' Meeting House, an Anglican church and a recreation centre, known as Ruskin Hall. Cadbury, an early conservationist, discovered in 1907 that Selly Manor, a Tudor house near Bournville, was about to be demolished. He arranged for it to be physically transported in numbered pieces to the corner of Maple and Sycamore Roads, near the Bournville village green, and rebuilt between 1912 and 1917. It is today a small, homely museum of rare oak furniture, much of it collected by Laurence Cadbury, the eldest son of George Cadbury's second marriage, including a twenty-two-foot refectory table in one piece. On the dark timber beams of the house can still be seen the chalk numbers that guided the workmen in re-assembling the house.

The world was fascinated by the Bournville experiment. A French model village was set up, and so was a 'German Bournville' – financed by the Krupp armaments family, which cannot have pleased George Cadbury. Another tribute which must have caused mixed feelings in this Quaker pacifist came from Australia's leading newspaper, *The Melbourne Age*. At the height of the debate in 1910 over building more battleships in response to the growing threat from Germany, the paper declared: 'Bournville is as important to England as a Dreadnought.'

In the middle of the First World War, George Cadbury – by then a newspaper proprietor and active campaigner for social advance – set out his radical vision to a committee of the Trades Union Congress. The TUC had honoured him as 'a pioneer of better conditions of life both at home and in the factory' and called Bournville 'the work of a great Englishman, filled with a generous and noble desire to serve his fellowmen'. In his letter to the committee, George observed that when wars came to an end the poor always suffered and predicted that the same would happen again without a united social effort.

'The little children of our land ought to live in healthier and brighter homes,' he wrote. Assuming that nine million households could be rehoused in cottages and gardens numbering ten to the acre, this would require

> not a million acres out of the 77 million in the United Kingdom – but probably not half this number would be found needful. From careful tests at Bournville we find that one acre of garden ground will produce 12 times as much food as one acre under pasture, so that while producing healthy children, cottage gardens also produce an increased food supply.
>
> The battle will be a severe one. Wealth gives enormous power. The wealthy hold the land, millions of acres of which provide for a mere handful of men sport, such as hunting, shooting and racing. This land might produce ten times as much food if properly cultivated, and many million acres set apart for deer forests might produce timber and provide healthy and profitable employment. Those who have fought our battles and saved the Empire ought, on their return, to find room in their own land and healthy homes to dwell in.

Needless to say, this trumpet call had no more effect than Lloyd George's election promise of 'homes fit for heroes', though other garden cities and suburbs were built in the 1920s, including Hampstead Garden Suburb. At the turn of the century, Cadbury's principal competitor, Joseph Rowntree, had built his own Bournville at New Earswick, near York, greatly influenced by his son Seebohm's famous book *Poverty: A Study of Town Life*, published in 1901.

The Cadburys were always intensely practical in their approach to industrial welfare: they simply believed that a healthy and contented workforce led to a more productive factory. It must have been highly satisfying to George and Edward Cadbury when in 1919 the comparative infant mortality statistics for Bournville and a poor district of Birmingham called Floodgate Street proved twice as favourable for the Cadbury community – 51 deaths per 1,000 babies against 101 per 1,000 in the city. Older children thrived better too: the average twelve-year-old boy in Bournville weighed eight pounds six ounces more than his Birmingham counterpart, while for girls the difference was nine pounds.

Meanwhile Edward Cadbury had been stamping his own influence on the Bournville experiment. Under his direction, the existing benevolent patriarchy blossomed into a miniature welfare state, with a company-subsidised pension scheme and a non-contributory sickness scheme which provided up to twelve weeks' sick benefit and another twelve weeks' half-benefit in the course of a year. (National sickness insurance still lay far in the future.) The company provided a fully equipped surgery with two qualified doctors – one of them a woman – and four trained nurses to treat sick employees. The medical staff would make home visits if necessary and three of the nurses were also qualified masseuses able to treat injuries such as sprains. In 1905 a works dental surgery was opened, staffed by a full-time dental surgeon; when it was found that 98 per cent of the youngsters applying for employment had tooth decay, Cadbury's provided free toothbrushes and tooth powder to four schools in the neighbourhood. There was also a convalescent home in Herefordshire with twenty beds, run by a qualified matron and nurse.

George Cadbury also privately made a number of buildings available for charitable use. In 1895, he turned his first house, Woodbrooke, over to the Society of Friends for use as a teachers' college, and in the grounds of his new, larger home, the Manor House, a building known as the Barn which could seat 700 was used for entertaining poor children from Birmingham. A house called The Beeches was built in Bournville to function both as a Salvation Army convalescent home in winter and as holiday accommodation for slum families in summer.

As early as 1900 there was an innovation at Bournville that would be rare even in these days of Health and Safety at Work legislation – Cadbury's engaged a full-time expert to prevent accidents in the factory. His job was to inspect the machines and ensure that guards were fitted where necessary. Clubs abounded – a youth club, social club, camera club and a musical society of nearly 200 members who could muster a choral society, a brass band and a mandoline and banjo band. The firm also negotiated with the railway companies to offer its employees cheap eight-day or fifteen-day return tickets to seaside resorts for their summer holidays.

These were all unprecedented benefits, but Edward had further ideas for improving the life prospects and efficiency of the workforce. In the 1900s most working-class children left school at twelve or fourteen and Edward thought this was far too young to stop learning. He introduced compulsory evening classes for all workers under eighteen. Their fees would be refunded by the company provided they could show at least 85 per cent attendance.

Courses for the boys included English, mathematics, history, geography, a choice of French or German, bookkeeping, shorthand and elementary science. For the girls the subjects were English, arithmetic, art, needlework, home dressmaking, physiology, cookery, laundry work, basic nursing and the care of infants. After the age of eighteen, both sexes could choose to continue voluntarily, and many did so, attending courses in history, citizenship, ambulance work, French, German, music, millinery, embroidery, art or any other subject taught in a public institution of learning in the city. Edward also made physical training compulsory for all under eighteen, and the company hired five gymnastic teachers to give their services for half an hour, twice a week.

All this now doubtless sounds like unacceptably imposed paternalism, but it did not seem so at the time, and it launched a kind of self-sustaining corporate family culture at Bournville that has never quite gone away. It was also extraordinarily ahead of its time in foreshadowing the 1990s emphasis on providing learning skills to enhance employability, though today the strategy is often being adopted to compensate for lack of a dependable career ladder.

Speaking in 1998 about his uncle Edward's ground-breaking book on industrial relations, Adrian Cadbury singled out the chapter dealing with the learning opportunities for employees as being a key influence on his own thinking as late as 1969, when he first became chairman of Cadbury Schweppes. The chapter begins with a letter to the parents of prospective Cadbury employees under eighteen years of age, explaining that company policy is for every boy or girl to receive education up to the age of sixteen 'in the ordinary things useful in everyday life' and then for a variety of courses to be made available from which they could choose, depending on what kind of career they had decided upon. It was only by treating the subject of education 'scientifically, as is done in Germany and other countries', wrote Edward Cadbury, 'that we can hope to keep our supremacy in the world, and take our lead among the nations'. Parents were assured that the firm would provide 'a good tea at 1d. per night' and that the classes would be run between 6.45 and 8.45 p.m. to allow their sons and daughters home at a reasonable hour.

Edward tried to approach every aspect of staff welfare scientifically, with a questioning mind. Although discipline was firm – Edward had a mania for punctuality and would wait by the staff entrance, fob-watch in hand, as late arrivals sheepishly trailed in, not saying a word but snapping the watch shut and replacing it in his pocket – the approach was always to try to find out why something had gone wrong or why an individual was behaving in an uncharacteristic manner. If a young worker were slow to learn, Edward would try to find out the reason before confronting him. Adrian Cadbury says of his Quaker forebears: 'They were concerned for the human condition but were intensely practical. They believed that you should look for what people can offer, that everybody can be good at something and that you should capitalise on that.'

If this was scientific management, it was very different from the technique under that label then being developed in the US by Frederick Winslow Taylor, for whom science in the workplace meant finding by measured observation the 'one best way' to perform each manual task, and laying down guidelines for each movement of shovel or spanner. Taylor was not in the least concerned with his workers' inner needs or in developing their initiative, only with maximising their earning power and the firm's productivity. Edward Cadbury wrote:

> In the case of the unskilled workman there is a great need for widening and deepening his outlook on life, since very often his work is monotonous and depressing, the sub-division of

processes being carried to such an extent that there is a narrowing of interest, while automatic machinery almost eliminates any demand for initiative and adaptation. The unskilled youth, therefore, is allowed a wider choice of subjects, especially in the fourth year, when he can take such subjects as music, art, handicrafts, science, literature, political economy and social philosophy. Thus he finds in his leisure time that opportunity for developing his mind and imagination which his trade calling denies him.

Edward was a short and stocky man who lacked his father's imposing presence and ease with others. He was shy and private by nature, but had a jovial side, with a loud, distinctive laugh. Competitors such as the Rowntrees, fierce opponents of trade unions, could not understand how Edward was not only in favour of union membership but became puzzled and positively frustrated when employees showed lack of interest in joining. His support of unions was a simple extension of his belief in what one man owed another in society: just as employers owed a duty to their workers to provide decent working conditions, so he believed employees owed it to themselves and each other to support their rights by being part of a union.

He was also perhaps the most effective businessman among his generation of Cadburys. When his nephew Charles Gillett, who eventually took over the export side from him in 1927, turned sixteen, Edward wrote to him outlining his four principles for business success:

> Firstly, strength of character and high purpose in life. Secondly, ability to concentrate on the work and problems before you. Thirdly, initiative, resource, and not being afraid to take risks and make mistakes. Fourthly, and this is an extremely important thing if one is to be successful, sufficient humility to be willing at all times to listen and to learn from the experience and opinion of others.

After his father's death in 1922 Edward introduced automation, which boosted profits nearly threefold, and pursued a more dynamic advertising strategy. Advertising and the use of publicity was an issue on which the Rowntree and Cadbury businesses were diametrically opposed. Joseph Rowntree thought advertising a complete waste of money but all the Cadburys back to John, founder of the tea and coffee business, had known the value of publicity and used it shrewdly, from John Cadbury's 'Chinaman' figure to the samples of 'pure cocoa essence' sent to the medical press.

Rowntree's were finally forced into advertising in 1891, when the firm needed to promote its Elect Cocoa against Cadbury's Dutch-milled product. Having fought shy of publicity for so long, they now went to the other extreme, hiring the firm of S. H. Benson (for which the novelist Dorothy M. Sayers would later write copy) to devise high-profile stunts such as mounting a huge tin of Elect Cocoa on the back of a car – still a novelty in York in the 1890s – sending free samples in return for a coupon from the *Daily Telegraph*, giving away tins of the product to women passengers on London omnibuses and chartering a barge at the Oxford and Cambridge Boat Race of 1897, covered with posters and drawn by two mechanical swans. So successful was the campaign that the public was drawn away from the 'unadulterated' Cadbury cocoa to the more flavoured Rowntree product, and in 1911 Bournville Cocoa was developed to meet the new taste.

Edward's strong leadership of the business, coupled with his ability to turn vision into practical social welfare measures at Bournville, meant that George Cadbury, while still an active chairman, could devote more time to the wider social and political concerns that had been pre-occupying him since the early 1890s. In 1892 Gladstone, knowing him to be a strong supporter of Irish Home Rule, asked him to stand for Parliament as a Liberal. Cadbury declined, saying he felt he could be of better service in religious work. Three years later the next prime minister, Lord Rosebery, also urged him to stand. He replied, 'My tastes do not lie in the direction of politics.'

He held intense political views, however, not least on the matter of the Boer War of 1899–1902, which like most Liberals he bitterly opposed, calling it 'the most diabolical that was ever waged. It is so evidently a speculators' war, and no one else can derive any benefit from it.' The war thrust him on to a wider stage than Birmingham, where in 1891 he had bought a group of four weekly suburban papers with the object of rousing people to the importance of civic government and how individuals could make a difference to their city. With rampant jingoism sweeping the country, only two major newspapers, the *Morning Leader* in London and the *Manchester Guardian,* were prepared to oppose the war after 1900. Birmingham in particular was hostile to both the great causes supported by Cadbury – Irish Home Rule and settlement with the Boers. The city was at the peak of its love affair with Joseph Chamberlain, a local screw magnate who had devoted his life and fortune to a political career and was at this time riding high as Colonial Secretary. George Cadbury was about the only Birmingham industrialist brave or confident enough to take issue with Chamberlain: almost to a man, the others changed their political coat with every alteration of Chamberlain's policy changes.

David Lloyd George, the rising star of the Liberal party, saw the need for a national newspaper to provide an effective voice against the war. The *Daily News,* whose first, if short-lived, editor had been Charles Dickens in 1846, was traditionally a pacifist journal but it had supported the imperialist line in South Africa since the appointment of E. T. Cook as editor at the time of the Jameson Raid. Perhaps as a result of changing its colours, it was losing money in the 1890s and looking vulnerable to an outside bid. Lloyd George persuaded George Cadbury and a Bolton textile heir called Franklin Thomasson to put up £40,000 between them to enable the paper to be bought by a syndicate. In December 1901, after Thomasson withdrew because of mounting losses and policy disagreements, Cadbury reluctantly agreed to buy him out and become sole proprietor. 'I was led into it step by step,' he grumbled to an MP friend.

He appointed Alfred George Gardiner, a thirty-seven-year-old journalist from the *Northern Daily Telegraph* who later became his biographer, as his first editor and Thomas Purvis Ritzema, owner of the *Northern Daily Telegraph,* to manage the paper. The *Daily News* now switched from supporting the war to arguing for a peace settlement and exposing some of the more inhumane British actions such as the con-centration camps for Boer women, summary executions and burnings of Boer farms. This dramatic change of tack created a sensation in public opinion and cheered the beleaguered opponents of the war: Sir Henry Campbell-Bannerman, the Liberal leader in the Commons, described it in a letter to his predecessor Sir William Harcourt at the beginning of 1901 as 'a happy change. We shall now have something besides the *Westminster Gazette* that we can read.' But it also chased off advertisers in droves, some of whom had been faithful to the paper for years.

On top of this the new proprietor laid down some rules that were highly eccentric by Fleet Street standards. One was that the paper would not publish any racing news or tipsters' columns, nor would it accept betting advertisements. Liquor advertisements were also banned. Circulation dropped heavily as a result. Cadbury fought these self-imposed handicaps by pouring money into new plant and machinery to double the size of the paper to sixteen pages and yielded to competition from the halfpenny press by halving its price to match them. Circulation went from a low point of 30,000 to 80,000, but the losses still mounted until they were running at nearly £30,000 a year.

With the end of the South African war, Gardiner's editorial focus homed in on other Cadbury crusades, chief among them the fight to establish a national old age pension in Britain. George Cadbury and his son Edward had financed a campaigning organisation called the National Old Age Pension League and when, in January 1909, the Liberal government introduced the first state pension for men and women over seventy, ranging between one shilling and five shillings a week according to their means, Cadbury made a ringing speech calling for a better deal.

> We want to see the whole scheme carried out – a shilling a day at sixty for every man and woman in England, from the Duke of Westminster downwards; only with this condition, that if the Duke wants his pension he must go to the post office and get it. If we asked for too much all at once, in all human possibility we should have got nothing. Now it is for us to

work downwards in the scale of age. There is no work in England so hard as that of the wife of the working man earning 20s. a week. She can never put aside the money for old age pensions, and yet she has earned it more than any man living.

Cadbury's *Daily News* set about the task of bringing the condition of the poor and ill-paid to the well-laden breakfast tables of the comfortable middle class, what would now be called Middle England. As part of its campaign to expose the cruelties and degradation of the sweatshops that proliferated in the industrial quarter of every city in the land, the paper organised an exhibition of sweated industries at London's Queen's Hall in May 1906. George Cadbury underwrote the whole cost of the exhibition, which for practical reasons had to limit itself to the plight of homeworkers rather than try to cover the whole range of slum factories.

These homeworkers, all women, were paid appalling pittances. The middle classes with a conscience who attended the exhibition in the capital's premier concert hall could read in their catalogues that artificial button roses were made for 1s. 4d. a gross, artificial Parma violets for sevenpence a gross, cardboard boxes for an hourly rate of just over a penny. Hooks and eyes, essential to Edwardian dresses, were carded at a rate of 1s. 4d. for 384 hooks and 384 eyes. Shirtmaking was paid by the piece at less than a penny an hour, matchboxes at 2½d. for a gross. Eleven-hour days spent making chains, a gruelling physical task, yielded an average wage of six to eight shillings a week. (A shilling, twelve old pennies, equals five pence in modern terms, without adjusting for a century's inflation.)

The exhibition-goers could watch the unrelenting pace at which these poor women had to work to scratch such a wretched living. The event attracted royal patronage – the exhibition was opened by Princess Henry of Battenberg, while the Princess of Wales, the former Princess May of Teck, was among the 30,000 visitors. Beatrice and Sidney Webb, founders of the Fabian Society, the Labour pioneer Keir Hardie and the novelist H. G. Wells were vice-presidents of the exhibition. It was one of the most influential public campaigns of Edwardian times, and aroused deep disquiet. Large employers had often not realised, or cared to question, what lay behind the system of contracting and subcontracting piecework. An Anti-Sweating League was formed, and a bill was put forward for a minimum wage in specific sweated industries, which became law as the Trade Boards Act. George Cadbury, now in his fifties, had carried forward his grandfather Richard's campaigns against child labour on an even wider stage.

Despite its high reforming profile and social influence, by 1907 the *Daily News* was losing more than £60,000 a year. Edward Cadbury, who had been a director of the paper from the start, identified the problem as the incompetence of the managing director, Thomas Ritzema. George Cadbury brought in his third son Henry to salvage the business, though Ritzema was still officially in control and it became an embarrassing and messy situation until Ritzema was forced into resignation.

Henry was the only one of George's sons never to work in the Cadbury firm. Still only twenty-four, he had struggled academically at Cambridge and then gone to be a farmer. He had no qualifications for running a newspaper, as he reflected ruefully during the fortnight in March 1907 that he had asked his father to let him think it over. He went for long evening walks round the farm trying to decide what to do, eventually agreeing to his father's request and moving into his parents' London flat in Whitehall Court to begin his new job. The first morning, he walked from the block of mansion flats in Northumberland Avenue to the *Daily News* offices in Bouverie Street, got as far as the door and had a panic attack. He turned tail and had walked back to Whitehall Court before he could summon up the courage to return and enter the door. Before long, however, he was checking on all aspects of the business, from distribution in Leeds to Ritzema's expense account, which was the final spur to his resignation. George Cadbury was relieved and surprised, confessing that neither he nor Henry's brothers had had any idea that he was 'such a first class man of business'.

Henry had stipulated that he would only do the job if his school friend Bertram Crosfield, who was to marry his sister Eleanor, joined him in the management. George agreed, giving the two men an eight-point list of suggested economies and improvements for the paper, including more sport ('this is a feature that practically everybody is interested in'); selling the company car used by the editor; reducing the space given to commodity and market reports; dismissing six or seven of the advertisement salesmen and putting the remaining four on commission ('they will probably do very much better than the whole staff as it is now'). He even suggested giving up the religious column to save the costs of its contributor.

Then, as Henry put it, 'the band began to play! In the last week of September we cleared out the whole of the management . . . I saw them all in 2 hours and gave them their notice . . . I think I didn't sleep for three nights with the strain of seeing personally all those people.' In January 1908 he moved out of his parents' flat and with his sister Eleanor took a flat in Church Row, Hampstead. Six months later the paper opened a second printing operation in Manchester to serve the north. By 1910, an election year, the total circulation had climbed to 540,000 from 150,000 when Henry took it over and the £60,000 losses were eliminated.

George Cadbury, who habitually wrote Henry four or five letters a week even after he retired as chairman of the *Daily News* in 1911, had by now completely succumbed to the lure of newspaper ownership, which he saw as a much more effective vehicle for social reform than giving to charity. When the *Morning Leader* and the *Star*, the Liberal evening newspaper, came up for sale in 1909, he formed a partnership with Arnold Rowntree of the rival chocolate family and another newspaper owner to buy the two, which had a combined circulation of over 500,000.

This immediately ran him into difficulties with the Society of Friends because the *Star* depended on its popular betting news for much of its circulation. At first reluctant to take on the papers for this reason, George was driven to do so by fears that they would otherwise fall into the hands of a Conservative proprietor. He decided, as he wrote to his son Laurence, an undergraduate at Cambridge, that he ought to be 'guided by commonsense, and it was evident that the *Star* with betting news and pleading for social reform and for peace was far better than the *Star* with betting and opposing social reform and stirring up strife with neighbouring nations . . .'

As a result of his friction with the Society of Friends, George formed a family trust in November 1911 into which 51 per cent of the *Daily News* shares were transferred. Edward took over as chairman while remaining in charge of Bournville, and Henry and Bertram Crosfield continued as joint chief executives until 1930, when ill-health forced Henry to retire. In a memorandum accompanying the deed of trust, George set out – perhaps to answer his critics – his philosophy behind acquiring the newspapers. It is not one that any modern newspaper baron would recognise. In it he said that he hoped the trust

> may be of service in bringing the ethical teaching of Jesus Christ to bear upon National questions, and in promoting National Righteousness; for example, that Arbitration should take the place of War, and that the spirit of the Sermon on the Mount – especially of the Beatitudes – should take the place of Imperialism and of the military spirit which is contrary to Christ's teaching . . .
>
> Much of current philanthropic effort is directed to remedying the more superficial evils. I earnestly desire that the Daily News Trust may be of service in assisting those who are seeking to remove their underlying causes. To this end if the funds permitted, it would be in accordance with my wish that the Trust should control, by purchase or otherwise, other newspapers, conducting them not with a primary view to profit but with the object of influencing public thought in channels all of which appeal to me, though . . . the trustees will be at liberty to follow their own conscientious convictions.

He then outlined a number of causes so radical even now that they would cause Tony Blair's New Labour government to break into a collective sweat: taxation of land values, appropriation of unearned income, altering the land laws to increase the number of smallholdings, cutting down military expenditure, 'relieving the labourer of all taxation for military purposes and placing such taxation upon the wealthy' and the acquisition by the state of 'all monopolies that can be better administered by the community for the benefit of all'.

To each son who was a trustee, he sent a copy of this memorandum together with a letter reinforcing his belief in the potential of the press as an instrument of reform.

> I want you to know that the money that I have invested in these papers would otherwise have been given to charities. I had a profound conviction that money spent on charities was of infinitely less value than money spent in trying to arouse my fellow-countrymen to the necessity for measures to ameliorate the condition of the poor, forsaken and downtrodden masses which can be done most effectively by a great newspaper.

Cadbury had long been a target for the non-reforming majority of the national press, especially after the Liberal landslide of 1906 to which the papers owned by Cadbury and Rowntree – 'the Cocoa Press', as one opponent dubbed them – were seen to have contributed. Now the acquisition by this pious Quaker magnate of two papers with popular betting columns stoked up their synthetic fury. The weekly *Spectator*, which was stridently anti-Liberal, attacked Cadbury week after week with the charge of 'organised cant and hypocrisy' and accused him of profiting from the vices of others – though in fact Cadbury never received, nor intended to receive, a penny of profit from the papers all his life. St Loe Strachey, the *Spectator* editor, portrayed Henry Cadbury as 'wrapped in a rhinoceros hide of self-righteousness'. The *Manchester Guardian* sardonically editorialised that 'a careless reader of the controversy might have supposed that they [Cadbury and Rowntree] had introduced a gambling newspaper for the first time into the white-robed company of the London daily press, instead of having made almost the first break with that press's disreputable practice'.

Press attacks, however, were something George Cadbury was well used to. By the time he acquired the *Morning Leader* and the *Star*, he found himself compelled to take the *Standard*, a London morning newspaper, to court in an action for libel. In September 1908 the *Standard* accused him and his company of acquiescing in slave-labour conditions in two cocoa-growing African islands, colonies of Portugal, at the same time that he was busily creating a welfare state for his British workers.

The background to this stretched back several years. Since the late 1880s part of Cadbury's supply of raw cocoa, bought in the London and Liverpool markets, had derived from plantations on the islands of San Thomé and Principe in the Gulf of Guinea, some 200 miles off the coast of west Africa. In 1901 William Cadbury, George's nephew, was visiting Trinidad and was told by a casual acquaintance that the labour conditions in these islands were little short of slavery. While the Cadburys were still trying to elicit information about the situation, they and other cocoa manufacturers received a letter from Lisbon offering a San Thomé plantation for sale. Among the saleable assets were listed a number of labourers, some at a higher per capita price than others.

Armed with this clear evidence that human beings were regarded as the property of the estate, William Cadbury visited Lisbon in 1903 and had a meeting with the Portuguese minister for the colonies, the British minister to Portugal, Sir Martin Gosselin, and representatives of the San Thomé planters' association. The planters denied any cruelty and invited Cadbury Brothers to make their own investigations on the spot. The colonial minister, Senhor Gorjao, promised that any existing abuses would be removed by a new law, the Labour Decree, that had been passed through the Lisbon parliament a few months earlier. Sir Martin Gosselin advised the Cadburys to give the new law a year to remedy the situation and then take up the invitation to visit.

The Cadburys accepted this advice, which necessitated the continued purchase of San Thomé cocoa in order to give them the right as customers to investigate after a year. They invited four other cocoa manufacturers in Europe and the United States to join in the investigation – at that time San Thomé cocoa accounted for about a twentieth of the world's supply. The Americans were not interested, but Fry of Bristol, Rowntree of York and Stollwerck of Cologne agreed to support the investigation and chose an independent observer, a Quaker named Joseph Burtt, to undertake the inspection after a year had elapsed.

Burtt did his homework thoroughly. He spent months in Portugal learning the language and finally set off for the islands in June 1905. Over six months he inspected more than forty plantations, then went on to Angola and finally returned to England in April 1907 after studying contract labour conditions in other African countries, including Cape Colony and Mozambique. His report, countersigned by another Birmingham worthy, Dr Claude Horton, who had accompanied him on the Angola leg of the journey, was damning. The labourers of San Thomé and Principe were obtained by force from the interior of Angola and driven in gangs, often shackled, to the coastal ports where they were made to sign contracts that most of them did not understand, assigning them to service in the islands for a period of years. At the end of these contracts the labourers were supposed to be asked if they wished to be repatriated to Angola or to re-contract for a further term: in fact, not a single man or woman had been repatriated up to that time, and children born in the islands appeared to be the absolute property of the estate owners. There was also a high mortality rate, most marked among the newly imported labourers – on one plantation, Burtt reported, eighty had died out of 150.

Burtt concluded his report:

> I am satisfied that under the servical [sic] system as it exists at present, thousands of black men and women are, against their will, and often under circumstances of great cruelty, taken away every year from their homes and transported across the sea to work on unhealthy islands, from which they never return. If this is not slavery, I know of no word in the English language which correctly characterises it.

The report was sent to the Foreign Office in July 1907, but the cocoa manufacturers were advised to take no action and not to raise it in the press, until His Majesty's Government could formally bring it to the attention of the Portuguese Government. With diplomatic procedures moving at their customary glacier-like pace, it was not until November that the report was presented to the Lisbon government by the new British minister, Sir Francis Villiers. Joseph Burtt and William Cadbury went to Lisbon at the same time to confront the plantation owners with it. Awareness of the treatment of cocoa labourers in the Portuguese colonies had by this time provoked the Liverpool Chamber of Commerce to urge the government to take action and the cocoa manufacturers to stop buying: a month later, having heard William Cadbury explain that the Burtt report was with the Foreign Office, the Chamber expressed itself satisfied that something was being done.

However, the Chamber's original resolution had received wide coverage in the press, which now began to stir the pot. The *Daily Graphic* published a letter accusing the Quaker chocolate firms of making their products from 'slave-grown cocoa, but they do not appear to care one pin'. Although the paper later published an apology for a 'grave injustice', stating that any appearance of inaction had been the result of Foreign Office advice, Cadbury Brothers now found itself under attack both in Britain, for failing to stop buying slave-produced cocoa, and in Portugal, for slandering a major Portuguese industry.

William Cadbury and Burtt made a third visit to Lisbon in December 1907 when they managed to extract a promise from the new colonial minister, Ayres de Ornellas, that the government would immediately make 'a thorough investigation of the whole subject in Angola, with the intention of replacing the present irresponsible recruiting agents by a proper Government system . . . [which] will also serve as a means of repatriation, and make it practicable for the native to return to his home in the interior'.

Burtt and Cadbury were favourably impressed by the minister's apparent determination to reform the system, but before it could be put to the test, King Carlos I of Portugal and the Crown Prince were both assassinated in Lisbon and a new government came into power, bringing more delays. Another year's grace was agreed by the cocoa firms, on condition that they would cease buying San Thomé cocoa at once if the reforms were not implemented by then.

Towards the end of that period, in September 1908, it was announced in the press that William Cadbury and Joseph Burtt were leaving for Angola and the islands to inspect the situation for themselves. The *Standard,* whose evening stablemate had earlier commended the cocoa firms for actively pushing for reform, now chose to publish an editorial on 26 September sardonically congratulating Cadbury on his visit, 'which does not come too soon'. The paper's editor, H. A. Gwynne, went on to compare the 'plenitude of the solicitude of Mr Cadbury for his fellow creatures' in Bournville with his indifference to the fate of 'those same grimed African hands whose toil is so essential to the beneficent and lucrative operations of Bournville'. Gwynne's editorial continued:

> We can only express our respectful surprise that Mr Cadbury's voyage of discovery has been deferred so long. One might have supposed that Messrs Cadbury would themselves have long ago ascertained the conditions and circumstances of those labourers on the west coast of Africa and the islands adjacent, who provide them with raw material. That pre-caution does not seem to have been taken.

The article pointed out that conditions in Angola and the islands had already been exposed in 1904 by the celebrated war correspondent H. W. Nevinson in an American magazine, and in a book in 1906 entitled *A Modern Slavery.* Nevinson was also writing for the *Daily News* at this time and the Cadburys had tried through their solicitors to stop him writing about the slavery issue in another journal – whether on grounds of breach of contract or to keep it quiet under the terms of their agreement with the Foreign Office is not clear. Nevinson himself criticised 'that peculiar hesitation which often characterises Quakers when action is called for', and the *Standard* now commented acidly on 'the strange tranquillity' with which his findings had been received 'by those virtuous people in England whom they intimately concerned'.

The newspaper was clearly alleging that Cadbury Brothers knew – or should have known – what was happening in the Portuguese colonies that supplied their raw material and had chosen to do nothing about it.

In March 1909 Cadbury's had publicly expressed its disappointment at the failure of the Portuguese government to honour its pledges of reform and announced that it would no longer be buying San Thomé or Principe cocoa. Now it issued a writ for libel against the *Standard* and proceedings began at Birmingham Assizes on 29 November 1909, before Mr Justice Pickford. George Cadbury had asked for the trial to be conducted in Birmingham, even though there was a risk of local prejudice among the jurors, because William, the family's chief witness, was unwell and needed to be close to home.

Several of the most celebrated counsels in the land were mustered on both sides. Appearing for Cadbury's were Sir Rufus Isaacs, later Lord Reading, and John Simon, later Viscount Simon, who had just taken silk and was to go on to a long and distinguished career as home secretary, chancellor and foreign secretary in several Labour and coalition governments. The *Standard* had retained as its star counsel no less a figure than Sir Edward Carson, the prosecutor of Oscar Wilde in a rather more notorious libel suit.

The case lasted seven days – 'a long ordeal', said George Cadbury later. The defence case, while presenting no evidence and relying on the formidable interrogative skills of Carson, intensified its plea of justification, from the Cadburys having done nothing to having deliberately avoided action in order to enable them to continue buying the San Thomé cocoa. The plaintiffs' team summoned Sir Edward Grey, the Foreign Secretary, to testify to the delaying advice he and the Foreign Office had given the Cadbury firm on a number of occasions. William Cadbury was fiercely cross-examined by Carson for more than three days but the celebrated Ulster prosecutor was unable to elicit any evidence of negligence, deliberate or otherwise. There was no reason for the firm to continue purchasing San Thomé cocoa – it had no financial interest in the estates and the quality of the cocoa, buying experts testified, was not such that it could not have been replaced easily from other sources. George Cadbury was also summoned as a witness to face

Carson. He could only answer that any profits that might have accrued from slave labour had all gone to charity.

Carson summed up with his customary silky menace: 'For eight long years that condition [slavery] was supported by money that came from the Cadburys – those perfect gentlemen. One million three hundred thousand pounds paid from this country by the Cadburys to the slave dealers in Portugal.'

The judge's summing up, however, was plainly in favour of the plaintiffs. He made it clear that there were several points on which the defendants could have brought evidence if the plaintiffs had been incorrect in what they said, but none had been brought. He instructed the jury to disregard what they thought of the *Daily News*, its campaigns or its politics and said it did not matter whether or not they considered the Cadburys' actions were the best that could have been done. The issue was whether their actions had been done honestly and with good intent, or as a cloak under which the buying of San Thomé cocoa could be continued. The judge also pointed out that the Liverpool Chamber of Commerce – 'not a philanthropic institution but . . . composed of business men' – had judged the Cadburys to have taken the right course.

He also noted that previous articles in the *Standard* and its evening sister had been favourable to the Cadburys in the matter, and he ended with a clear direction to find for substantial damages if the defendants failed to prove that the plaintiffs were dishonest persons. Astonishingly, however, after fifty-five minutes the jury returned with a verdict for the Cadburys but damages of one farthing – the most contemptuous award in the old legal lexicon (most notoriously in post-war years awarded in the 1960s to a London doctor acquitted of assisting Nazi experiments in Auschwitz).

Mr Justice Pickford ignored this and awarded the costs of both sides, which were heavy in view of the calibre of counsel, against the *Standard*. The press was baffled by the jury's quixotic verdict, which clearly had some political undertow. The *Birmingham Daily Mail* called it 'utterly inconsistent and inexplicable' and both the *Times* and the *Morning Post*, no friends of the Liberals, stressed that Cadbury's had vindicated their good name and been cleared of any suspicion of hypocrisy or double-dealing.

Years later, during the First World War, the Foreign Office issued a report which showed that repatriation from the islands was at last taking place and A. J. Balfour, apparently trying to mend fences with the Portuguese, expressed the hope to the Lisbon government that the report would 'remove the boycott which has been maintained by British firms against the produce of the regions in question . . .' The Cadburys, however, were not satisfied. They proved the Foreign Office report to be a whitewash in one verifiable area – that the death rate of the labourers was 10 per cent and not 5 per cent – and demanded a public correction. It was never made. None of the British cocoa firms, including Cadbury's, ever again bought from those islands, switching their sources to the Gold Coast of West Africa (now Ghana).

If George Cadbury was cast down by the Birmingham jury's contemptuous attitude, he did not mention it in any letters that have survived. As he wrote to Henry after the trial, he thought the verdict might actually go against him when he observed the

> evident bias shown by their laughing and by their gestures at any hit made by Sir Edward Carson. . . but the noble summing up of the judge was absolutely impartial; he quite grasped the subject and it has cleared away a great many of the slanders that of late have been hurled against us, and which would have abounded on every side during the coming election.

(This referred to the general election of January 1910, fought on the heated issues of Lloyd George's 'People's Budget'; the power of the House of Lords, which had tried to block the budget; and Irish home rule. The Liberals were returned with a reduced majority.)

For the remaining thirteen years of his life, George Cadbury at last was content to leave the public stage and devote himself more to family life and his thirty-nine grandchildren. His own youngest daughter Ursula was only three at the time of the libel case, having been born in

1906 when her mother Elsie was nearly forty-eight and George was sixty-seven. (She was still living in rural Essex in 1999.)

At seventy, George had only just given up his rigorous early Sunday mornings teaching adult school. He had rejected a peerage several times, being resolutely opposed to honours, and declined a privy councillorship from Campbell-Bannerman in 1907 saying 'I do not think it would be in the interests of the poor suffering people whose cause you and I are pleading, to accept it . . .' He even refused an honorary doctorate of law from Birmingham University. (The first Cadbury to accept a knighthood was Egbert (Bertie) in 1957; the most recent Dominic in 1997. In Quaker custom, however, titles are not used – not even 'Mr' on an envelope. Sir Adrian Cadbury receives letters from his relatives simply addressed to Adrian Cadbury.)

The marriage of George and Elsie was exceptionally close: when they were apart, they wrote to each other nearly every day, sometimes twice daily. Elsie led quite an independent social life for the period; she was more gregarious than her husband and often attended dinner parties, royal garden parties, civic and government receptions on her own account, sometimes taking her older stepsons and daughters with her. Every year from 1905 Elsie would take George Jr. to the royal garden party at Windsor Castle or Buckingham Palace. She also made trips to Europe on her own, in the winter of 1900 visiting Berlin and Stockholm while her husband sent her detailed letters about the children's doings.

At the Manor House in Northfield – the multi-gabled, many-chimneyed house with a quarter-mile driveway that George bought for his expanding family in 1894 after handing Woodbrooke over to the Society of Friends – weekend house parties attracted a mix of writers, MPs and well travelled people. On one weekend in October 1905 G. K. Chesterton and his wife were guests along with Noel Buxton, the MP for Whitby, and Charles Masterman, a Liberal politician-writer with Christian socialist sympathies noted for his 1902 collection of essays about slum life, *From the Abyss*, and *The Condition of England* (1909), which portrayed a land in the throes of acquiring social improvements without comparable spiritual renewal. Chesterton, wrote George, 'is very amusing and knows so much about everything. Last evening he drew some wonderful pictures right off for the children.'

Chesterton was, however, equivocal about the Cadburys and later resigned from the *Daily News* after penning an enigmatic attack in verse on his employers, part of which ran: 'Cocoa is a cad and a coward, Cocoa is a vulgar beast, Cocoa is a crawling, cringing, lying, loathsome swine and clown.' Arnold Bennett also left the paper in 1919, partly, he said, because 'now that Gardiner has gone my original distaste for the Cadburys has free rein'.

Christmas was always a massive gathering of the extended family, with thirty-four people sitting down to Christmas dinner at the Manor House in 1910 and 150 attending a dinner party a few days later – enough to tax even the resources of the home farm and between twenty and thirty domestic staff.

All these social activities of Elsie's were fitted around a diary filled with public service in the fields of education, health and young women's welfare. She founded the first YWCA in Birmingham and the Union of Girls' Clubs, which fostered leisure activities for young women. Just days after their honeymoon in 1888, George introduced her to the adult schools and she taught there for the rest of her long life.

She sat on numerous education committees in the West Midlands and was a founder member of the board of governors of Birmingham University in 1900. (Unlike her husband, she did not turn down the honorary degree the university awarded her in 1919.) From chairing a humble hygiene sub-committee on Birmingham City Council, she went on to organise clinics for local schoolchildren to receive dental treatment and care for minor ailments, expanding this over twenty years into a full school medical service. Elsie also diligently visited each new family moving into Bournville and kept in contact with them, celebrating births and offering bereaved families a holiday at Winds Point, the Cadburys' country house in the Malvern Hills.

Still owned by the George Cadbury trust and used as a holiday home by the family today, Winds Point was the haven at the centre of George's busy life. He and his brother Richard had bought it in 1897, ten years after the death of its most celebrated owner, Jenny Lind, the soprano known as the 'Swedish Nightingale', who towards the end of her life was professor of singing at London's Royal College of Music. Lind and her husband Otto Goldschmidt had transformed it from a cottage on the edge of a stone quarry to a gabled and balconied jumble of a house built like an overgrown Swiss mountain chalet. It had tremendous charm and occupied a superb position about four miles from Malvern on the crest of a hill facing the ancient earthworks of Hereford Beacon and backed by thickly wooded grounds rising to the ridge that led to Worcester Beacon.

From Hereford Beacon, which George loved to climb in the early morning, the countryside, still largely undeveloped in the late nineteenth century and polluted only by the smoke of an occasional steam train, spread out to the towers of Gloucester Cathedral in the south, Hereford Cathedral to the west and Tewkesbury Abbey to the east. Every vista was bounded by hills; the Black Mountains of Wales, the Cotswolds and the Lickey Hills, beyond which lay Bournville and Birmingham.

George made extensive alterations and improvements to the property, but carefully preserved the little octagonal nook in the drawing room, decorated in white and gold and known as 'the Golden Cage', where Jenny Lind had kept her piano and would sing to her own accompaniment. The Golden Cage is still there today, as are the rails fitted to one of the bedroom balconies so that Laurence, George's eldest son by Elsie, could run his bed out on hot nights, though the mechanism no longer works. The Cadburys levelled off the bottom of the stone quarry and turned it into a tennis court, landscaping the rest into a magnificent rock garden and scooping a swimming pool out of the granite. An observation point on the peak above was fitted with a telescope for guests to enjoy the panoramic views.

There were guests by the score in the 1900s, even more than at the Manor House, among them the Liberal prime minister, Sir Henry Campbell-Bannerman; the celebrated cleric Dean Inge; Bramwell Booth, son of the Salvation Army founder, and the eminent physicist Sir Oliver Lodge, first principal of the new Birmingham University. Staying at Winds Point, however, had a certain amount of enforced therapy about it. George Cadbury, himself an early riser and early to bed, believed people came to Winds Point to rest and rest they would, with no night-time distractions – not even reading. At 10 p.m. each evening, the gas generator which ran the electricity supply slowed down, dimming the light to a point where guests were forced to light a candle to read or else go to bed.

As his otherwise admiring biographer A. G. Gardiner observed: 'It was this care for you that made George Cadbury a little trying to disorderly people who loved freedom more than good habits. Life was systematised down to its smallest detail, and moved with the precision and calm of an eight-day clock.' Alcohol did not appear on the table at Winds Point, and for some time tobacco was not tolerated either, though eventually a smoking room was installed.

In his seventies George was still an active chairman of Cadbury Brothers, which had become a publicly quoted company in 1912, and he continued to go into the Bournville works daily, riding the two miles from the Manor House on his bicycle and dealing swiftly and comprehensively with his vast correspondence. No letter, however insignificant its subject, went unanswered by return of post.

On the morning of 31 January 1913, while dictating to his secretary, he suffered a stroke and lay unconscious at the Manor House for six hours. By the next morning, with his children gathered around him – some of whom had been summoned from various parts of the country – he was able to joke: 'This is the first time you have seen me in bed at this time of the morning.' After convalescing at Bordighera, their favourite Italian resort, he seemed to make a full recovery, but at seventy-three his daily round was now reduced, public speaking was banned by his doctor and in particular, the rides into Birmingham on cold dark Sunday mornings to teach the adult school were abandoned on medical orders. He still visited the works daily, however, and loved to take his grandchildren on a tour of the chocolate works, dipping his finger into the liquid chocolate and letting them taste it, and allowing them to climb into the engine driver's cab in the Bournville railway yard. When he came home from the works, his grandson John Crosfield remembers, he would visit the nursery with his pockets full of chocolate neapolitans and hand them out.

The First World War divided the Quaker movement. Some Friends refused to participate at all, though many, including successive generations of Cadburys in 1914–18 and 1939–45, served in the Friends' Ambulance Unit as non-combatants. Laurence Cadbury joined this in 1914, having first wanted to enlist in the army, and commanded an ambulance unit through to 1919, when he was awarded the Croix de Guerre. His sister Molly also served with the ambulance unit in France, but Bertie broke with the family's pacifist tradition by joining first the Royal Navy and secondly the fledgling Royal Naval Air Service, in which he engaged in a number of daring attacks against Zeppelins and was recommended for a VC, eventually being awarded the DFC and DSC.

On balance George thought the war a necessary evil to repel the German threat to Europe, and he was appalled to be visited in 1916 by an officious detective inspector who demanded to see his cheque books on the grounds that he might be subscribing to anti-war journals or organisations. He told the inspector he had no objection to opening his books (although he received a quarter of Cadbury Bros. profits he gave away three quarters of it) and then took satisfaction in telling the man of Bertie's decision within a week of the outbreak of war to quit his law studies and join the Navy on a minesweeper.

George and Elsie's proudest moment at Bournville came in May 1919, when they escorted King George V and Queen Mary round the works and the village. The family story goes that George Cadbury in his formal frock coat was walking with his top hat in his hand in deference to the Queen, but the sun was extremely hot and the Queen said, 'Mr Cadbury, please put on your hat.' As he hesitated, Elsie said sharply, 'George, put on your hat!' and the King, who was in army uniform and also bare-headed, promptly replaced his cap. A year later, at an afternoon party in Buckingham Palace, Queen Mary jokingly recalled the incident and said she hoped he hadn't suffered any ill effects from the sun.

In 1922 George was eighty-three and had seen Cadbury Brothers transformed out of all recognition from the cottage industry he and Richard had transferred to the fields of Bournville in 1879. The introduction of milk chocolate in 1905 against opposition from some family directors (see Chapter 3) and the huge popularity of Cadbury's Dairy Milk had given the firm undisputed market leadership, and a merger with J. S. Fry in 1919 under a holding company called The British Cocoa and Chocolate Company, chaired by Barrow Cadbury, had doubled its market share.

George's last appearance at the Bournville works was in October 1922. He had been weakening in health for some time and even a visit to Winds Point the previous summer could not restore his energy. On 20 October he collapsed with congestion of the lungs and four days later died just as the siren from Bournville signalled the end of the day's work. By his own wish he was cremated and his ashes placed in an urn to be sealed in a memorial on Bournville village green. On the green, where in 1914 the works employees had subscribed for a pretty little octagonal wooden rest-house as a silver wedding gift for the Cadburys, some 16,000 people gathered for the final ceremony and the rest house was submerged in flowers.

Tributes poured in from around Britain and abroad, not only to his remarkable achievements as a pioneer of industrial welfare, but even more to his exceptional character. 'Perhaps the greatest thing that can be said of him is that he increased the sum of love in the world,' said a descendant of the Quaker founder George Fox. A wreath from Austria bore the inscription 'To the revered memory of Mr George Cadbury, the life-long friend of all nations. Blessed are the peacemakers.' In the course of his funeral eulogy, the minister Dr Henry Hodgkin described Cadbury as a man who never showed the slightest trace of superiority to anyone, a man of vision and of purpose, 'a man who knew how to trust others', a man of wide sympathies and above all, a man of love, fuelled by his deep religious practice and following of Christ's teaching.

'His life,' said the minister in a tribute that probably ranks as unique for any business tycoon, 'had a sweetness and charm that is not always preserved by those who succeed in this world.'

Chapter 3:

'A Glass and a Half of Milk'

THE COCOA WARS of the last quarter of the nineteenth century, when Cadbury's, Rowntree's and Fry's engaged in vicious accusation and counter-accusation over so-called adulteration, had calmed down by the 1900s. Ironically, public taste for the 'absolutely pure' cocoa on which the Cadbury brothers had built their market lead, Cocoa Essence, was by this time giving way to a more spicy, flavoured product, typically treated with alkalis to intensify the chocolate flavour. Rowntree's Elect Cocoa, made to this formula, had seized the market lead, and to meet the challenge Cadbury's scaled down the production of Cocoa Essence and in 1911 developed their own treated brand, Bournville Cocoa, which had a more pronounced chocolate flavour than the Rowntree's product and was an immediate success. In 1905, however, Cadbury's made a technical leap in another product area which was to revolutionise its fortunes in the new century.

The search for a better milk chocolate formula had been going on among British and American manufacturers since a Swiss chocolate maker called Daniel Peter, working with the chemist Henri Nestlé, produced the first version in 1875 by blending condensed milk (a Nestlé invention) with cocoa powder and sugar, and driving off the water content to produce a crumb-like substance that was then mixed with additional cocoa butter, chocolate liquor and vanilla. Milk and chocolate had been notoriously difficult to blend because milk is mostly composed of water and cocoa butter mostly of fat.

Some credit Sir Hans Sloane, the seventeenth-century London landowner and progenitor of the British Museum, with having invented the idea of mixing the powdered bean with milk after a visit to Jamaica. Sloane, who gave his name to Sloane Street and Sloane Square in London's fashionable Knightsbridge, is reputed to have sold his formula to a Soho grocer who then sold it on to the Cadburys. Whether this story is true or not, Cadbury's did produce the first British milk chocolate in 1897, made with powdered milk, cocoa and sugar, but it was unpleasantly dry and gritty and the firm did not regard it as successful.

It was George Cadbury Jr., who had been so unwillingly plucked out of his scientific studies at Cambridge to learn about chocolate technology at Germany's Stollwerck plant, who made the breakthrough at Bournville in 1904. George's scientific training contributed to a great deal of rationalisation and standardisation of the manufacturing processes at Bournville, and early in his enforced career he had introduced a key appliance for covering or 'enrobing' centres with liquid chocolate. This led in 1927 to the installation of automatic moulding machinery, doubling output. He also applied scientific method to the chocolate recipes, and one of his key tasks in this area was to improve the unsatisfactory formula for milk chocolate.

He set up a laboratory and appointed a qualified analytical chemist, N. P. Booth, in 1901. Within three years his team had produced what would become Cadbury's Dairy Milk, a formula based on the Swiss method of condensing the milk to one-eighth of its volume, grinding the chocolate into fine particles and keeping the milk and chocolate mixture warm and moving before being moulded into blocks. Across the Atlantic, Milton Hershey in his brand-new factory on the outskirts of Chicago was also trying to find a formula that successfully blended fresh milk with chocolate and in late 1905, just after Cadbury's, he discovered it by boiling a heavily sugared milk mixture very slowly under low heat in a vacuum. The resulting taste was slightly soured, a distinctive difference to this day between American and European milk chocolate.

The Cadbury family board, all but one of whom Sir Adrian Cadbury remembers meeting when he was a boy, was initially divided on whether to launch milk chocolate at all. William Adlington Cadbury, George's nephew and chairman of the firm, was adamant that the company's future lay with 'good dark chocolate', and the board also jibbed at George's request for plant capable of producing twenty tons of milk chocolate a week. The directors thought five tons was ample capacity. George won: in time production was to reach five hundred tons a week.

When Dairy Milk was launched in 1905, it wiped the floor with every other chocolate on the market, and by 1913 was the biggest-selling line for the company, remaining its top brand ever since. Cadbury's first factory away from Bournville was set up in 1911 at Knighton, in the dairy country of the Shropshire/Staffordshire border, to process milk for the new product. Pure ground cocoa was transported from Bournville to Knighton to be mixed with condensed milk and sugar, then dried in ovens until all the moisture had been removed and the mixture was reduced to a crumb-like consistency. This was then returned to Bournville to be made into Dairy Milk chocolate. As demand soared in the 1920s, a second milk-condensing plant was built at Frampton on Severn and by 1925 two more were opened at Marlbrook and Bangor-on-Dee. During the First World War, these plants along with Bournville changed over to food production: butter, condensed milk and cocoa-and-milk powder, cheese, fruit pulp, biscuits and dried vege-tables, much of which went to supply the army in France.

Neither Fry's nor Rowntree's ever produced a milk chocolate to match the success of Cadbury's Dairy Milk, although in the mid-1930s Rowntree's, which had hit back with the hugely popular Kit Kat biscuit bar, invented an aerated milk chocolate, the Aero bar. This caused a legal conflict between Rowntree and Cadbury, only finally resolved by the out-break of the Second World War. Ironically, when the US company Mars first set up in Britain, in a small kitchen at Slough in 1933, its candy bars were coated with Cadbury's Dairy Milk, and this arrangement went on for some years. Although it gave Cadbury's a useful volume of business, Sir

Adrian Cadbury observes that had he been running the company then, he would 'never have let any competitor have my chocolate'.

The 'glass and a half of milk' – the amount of fresh milk claimed to go into every half-pound bar of Cadbury's Dairy Milk – became one of the most successful advertising slogans and visual logos ever devised. Introduced in 1928 under the dynamic sales leadership of Paul Cadbury, no one in the firm today can trace its origins precisely, or knows who first devised it. Sir Adrian Cadbury, a usually omniscient authority on the firm's history, thinks it probably came from something as mundane as a printer's mock-up for a label or trade brochure. The slogan above the picture of milk pouring into the chocolate bar has gone round the world for over seventy years, a powerful image reinforcing the idea of the product's food value and nutrition. It is, says Adrian Cadbury, technically correct in its claim, although the precise recipe for any chocolate is closely guarded by its makers, and there were many stories between the wars of industrial spies infiltrating the great chocolate companies, paid by their competitors.

Each chocolate's particular flavour is a combination of the type of cocoa bean, the way it is roasted and how the various ingredients are treated or 'cooked'. When Adrian Cadbury was learning the chocolate-maker's art on the production lines in the 1950s, he recalls that there were always two different teams working on each flavour, so that the people in one team never knew what the people in the other were contributing. 'The process is difficult to copy,' he says. Even standardised formulas vary and modify over time, so that now, Adrian's taste-buds tell him that the Cadburys Dairy Milk made in Ireland and New Zealand comes closest to the taste of George Cadbury Jr.'s original.

The First World War brought one member of the family to prominence in a most un-Cadbury-like activity – armed combat. Egbert, always known as Bertie, born in 1893, was the youngest of the sons of George and Elizabeth (Elsie) Cadbury, and also the tallest of the family at six foot three. Bertie was the most colourful Cadbury of his generation, and it is perhaps no coincidence that his son, Peter Egbert Cadbury, born in 1918, attracted the most publicity in his turn among the mid-century Cadburys, becoming a controversial entrepreneur in television and the leisure industry, and constantly figuring in the gossip columns.

Bertie became skilled at sports from golf to fishing and followed his brother Laurence up to Cambridge in 1912 after a second attempt at the entrance examinations for Trinity College. In August 1914, he immediately gave up his law studies to sign on as an able seaman in the Royal Navy, writing many years later: 'We were all in a desperate hurry to enlist because we thought the War would be over by Christmas and unless we were quick we might miss the fun. We all thought we should be back at Cambridge for the Lent Term.'

He had a rough few months serving in minesweepers, on one occasion writing to Laurence about his ship's narrow escapes in mine-infested waters: 'Don't tell Mother or Father or they will have hells [sic] own needles.' In May 1915 he swapped minesweepers for the infant Royal Naval Air Service as a flight sub-lieutenant and for over a year chased Zeppelins without a kill. Germany's fighting airships were much faster than the aircraft flown by the RNAS and the newly formed Royal Flying Corps, which had primitive and very short-range armaments – little more than service rifles, shotguns with chain ammunition and something called 'Ranken darts'. Then in October 1916, during the first major Zeppelin raid on Britain, over Lowestoft, Bertie and two other pilots shot down a Zeppelin, the 121, at close quarters. Bertie was awarded the Distinguished Service Cross. Eight months later, he chased two Zeppelins out to sea but at eighty to ninety miles an hour could not catch them, and at twenty miles out a petrol pipe fractured in the cockpit. Bertie stuck a finger over the broken end and just made it home to Yarmouth, soaked in petrol. 'Not a very pleasant trip,' he noted laconically in his diary.

When the Royal Air Force was formed in April 1918, the station at Great Yarmouth became a wing of the RAF with three squadrons, one of them commanded by Bertie, now a captain. On 5 August, while Bertie was listening to his new wife Mary singing at a charity concert at Yarmouth, he was summoned to the base to learn that three Zeppelins were fifty miles out to the north-east, over the North Sea. Racing several fellow-pilots to the base, where there was only one plane – a De

Havilland DH4 fighter, not a seaplane – with the necessary speed and climb to catch the Zeppelins, he 'took a running jump into the pilot's seat', beating his closest competitor 'by one-fifth of a second'. With him was his observer, Bob Leekie, DSO, DSC. They chased the Zeppelins, which were in V formation, and shot down the leading airship.

As Bertie prepared to pursue the other two, his engine cut out and he had just managed to restart it when the observer's gun jammed after opening fire on a second Zeppelin. He and Leekie were forced to abandon the chase and the next half-hour, he wrote, 'diving through 12,000 feet of cloud in inky blackness on a machine that I had been told could not land at night, even if I ever made land again, was the most terrible I have ever experienced'. He landed at Sedgeford, missing another circling aircraft by inches, only to find that two of his 100-pound bombs had failed to release and too heavy a landing could have set them off underneath him.

The Zeppelin they had shot down was the new 170, the pride of the German Airship Service, which was carrying Fregatenkapitän Peter Strasser, the head of the service. None of the Zeppelins succeeded in dropping a single bomb that night, and the Commodore of Lowestoft recommended Bertie for a Victoria Cross for his courage in attacking two Zeppelins out to sea in an aircraft with no flotation gear. Bertie and Leekie were in fact awarded the Distinguished Flying Cross.

When war broke out, Bertie's elder brother Laurence, born in 1889, had just begun work at Bournville, interrupted by a year travelling round America. He was the first graduate in the family to work in the business. The children of both George Cadbury's marriages had been brought up together as one family, but inevitably Elsie's three sons Laurence, Norman and Bertie, tended to do things together and to share adventures. At school Laurence showed an interest in engineering and mathematics but when he reached Trinity College, Cambridge, he decided to read economics, then a new subject on the university's syllabus. Curiously, it was classified as an offshoot of the school of moral philosophy and Laurence's first tutor was a moral philosopher with no knowledge of economics, although the senior professor was the famous economist Alfred Marshall, author of *Principles of Economics*.

Laurence had been fascinated by guns since he was a small boy, and now, in 1908 as an undergraduate, he began collecting antique firearms along with many other objects. Attempting to test an ancient gun with a powder charge one day, he blew out the entire window frame of his college room. He developed a knowledgeable interest in Jacobean oak furniture and always insisted on personally collecting any purchase from the dealer in case an unscrupulous vendor had a quick copy made before delivery. Some of his best pieces, including a twenty-two-foot-long refectory table carved in one piece, are preserved in the Selly Manor Museum, the Tudor house that his father had transported bodily to Bournville and reconstructed, under Laurence's supervision, between 1912 and 1917.

Laurence was an obsessive collector who 'kept everything', according to his son Adrian – tin trunks full of dance programmes from university, First World War correspondence, and the largest collection of antique cannon outside the armoury in the Tower of London. This was kept in the grounds at The Davids, the home of Laurence and his wife for more than forty years. He was also an adventurous traveller, raced at Brooklands in a twenty-horsepower Vauxhall and went prospecting for gold in the Yukon during his year out in the States, where he also gained experience of automation at the National Cash Register Company. He was preparing to introduce it at Bournville when war broke out on 4 August 1914. Like Bertie, he was in a hurry to volunteer before it was 'over by Christmas', and formed a Quaker ambulance unit – the first of many to serve with the French army – with his friend Philip Noel-Baker, later a well-known writer and Labour politician. Laurence's cousin Paul, Barrow's only son, also volunteered for the Friends' Ambulance Unit: he had been up at Cambridge just one day when war was declared. Laurence was transport officer for the unit and took his Vauxhall to France with him. He was eventually awarded the Croix de Guerre as well as a military OBE for his war service.

Laurence and Bertie introduced new ways of doing things when they and Paul returned to the family business in 1919 – Laurence and Paul to Bournville, where Paul was to drive the great marketing campaigns of the 1920s and 1930s, and Bertie to Fry's, which had just been merged with Cadbury's under a new holding company, the British Cocoa and

Chocolate Company. Laurence's first action at Bournville was to bring in automated production lines; something his father had resisted because he did not want to put any employees out of work. The innovation immediately created expansion as well as saving production costs: two new six-storey buildings were needed to accommodate the long production lines, providing two-and-a-half times the old floor space. Productivity per employee also increased by two-and-a-half times and employment actually rose by 10 per cent. In 1927 Laurence introduced automatic moulding machines from Denmark, which cut production costs by 40 per cent and enabled Cadbury's to reduce the price of its popular half-pound Dairy Milk bars from two shillings in 1921 to eight pence in 1934. Sales rose from seventy tons a week in 1921 to 250 tons a week in 1936: chocolate was clearly one luxury that depression-hit Britain still felt it could afford.

Laurence's modernisation plans were sometimes too much for the Cadbury's board, which turned down his proposal to demolish the old power station and replace it with a new one. Soon after this setback, the power station was destroyed by fire and when the Bournville fire brigade arrived they found Laurence already on the scene wearing his First World War tin hat. He said he had seen the flames from his house and had driven over as fast as he could, but apocryphal stories soon circulated round Bournville about the convenience of the fire, which meant that Laurence got his modern plant.

At the end of the war Bertie had to choose between staying in the RAF, which he was urged to do, or seeking a business career, for which he engagingly admitted he had no qualifications. There was no suitable post at Bournville, so he asked his half-brother Edward and brothers on the Bournville board whether they could find him a vacancy at Fry's, now under Cadbury's umbrella. 'But they quite understandably refused to help,' he wrote. 'They thought that having only so recently joined up with Fry's, they did not want to appear to be anxious to foist unemployed members of the Cadbury family on the Frys. So my family refused to sponsor my application and I was left to my own devices.'

He finally managed to persuade Roderick Fry, the chairman, to give him an interview and was offered a job in May 1919 at £300 a year to work in four different areas of the business – employment, wages, engineering and power production. So began, he recalled sunnily in 1963, 'the happiest and most interesting business life that has ever been enjoyed by anyone. I formed a great attachment and affection for the old Fry directors, no one could have been kinder, more helpful or considerate, than they were to me.'

Fry's business had been going downhill for some time before the war. Although the legal battles over cocoa adulteration claims were well in the past, new wrangles had surfaced over pricing. Up to 1910 the big three cocoa manufacturers observed a sort of gentlemen's cartel on prices, a common practice among early Quaker traders, who did not approve of competitive pricing. To a lesser extent such co-operation among the cocoa companies also applied to advertising campaigns, although Rowntree board minutes suggest that Cadbury's did not always play by the rules. But the big three were becoming wary of the public getting wind of the agreements: since the rows over 'the Cocoa Press' and their ownership of newspapers, anything that smacked of collusion was to be avoided.

In the years before the First World War, while Cadbury's and Rowntree's battled it out between their premium cocoas, Fry's had chosen to go for the cheaper end of the market, although this was shrinking as working people gained more purchasing power. They had other problems of production and logistics, caused by the Fry family's decision to stay in the congested centre of Bristol, adding more and more haphazard buildings to the factory – even a chapel was converted for manufacturing use – while Cadbury's expanded and modernised in their green-field site at Bournville. Fry's also made some disastrous decisions in the first years of the war, choosing to scale down their hugely successful Chocolate Cream brand when wartime sugar rationing was imposed. Instead, they cut corners on quality to produce a plain chocolate which proved gritty and unpalatable.

In 1916, with their sales falling behind Cadbury's, Fry's opened merger negotiations with Bournville. Rowntree's, though not in Fry's parlous position, went further, raising the possibility of combining all three firms. Seebohm Rowntree, the chairman's son, and Arnold

Rowntree, his nephew, were in favour of this radical step and a meeting between senior directors of all three companies was arranged for March 1918 when suddenly Joseph Rowntree vetoed the idea. Although his reasons were never made clear, he had been working to democratise the company through an elected works council and had plans for a profit-sharing scheme, which was later adopted. He may have feared that these reforms would not survive a merger: Cadbury Brothers, for all the pioneering work conditions at Bournville, and a consultative system that operated well enough between management and employees, preferred to retain decision-making authority, including the disposition of profits, in their own hands.

Years later, in 1930, Seebohm Rowntree as chairman went cap in hand to Bournville to discuss a merger with the four leading Cadburys – Edward, Paul, William and Laurence. The answer then was no, probably because Cadbury's thought it could let its rival twist in the wind and then pick it up cheaply later. If so, the strategy backfired, because after reaching the pit of its fortunes in 1931, when it was forced to cut back production to a three-day week, Rowntree's came under new and dynamic management from George Harris, who had married into the Rowntree family. Harris was responsible for introducing a stream of new products that remain star sellers to this day – Black Magic, Kit Kat, Aero, Dairy Box and Smarties.

But in 1918, Cadbury's was being forced to make a decision about Fry's. Nestlé, the Swiss chocolate-maker, was making overtures to the ailing Bristol firm. (Seventy years later, in 1988, Nestlé would finally succeed in acquiring what was by then Rowntree Mackintosh, a coup that gave it a quarter of the UK confectionery market.) Cadbury's was also sharply aware of growing American competition from Mars and Hershey. Stopping short of a full merger or takeover (which eventually happened in the 1930s, when the old J. S. Fry was liquidated and a new J. S. Fry formed as a Cadbury subsidiary), a consortium arrangement was agreed under a holding company, the British Cocoa and Chocolate Company. This held the ordinary shares of both companies and issued its own equity to Cadbury and Fry shareholders in proportion to the value of their stock.

Cadbury's equity was valued at four times that of Fry, but Barrow Cadbury, who became chairman of the new holding company, was disposed to be generous to the Fry family and allocated them one-third of the equity. (John Crosfield, a grandson of George Cadbury, says that Barrow was probably 'too saintly for business', but over the merger he did join Edward and William in resisting opposition from George, who was still chairman in 1918.) Cadbury and Fry family members sat together on the board of the holding company but in practice, the two companies continued to be run as if they were independent of each other until the final merger in 1936.

This was the situation in which Bertie began his career with the Cadbury-controlled Fry's. Quickly realising that no amount of technical help offered by Bournville would be accepted by the Fry's board, he devoted most of his time at Fry's Union Street factory to developing sports facilities for the workforce. At last in 1920 the directors realised the impossibility of continuing in their tangle of old industrial buildings in Bristol, and moved the factory to a site outside the city, named Somerdale through a public competition. Somerdale remains an important centre for the production of Cadbury's Crunchie bars and Fry's products.

When George Cadbury died in 1922, his nephew William Adlington Cadbury, who had seen through the arduous negotiations with Portugal over the 'slave' plantations, and had served as Lord Mayor of Birmingham for the previous two years, succeeded him as chairman. Although at fifty-five William was already suffering from the lameness that would handicap him for the rest of his life, he remained head of the company during its great expansionist days between the wars, retiring only in 1937. His elder brother Barrow, now sixty, was also a Cadbury Brothers director, as were the three sons of George's two marriages: Edward, forty-nine, George Jr., forty-four, and Laurence, thirty-three.

Barrow, though never head of the company, was now the patriarch of the family (he lived to ninety-five) and looked the part with the great weeping moustache he had worn since his twenties and which became ever more luxuriant, flowing into a trimmed beard, as he grew to middle age. He was one of the last in the family to work a traditional apprenticeship, with a firm of cocoa brokers in London's Mincing Lane, and then, aged twenty, he made a two-month tour of the United States and Canada to study chocolate production in North America. More than sixty years later he recalled his crossing in 1882 on the White Star liner *Republic*, the last steamship to be equipped with four masts and a full set of sails, one of which burst with a loud explosion during an Atlantic gale. On his return he began work at Bournville, living with his father Richard at Moseley Hall and sharing his office, which was linked by a private passage to George's. Barrow underwent the usual training in all the production and packing departments before moving to sales and taking over responsibility for the travelling sales reps. In the 1880s there were only fourteen of these covering the whole country, and they would all turn up to the annual Bournville Christmas party clad formally in frock coats and silk hats.

Barrow also had responsibility for the accounts and personally entered up the firm's income and expenditure each week in a ledger. Such was the trust between the brothers Richard and George that cheques drawn on their private accounts were left in plain view along with those to be entered in the firm's ledger. After Richard died and Barrow became responsible for the much enlarged cashiers' department in the 1900s, he introduced new office technology to Bournville including the telephone, accounting machines, punched cards and type-writers.

Barrow had been left a huge block of Cadbury shares by his father but made an early decision to give most of his wealth away to a charitable trust, which is still administered by the family today. In this he was fully supported by his wife Geraldine, a fellow-Quaker whom he had married in 1891. Geraldine's father Alfred Southall exceeded even George and Richard Cadbury in his spartan habits; not only refusing to wear an overcoat in cold weather but also finding no need for carpet and curtains in his home. His daughter, though not so extreme in her plain living, had no desire to be the heir to a Cadbury fortune; indeed, she positively feared the prospect in her early years of marriage.

Geraldine, like George's second wife Elsie, would become one of the outstanding Cadbury wives in her own right as a social reformer and like Elsie, was honoured as a Dame of the British Empire. In 1947, six years after her death, James Chuter Ede, home secretary in the Attlee government, said that she 'did probably more for delinquent children than anybody in this country or any other. She was ahead of her time, but her faith will be justified.' Geraldine herself regarded Elizabeth Fry, the great Quaker prison reformer, as her 'patron saint', and in 1905 became involved with the new children's court, the first in Britain, set up by Birmingham's Watch Committee. Up to that time, children were tried in adult courts, often without their parents or guardians being present, and were liable to be given harsh prison sentences for the most trivial offences such as stealing fruit or playing football in the street.

Even with the new, more humane children's court, however, there was still nowhere except prison for a child to wait before its trial or before being sent to reform school. Geraldine and Barrow, who had already provided a well-equipped kindergarten for slum children in Greet, a poor suburb of Birmingham, now built and equipped a children's remand home, also the first of its kind in Britain. It had the atmosphere of a kindly boarding school and dormitories to sleep six to eight children each, the beds covered in cheerful red blankets. Both the warden and woman superintendent were chosen by Geraldine, and child offenders were henceforth treated quite differently. 'They're not bad kids,' the warden told one visitor. 'Most of these children here only need a good chance and they will turn into good citizens.'

Geraldine set one long-remembered example of compassion in action. She happened to be visiting the home one day when a small girl was brought in filthy dirty, her matted hair alive with lice. The superintendent declared that she could not touch the child's hair, she must be dealt with somewhere else. Without speaking, Geraldine took the child by the hand, led her to the bathroom and asked for a sturdy apron, scissors, brushes and soap. She then proceeded to do the job herself.

Geraldine and Barrow had three children, Dorothy, Paul and Geraldine Mary. Despite their parents' strong Quaker beliefs, they had a more relaxed childhood in their Edgbaston home than previous generations. Music was allowed, and Dorothy learned the piano while Paul had cello lessons. Dorothy Cadbury, born in 1892, was the first –

and only – female Cadbury to work in the company, which she joined in 1917, and she did it the traditional way, gaining experience in the various production processes, piping cream into moulds for twenty-five shillings a week and operating the wrapping machinery. She and her brother Paul were both appointed managing directors of Cadbury Brothers in 1919 and Dorothy was active in the firm all through the inter-war years, taking responsibility for the women in the workforce and their separate works council. In 1941, she found herself, for the space of just one meeting, acting chairman of the Bournville board; her brother Paul became chairman in 1959. Dorothy, who never married, retired from Cadbury's in 1952 and continued to look after her widowed father Barrow.

Paul came back from the Great War to marry a nurse he had met in the Friends' Ambulance Unit, Rachel Wilson, and to start his career at the top of the family firm, as a managing director. It was in the 1930s, however, that he made his greatest contribution. Between 1933 and 1939, said his son Charles, he was 'the power house', launching an aggressive marketing policy – 'two ounces for twopence' was one successful slogan – and building a dynamic sales force whom he called 'my boys'.

Cadbury's needed to be aggressive, because Rowntree's under George Harris had become a force to be reckoned with. Harris had powerful friends in industry, among them the American chocolate tycoon Forrest Mars, Simon Marks of Marks and Spencer and John Benjamin Sainsbury of the Sainsbury grocery chain. From all these marketing geniuses he learned about sales professionalism, the importance of the customer and of consumer research, then in its infancy. Aero chocolate, introduced in the mid–1930s, was Rowntree's longed-for challenger to Cadbury's Dairy Milk. It was advertised in a pseudo-scientific manner which claimed that its cellular, 'bubble' structure enabled it to be digested twice as fast as 'old-fashioned milk chocolate'.

In 1936, at the annual chocolate industry conference in Cheltenham, Cadbury's formally warned Rowntree's that its Aero advertising was offensive and prejudicial to good relations between the manufacturers. Paul Cadbury followed this up with a threat of litigation over the patents for the Aero process, and in 1937 the two firms were close to legal warfare. Cadbury's had developed its own process for aerating chocolate, but finally agreed not to market a cellular chocolate until after June 1938. Then the outbreak of war in September 1939 made the whole issue irrelevant.

Paul, like all the Cadburys since George – who believed in spending money 'while it is fresh' – established a charitable trust for his share of the family wealth. Like all the Cadburys too, he was deeply involved in Birmingham civic life, but although he gave money generously to the the handicapped and family welfare, his primary interest lay in town planning beyond the boundaries of Bournville, of which he was a leading trustee. During the Second World War he served on Birmingham City Council and was chairman of a research committee which produced a report in 1941 called *When We Build Again* as well as acting as honorary secretary of another group on postwar reconstruction in the West Midlands. After the war his book on the future of Birmingham town planning, called *Birmingham 50 Years On*, led to him being described by the Lord Mayor in 1965 as 'Father of the inner ring road plan and of the new Birmingham' – an accolade that today rings rather less triumphantly than it did in the 1960s.

By the 1930s, Cadbury's had become one of the most famous trade names in the country, and its Bournville works was one of the largest of any manufacturer. The novelist and playwright J. B. Priestley, visiting Birmingham in 1933 for his book *English Journey*, arrived in the city with preconceptions of metal-bashing mills, 'a city of big profits and narrow views which sent missionaries out of one gate and brass idols and machine-guns out of another'. The Birmingham Watch Committee, along with many other bodies of its kind, was something of a national butt for narrow-mindedness, but Priestley acknowledged, as he trundled into the city on a slow bus, that Birmingham was also a fertile source of scientific innovation from the steam engine to gas lighting to electro-plating, as well as a noted home of political free-thinking. (In what now seems a description of civic Arcadia, before Goering's bombers and the post-war planners' new brutalism got to work, Priestley also hymned the confident Victorian architecture of corporate Birmingham – 'an English provincial city that has the air and dignity that a great city should have'.)

Priestley was impressed by Bournville, by 1933 less a village, as he noted, than a small town in size and population. Like many others, he had thought of it as a company town and was surprised to find that the Bournville Trust acted like a local authority, leasing land to four public utility housing societies for building houses and renting or selling them to their members. Cadbury's employees were mingled with people of varied social and educational backgrounds from Birmingham and the surrounding area – artisans, teachers, professional and clerical workers. And the health record of the place, he noted, was still as striking in comparison with the rest of England as when George Cadbury had first ordered statistics to be drawn up: over the seven years ending in 1931, Bournville's death rate was half that of England and Wales, and infant mortality two-thirds that of neighbouring Birmingham. Although preferring, as he said, houses arranged around courtyards and small squares instead of detached and semi-detached villas lining roads as if 'sprinkled . . . out of a pepper-pot', Priestley's good socialist instincts had no doubts about the merits of the place: 'It is neither a great firm's private dormitory nor a rich man's toy, but a public enterprise that pays its way. It is one of the small outposts of civilisation, still ringed around with barbarism.'

The chocolate factory itself was also, to his eyes, the size of a small town engaged in the production of cocoa and chocolates of many kinds. He was shown round the works, from the crushing of the cocoa beans to the overalled men and young women looking after the '101 machines that pounded and churned and cooled and weighed and packed the chocolate, that covered the various bits of confectionery with chocolate, that printed labels and wrappers and cut them up and stuck them on and then packed everything into boxes that some other machine had made'. He learned 'the life history of an almond whirl', down to the 'little mechanical device that makes that whirl on the top', and saw 'thousands of marshmallows hurrying on an endless moving band of silvered paper to the slow cascade of chocolate that swallowed them for a moment and then turned them out on the other side, to be cooled, as genuine chocolate marshmallows'. He also saw solemn conclaves of men who looked like scientists and engineers deliberating over bits of coconut dipped in chocolate and other trifles: 'When you buy a box of these things, you have also bought the services of a whole army of people . . . I will never feel quite the same now about a box of chocolates.'

The Bournville production lines that Priestley saw in 1933 would still have been recognisable to Adrian Cadbury when he was learning the ropes of chocolate manufacture in the 1950s. On a visit to Bournville in 1998, the former chairman was greeted by a retired colleague, now a demonstrator in the mini-theme park of Cadbury World, and the pair reminisced as the veteran chocolate-maker poured molten white chocolate on to marble slabs to cool it, folding and patting the solidifying pool with spatulas like huge butter-pats.

But Priestley's view was not all rose-tinted. Noting the enormous range of leisure facilities – recreation grounds and concert hall, continuation schools, music, drama, hobbies and lectures all humming away after working hours – and the provision of medical care and pensions long before the welfare state was dreamed of, he marvelled at the sight, in a factory run for private profit, of 'nearly all the facilities for leading a full and happy life'. Once you had joined the firm, you need never move out of its protective shadow: 'No factory workers in Europe have ever been better off than these people.'

It was only, he suggested, when one took a longer view that the doubts began. 'Is it good for people to see the factory as the centre of their lives even if that factory offers them so much, and so much that is genuinely significant?' When Cadbury's had opened a factory in Tasmania in 1922 to serve the Australian market, complete with its own Bournville-type village, Priestley noted that the Australian employees had refused to accept recreation grounds and concert halls, saying they would rather have the money in higher wages to spend as they wished. That was a true spirit of independence, said Priestley: the Australian was 'selling his labour and nothing else'. Priestley saw the benevolence of the Cadburys as a velvet chain binding their employees and leading them to suppose that life revolved around the production of cocoa and chocolate. If he had his way, he wrote, he would rather see workers combining to provide Bournville-type benefits for themselves, away from the factory, 'using their leisure, and demanding its increase, not as favoured employees but as citizens, free men and women'.

The Cadbury brothers and cousins – William, Barrow, Edward, George Jr., Paul and Laurence – were still firmly in control at Bournville, and Bertie was enjoying himself at Fry's, but the protean reach of old George Cadbury into the world of newspaper publishing meant that the risky politics and economics of Fleet Street constantly intruded into the relatively well-ordered world of Bournville. Laurence, a shy and reserved man of intellectual and cultural interests who would never have chosen a career in newspaper publishing (and who was, anyway, more Tory than Liberal in his political sentiments), found himself catapulted in 1930 into the chair of the Daily News company when his half-brother Edward retired. Henry, the unlikely businessman who had ruled the *Daily News* with a surprisingly decisive hand, had already retired because of poor health, and Edward had co-opted on to the board Laurence's old economics tutor at Cambridge, Sir Walter Layton, then editor of the *Economist*.

Laurence's first action, on Layton's advice, was to acquire the only other national daily to support Liberal values, the ailing *Daily Chronicle*, which was losing over £8,000 a week. The two papers were merged and in June 1930 appeared as the *News Chronicle*, which quickly achieved a circulation of 1,200,000, twice that of the old *Daily News*. It was to become a favourite of Fleet Street professionals for its first-class writing and radical opinions. Its ultimate fate in 1960, sold to the *Daily Mail*, which then closed it down, was a devastating failure for Laurence, who was universally pilloried for the decision. Perhaps the real source of the tragedy – and both in human and historical terms it was a tragedy for the industry – lay back in the Boer War when George Cadbury allowed his conscience over jingoism to lead him into the quicksands of newspaper ownership. The Liberal party as a political force did not long survive its greatest parliamentary triumph in 1906, and with the hindsight of ninety years, the Cadburys would have done better to stick to what they did best.

Layton became executive chairman of the company, which also published London's evening *Star*, and Bertram Crosfield, Henry's old friend, took over both papers as chief executive. Laurence held the purse strings and ultimate power, although his relationship with Layton was always ambivalent, still coloured by their student–teacher past. Layton also nurtured vain ambitions to buy the paper from the Cadburys, and longed at times to control it absolutely. Laurence once complained that he was treated like 'a nagging outsider'.

For years Laurence followed the same divided weekly schedule, spending Mondays and Tuesday mornings in Bournville, catching the London train on Tuesday afternoon to spend Wednesday at the *News Chronicle* and Thursday at the Bank of England, where he was appointed a director in 1936. He would then return to Bournville on Friday. (One of the changes he suggested at the bank was to replace the crackling white five-pound note with a smaller, multicoloured version resembling the Scottish fiver: opposed for many years by the bank's board, the change was finally introduced as a fraud-combating device in 1957.)

Adrian Cadbury's second wife Susan, who used to be Laurence Cadbury's secretary, recalls how he used to take his own farm eggs to London with him, in an eggbox tied with an elastic band, and another container with rashers of bacon, all of which he carried in his briefcase. In his London flat in Curzon Street, Mayfair, he would make breakfast to his own eccentric recipe, sprinkling the bacon with Bisto powder before putting it under the grill on a Pyrex plate, and eating the result with a boiled egg. He usually dined at one of his clubs, the Athenaeum or the Oxford and Cambridge. He travelled to the bank by No. 9 bus from Piccadilly, and when the Red Arrow single-deckers came in, complained about the inconvenience of having to proffer the exact fare. When he returned home, the £25 spending money which Susan handed to him in an envelope each Tuesday was often barely touched.

Newspaper circulation wars in the 1930s were rougher than ever before. The infant *News Chronicle* was faced with competitors like Lord Beaverbrook's *Daily Express*, flying the Empire flag for all it was worth, and Lord Rothermere's *Daily Mail*, which was touching two million copies a day. The *Daily Herald*, backed by the Labour party, seemed able to sustain the most enormous losses, while the tabloid *Daily Mirror* pandered to the depths of triviality with such 'stories' as having a film starlet sit on a fertile hen's egg to see if she could hatch it. In this climate, and with *The Times* under editor Geoffrey Dawson watering down anything seriously critical of Hitler's Germany, the *News Chronicle* shone like a small beacon of honesty and quality. It boasted the best team of political writers in Fleet Street, including Vernon Bartlett and A. J. Cummings.

But the *News Chronicle*'s brave stand against appeasement involved personal attacks on Neville Chamberlain as prime minister that caused a family rift among the Cadburys. Paul Cadbury angrily told his cousin Laurence that he was giving up the paper in favour of the *Birmingham Post*. By this time, with Layton seconded to a government job, Laurence was at last able to take full control of the paper, apart from a surreal couple of months in the summer of 1941 when he was hauled into high-level international diplomacy. On 22 June 1941 Germany invaded its erstwhile ally, the Soviet Union, and a few days later Laurence was summoned to Whitehall in his capacity as a director of the Bank of England by Hugh Dalton, minister of economic warfare. Dalton asked him to head a British economic mission to Moscow with the task of assessing what the USSR needed to fight Germany and how materials could be provided and paid for.

Laurence flew to Moscow on 27 June, to be received by Stalin's number-two, the foreign minister Vyacheslav Molotov, who had been involved in shaping the infamous Nazi-Soviet non-aggression pact in 1939 under the noses of an Anglo-French delegation trying to set up their own alliance with the USSR. Laurence noted amusedly in a letter home that the British ambassador, Sir Stafford Cripps, looked depressed and dejected, 'as well he might be after seeing his policy of appeasement fail so ignominiously'. Relations were still wary between the two countries, but within two weeks an Anglo-Soviet pact of mutual assistance was signed, to be extended to a twenty-year alliance in 1942.

As the exchange of information became more relaxed, relief that the power of the Soviet Union was now turned against Hitler was reflected in a rush of goodwill to the new allies. In one of his letters, Laurence described 'Uncle Joe' Stalin as 'quite a benevolent old gentleman, his hair very slightly grey, a shrewd twinkle in his eyes and a quiet, rather aloof, unassuming manner'. The Soviet leader was dressed for the signing of the pact on 12 July in a grey alpaca jacket with no decorations, and dark trousers tucked into high boots. Perhaps sardonically, Laurence recorded that Stalin's 'strong, short, rather peasant hands . . . do not seem to be either dripping with or stained with the blood of his liquidated rivals'.

The talks were repeatedly stymied over the question of Russian payment, with the Soviets bringing up one obstacle after another, from fears of a German blockade of the USSR that would prevent the shipping of gold, to technical problems of accountancy between the Soviet central bank, Gosbank, and the Bank of England. Eventually the agreement was signed and Laurence flew home in a Catalina seaplane without seats in which he took turns in one of the pilot's seats during their four-hour rests. The flight was rough and plagued by icing problems, and at one point the plane crash-dived to fifty feet above the sea to avoid a pursuing Heinkel fighter.

Back in the calmer atmosphere of Fleet Street, Threadneedle Street and Bournville, Laurence found that the new climate of cross-party co-operation under the coalition led by Winston Churchill suited his own temperament, and the hunger for news of any kind meant constantly rising circulation. But in the world after the war, Laurence would not be able to save a dying paper in a dying political culture. The post-war years would also bring a string of personal tragedies to Laurence and his wife Joyce, and eventually, under the pressures of growing international competition, force the sixth generation of Cadburys to relinquish personal control of their famous business.

CHAPTER 4:

MOULDING THE MODERN FIRM

IN MAY 1940, as France surrendered to the Nazis and Britain suddenly faced the threat of invasion from just across the Channel, part of Bournville was secretly being turned over to the manufacturing of munitions and war materials ranging from rockets to gas masks. With chocolate output severely cut by civilian rationing (three ounces a week for all confectionery) and restrictions on the import of cocoa and sugar, as well as on domestic milk supply, where more was now needed to replace imported butter and cheese, there was plenty of spare capacity, and the mould-makers' department was immediately pressed into service for light metal work. The first job, begun immediately after the fall of France on 10 May, was to build fifty-three vertical milling machines for rifle factories. Companies and government departments that moved into the site included Joseph Lucas Ltd., the Birmingham motor and aero parts manufacturer, the Austin Motor Company and the ministries of food and of works.

In July a new subsidiary company called Bournville Utilities was set up to manage the operations, although no word of its activities was published in the Bournville works magazine until July 1943, and then only in a vague reference to 'products other than cocoa and chocolate'.

Full details were only made public in the May 1945 issue of the magazine, after the war was over. As it turned out, however, German intelligence was fully aware of Bournville's non-chocolate activities, in spite of the factory being painstakingly camouflaged with strips of brown and green hessian attached to wire netting: a Luftwaffe map discovered after the war showed the site in alarming detail, though it was never directly bombed.

The formation of Bournville Utilities, which was run by Laurence Cadbury and occupied over half the area of the chocolate works, seems initially to have been the source of some disagreement among the family directors. The Quaker ethos of non-violence was still very strong in the family, and once again, as in the First World War, the main Cadbury war effort was directed into the Friends' Ambulance Unit, which Paul took the lead in reconstituting, and which eventually had active units in nearly every theatre of war, including China. Paul seems to have been opposed to the use of Bournville for war production, although the reason may have had more to do with who would manage the seconded Cadbury workers than with Quaker principles over munitions: aside from aircraft parts, most of what was produced at Bournville was defensive in purpose rather than offensive, such as gas masks and anti-aircraft rockets, though the filling of rockets was only taken on after a good deal of hesitation from the family.

Paul's cousin George Cadbury Jr. wrote on 1 June 1940 to Edward, who had become chairman on William's retirement in 1937, about a memorandum received from Paul which raised 'difficult questions'.

> I am afraid I find it difficult to agree with all he [Paul] says, In the first place I find it very difficult to see in what way Hitler can be opposed except by force. The Danes, who had disbanded their army, have been overrun and as far as we know treated just as brutally as any other nation. The hideously cruel treatment of fleeing men and women makes one feel one must oppose the demon by all means in one's power. I am afraid, therefore, that although I feel all war to be wrong and that one should do one's utmost to eliminate war,

I cannot say I would not help to oppose Hitler and the demon of Nazi-ism.

The immense bravery of our young men makes me feel I must back them up, although killing and warfare is repugnant to me. In my younger days I would willingly have gone to prison rather than fight, but now the merciless killing of women and children, which may easily come to this country, makes me feel that civilisation itself is in danger of being extinguished . . .

I also have a strong feeling of duty to our workpeople. I cannot hand that over to deputies. It would be much easier to resign or even salve one's conscience by forgoing part of one's salary, but I feel that would not satisfy me. I think my duty is to stand with Laurence in managing Bournville and looking after the welfare of our people in these difficult times.

We have stood for something in industry and I could not lightly let my life's work go.

It comes, therefore to this.

I cannot feel on conscientious grounds that I should not respond to the nation's call.

I cannot see how it would be possible to divide Bournville into two parts.

If it is agreed to try, I feel I must take responsibility on both sides . . .

I am afraid we shall not all see eye to eye on these matters. We must be tolerant of each other's views as we always have been. I am prepared to do my part whatever it may be, but I feel that does entail managing Bournville and its workers whatever happens.

Sir Adrian Cadbury knows of no fundamental moral disagreement in the family over the wartime use of Bournville, but suggests that operating two very different manufacturing businesses on the same site would have raised problems of logistics and security. There was also concern that the Bournville workforce, many of whom were being retrained from such tasks as packing chocolates to filling respiratory canisters, should continue to be managed in the Bournville way and under Cadbury's aegis.

Over the five years of its existence, Bournville Utilities turned out millions of jerry cans for use in the desert war, where petrol had to be transported long distances overland; wings and fuel tank doors for Lancaster bombers; gun mounts, fairings and doors for Spitfires, and anti-aircraft rockets, among much else. The aircraft parts section was run by Lucas for the Ministry of Aircraft Production, and the manufacture of self-sealing aircraft tanks for Spitfires and Lancasters was taken over from Dunlop, releasing the rubber company's plant to concentrate on the production of tyres. Bournville's biggest single war job was the assembly of more than five million service respirators and 6.3 million canisters for use in the event of full-scale gas warfare, which mercifully never happened.

Chocolate production during the war was restricted to a small range of moulded block chocolate (milk chocolate was at barely half the pre-war level because of the diversion of milk into other foodstuffs), large quantities of cocoa and ration chocolate for the armed forces and two-pound blocks of chocolate, together with powdered citric acid, packed in tins for provisioning lifeboats on Royal Navy and merchant navy ships. There were no more fancy assortments, which were labour-intensive to produce. After the war, Cadbury's production would be on a far more modest scale than that of the 1930s, with only about sixty product lines compared with 237 before the war. With a highly automated production process, it would have been uneconomic to attempt the pre-war range, but sales were not affected; indeed, they rose from £14m a year in 1939 to £85m a year in 1959, while the workforce expanded worldwide from 16,000 to 27,000 over the same period.

Laurence Cadbury had succeeded his half-brother Edward as chairman of Cadbury Brothers in 1944, when he also became chairman of the holding company that controlled Fry's. He held both of these posts until 1959. When the war ended, he presided over a rebuilding of the Bournville factory to include more floors, and every Friday, on his return from the *News Chronicle* and Bank of England in London, he would make a personal tour of inspection round Bournville, nodding greetings to familiar employees.

At home, he was the head of a typically large and good-looking Cadbury family – four sons and two daughters – whose births spread over twenty years from Julian, the eldest, to Jocelyn, the youngest, born in 1946. During the war the three youngest children – Veronica, Anthea and Dominic – had been evacuated to Canada, returning in 1944. His wife Joyce came from a Unitarian rather than a Quaker family and gave up her scholarship to Girton College, Cambridge, after a year reading English in order to marry Laurence in 1925. She was nineteen and he was thirty-seven, almost twice her age. They set up home at The Davids, just across the Bristol Road from the house where Laurence had grown up, the Manor. (Cadburys tend to stay rooted to their homes: Sir Adrian, like his father, has only ever lived in one house since he was first married in 1956.)

The Davids got its curious name from the previous owners, a pair of brothers whose surname was David. Laurence and Joyce extended it to a large, rambling house with sixteen and a half acres of wooded grounds which, Adrian recalls, 'we used to think quite a normal sized garden for a family home'. After it was pulled down in the early 1990s, seventy-five houses were built on the site. Family life was close and happy, bordering on the idyllic as the children grew up. Laurence encouraged them to read, learn poems by heart and discuss books at meals, except for breakfast, when he did not approve of talking of any kind: he used to prop his copy of *The Times* on a reading frame large enough to discourage contact and breakfasts were silent affairs, presided over by a gigantic stuffed figure of a bear in the dining-room.

At other meals, however, he wanted lively and informed conversation. Like Dickens' Mr Gradgrind, he preferred facts to opinion and liked being told new pieces of information. Sometimes he would quiz the boys on books or literary allusions and when Adrian, who for some reason he always called Bill, got something right he would say, 'Bill gets the bag of nuts.' When the children were very young he would place a penny on the dining table and gradually move it towards the child who had managed to avoid making a mess. Other financial incentives were on offer as they grew older. Laurence hated pigeons and particularly cuckoos, whose call irritated him: there was a standing reward of half a crown for the shooting of a pigeon and ten shillings for a cuckoo, though cuckoos always managed to avoid their fate and that reward was never claimed.

Julian, the eldest son, born two months before his mother's twenty-first birthday, had engineering flair like his father and the two loved to use the workshop Laurence had fitted up in the basement of The Davids. As well as making petrol-engined boats controlled by radio, Julian cast his own lead soldiers and during holidays from Eton in the war he helped to produce aircraft parts at Bournville Utilities. Early in 1945 he joined the Royal Engineers and after technical training at Trinity College, Cambridge – his father's and uncle Bertie's old college – he was commissioned in the summer of 1946 and posted the following year to the First Airborne Squadron, Royal Engineers, of the Sixth Airborne Division of Arnhem fame. He was stationed in Palestine at the height of the revolt against the British Mandate, and around the Suez Canal until his national service was over in the summer of 1948, when he was demobilised with the rank of captain. During his time with the sappers he became expert with explosives and the disposal of mines and salvaged the Allenby Bridge over the river Jordan, which had been blown up by insurgents and was regarded as irreparable. He was also mentioned in dispatches for a daring rescue of a fellow-soldier the day before his demob.

Julian returned to Cambridge and spent the next two years reading economics. It seemed as if he had got engineering out of his system, because now he was bent on a business career. In 1950 he was about to join Bournville and had begun to prepare himself for a trip to study cocoa-growing regions on behalf of the firm. W. N. Hallett, engineering director at Bournville, said: 'We must have him here. He has the right sort of enquiring mind and asks the right questions.' It was not to be. Julian had not lost his passion for things mechanical and had owned a succession of motorcycles from his schooldays. Towards the end of July 1950 he went to stay with a school friend in the South of France, riding his 1,000cc HRG Black Shadow. Near Moulins a French truck coming out of a side road failed to stop at the halt sign and hit Julian's bike. He was killed instantly.

Julian's death changed the course of Adrian's life. The two oldest brothers had always been close: now Adrian, who was in his first year at Cambridge and had not yet decided on a career, made up his mind that he should work for the family firm. Having done his national service in the Coldstream Guards, where he found out that he was 'more effective at getting things done than many of my brighter contemporaries', he had switched his degree course from modern languages to economics and studied under his father's old tutor, Professor Pigou, as well as Richard Kahn and Nicky Kaldor, later an adviser to Harold Wilson's Labour government of the 1960s. An exceptional sportsman like his father, he gained a rowing Blue and rowed in the 1952 Boat Race when Oxford won by twelve feet in a snowstorm, one of the smallest margins on record. He also skied for Cambridge against Oxford in 1951: skiing, as he has observed, is one of the few sports that combine seasons conveniently with rowing.

Starting at Bournville in 1952 under his father's chairmanship, Adrian spent the first eighteen months on the traditional induction round of working in every department of the factory and its administrative offices. His cousin Paul Cadbury, still in charge of sales, became a valued mentor. Paul and his cousin Michael, who became one of the most practising Quakers in the family, walking to Meeting every week well into his eighties, were 'very moral people', Adrian recalls. In 1965 he would have proof of that exceptional integrity when Paul passed over his eldest son Charles in favour of Adrian to succeed him as chairman.

A characteristic of the Cadbury family in business has been the way each generation from the brothers Richard and George onwards has contributed complementary skills, whether in engineering expertise, sales flair, financial acumen or interest in technological advances. This range of talent in generation after generation, defusing succession rivalry, is rare among family businesses and was a key factor in sustaining the Cadbury control for so long. It was reinforced by the Quaker ethos which worked on the pragmatic belief that looking after employees' welfare was good business as well as morally desirable.

'They were concerned for the human condition but were intensely practical,' says Adrian of his Quaker forebears. 'They believed that you should look for what people can offer, that everybody can be good at something, and that you should capitalise on that.' When Adrian became chairman, he constantly returned for guidance to his uncle Edward's pioneering 1912 book about the foundation of Bournville, *Experiments in Industrial Organization,* with its emphasis on developing the abilities of the workforce, especially those of the less skilled. When his younger brother Dominic rose to the top job in Cadbury Schweppes, Adrian urged him to take the book as his guide, and whatever continuity of culture remains in Cadbury Schweppes from the old Quaker chocolate firm is due in large measure to Uncle Edward's blueprint for a new kind of industrial relations.

In 1954 Paul took Adrian on a tour of the cocoa-growing areas in the Pacific – the journey that Julian had planned for himself – and of the company's Australian and New Zealand factories. Adrian then joined the buying office at Bournville, where he fully expected to remain for his career, as Paul had done in the sales office. In between he had spent six months on the family's other business, newspaper publishing, finding out how different the world of Fleet Street unions with its overmanning, 'Spanish practices' and restrictions on non-members was from Bournville, where Edward in 1912 had lamented the lack of interest among employees in banding together for their own benefit. Adrian's fluency in French and German, acquired during three childhood winters spent at a Swiss school to improve his health, gave him a usefulness in the newsroom beyond that of most heirs apparent. Later he wrote that the clearest lesson from his brief time in newspapers was 'what the consequences are of losing management control of a business'. Within six years this was to become brutal reality for his father.

Adrian's assumption of a career in Cadbury's buying office was soon disrupted as he was moved to the wages department, learned time-study techniques and was thrown into trade union negotiations. Cadbury's works councils were still segregated by gender in the 1950s, as was policy generally, with men only allowed into women's recreation areas at strictly limited times. Adrian was made a member of both the men's and women's works councils as management representative. Now he began to 'move up the ladder faster than I intended', acting as head of his department when the incumbent became ill and eventually becoming personnel director and the youngest member of the board. The buying office, meanwhile, turned out to be a backwater for promotion, his cousin John never progressing beyond buying director.

The board that Adrian joined in 1958 at the age of twenty-nine was still entirely family-run and basically structured in the same way as in 1899, with all its members known as managing directors and directly involved in the day-to-day running of the business, each with a finger in a number of pies rather than specific functional responsibilities. Although it met weekly, there was little time for long-range policy-making or planning discussions. The system had worked brilliantly in the pre-war world, but as the 1960s dawned, it became clear that the trading environment was changing and so was the nature of the competition; companies needed active growth strategies beyond yearly incremental profits, and the rise of the multinational was bringing competition in global markets. Cadbury's responded by diversifying into food products such as Smash instant mashed potato and Marvel instant milk, buying Pascall Murray, the mints makers, and a small meat company. In 1962 the British Cocoa and Chocolate Company, the holding company that spanned Cadbury's and Fry's, was floated on the stock market. It could no longer, thought Paul Cadbury, be considered a family business, but in many ways it remained one.

In 1960 Adrian had written a paper for the board which proposed clearer responsibilities for managers, less of a hands-on role for the directors and a sharper decision-making structure. It was not until he was unexpectedly made chairman in 1965, however, that he could begin the reorganisation in earnest, bringing in the US management consultants McKinsey to help restructure the business. The changes involved finally integrating the Cadbury and Fry interests (still being run separately nearly fifty years after the 1919 merger); separating the food and confectionery divisions; making board meetings monthly and changing the company name to Cadbury Group Ltd. This would help brand the shares along with the household-name products, not a strategy fashionable today, when large mergers often lead to abstract new names such as Diageo, probably unrecognisable by the average drinker of its most famous brand, Guinness stout.

While the youngest member of the board was drawing up his proposals in 1960, the walls were closing in on the Cadbury family's other business, the company that was still called the Daily News Ltd. The papers were always a burden to Laurence Cadbury – indeed, to most members of the family involved with them – and his heart was in Bournville rather than Bouverie Street. The *News Chronicle* had been profitable under Walter Layton despite the decline of the parliamentary Liberal party, but since the war its editorial politics had undergone a change, partly dictated by events. Many of the causes George Cadbury had propagated through its columns, such as public ownership of leading industries, had been turned into reality by the postwar Labour government, and Laurence felt that for the *News Chronicle* to go on crusading under a progressive banner would be redundant and probably lose the paper circulation.

Unlike his father, he had no taste for using the pulpit of the press in pursuit of social reform, though he took a keen interest in the editorials, having them read out to him over the telephone when he was not in London to see the proofs. In 1950, the year he became chairman of the Daily News company on Layton's retirement, he instructed the paper to support the Attlee government, back in office by the skin of its teeth, because he thought its precarious single-figure majority would force it to drop its nationalisation programme. Frank Waters, the managing director brought in from *The Times* after Bertram Crosfield's retirement, thought Cadbury suffered from 'weakness and timidity and a lack of news instinct', but he, too, worried whether a radical paper could play any valid role under a socialist welfare state.

Ten years after the death of the *News Chronicle*, Tom Baistow, one of its former journalists, writing in the *New Statesman*, analysed his old paper's terminal decline as due, in large part, to 'a sudden and severe change of personality by ham-handed, pre-frontal leucotomy in the early 1950s when Laurence Cadbury, a Conservative industrialist, took over the chairmanship from Lord Layton, an enlightened if rather woolly Liberal'. This is undoubtedly a biased over-simplification. Liberalism was dying in Britain as a serious political force, and therefore as a selling proposition for newspapers. In retrospect, however, it is still puzzling that Laurence Cadbury, a shrewd business manager, should not have seen ways to save the paper's haemorrhaging costs by concentrating resources on one production centre instead of printing in both London and Manchester. But probably little could have been done to reduce the main cost centre, the Byzantine restrictive practices of the 1950s print unions: it would take the best part of forty years, computer technology and an aggressive Australian newspaper proprietor called Rupert Murdoch before those were finally swept away.

There had been glimmerings of offers to save the papers before things came to a head in 1960. One emerged, improbably, from Lord Beaverbrook, owner of Express Newspapers, who is reported to have offered Lord Layton funds to buy the papers. Layton had long wanted to own them but he was now sixty-eight and felt the time was past. He is supposed to have told Beaverbrook that Laurence Cadbury would not sell. But Layton did enter negotiations with Odhams Press, with Cadbury's backing, to see if a composite paper of the left could be created with the *Daily Herald*, a scheme that was sunk by the opposition of the Transport and General Workers' Union and the Trades Union Congress, though the *Herald* later tried to lay the blame on Cadbury.

The sale when it did happen was as swift as an executioner's axe. At 6 p.m. on Monday, 17 October, the staff of the *News Chronicle* were told to stop producing Tuesday's paper. They then learned from a meeting of their National Union of Journalists' chapel that all 3,500 staff on both papers had lost their jobs – the biggest mass redundancy in the history of Fleet Street. Both papers, their prime sites and their printing plants had been sold for £1.5m to the *Mail*, a stridently Tory-supporting paper which was closing them down overnight. The *News Chronicle* title would be absorbed into the *Mail* and the *Star* into the *Evening News*. Only twenty-four hours earlier, a *Mail* spokesman had denied that any form of merger was on the cards.

Compensation was meagre – a pension fund had only been started in 1958 – and although Laurence Cadbury immediately stated that the whole purchase price was to be devoted to staff compensation and pensions, the result became known bitterly as 'the cocoa handshake'. There was much acid comparison of Cadbury the benevolent Quaker employer of Bournville tradition, with the fate of his newspaper employees. Originally the Daily News company intended to give notice to its staff before ceasing publication, but the *Mail's* owner, Lord Rothermere, asked the company to defer it to the end of the week and said he would take on the additional costs. Ironically, the *News Chronicle* presses still rolled that Monday night – printing extra copies of the *Daily Mail.*

After the closure, the NUJ brought forward more claims that offers for the papers had been made in the past few months, one from Australian Consolidated Press and a smaller bid by the Canadian Roy Thomson, who was in Britain looking for acquisitions and subsequently founded his UK fortunes with *The Scotsman.* Sir Frank Packer, the managing director of Australian Consolidated Press, said his company had offered £10,000 for an option to buy the Cadbury papers for £2.5m. But Cadbury, he claimed, was not willing. Cadbury for his part denied that an option arrangement had been agreed, merely discussed, and his son Adrian maintains that none of the offers were substantial enough to be taken seriously by his father.

Forty years on, the death, or 'murder' as it was called by some, of the *News Chronicle* is still an emotive landmark in journalistic history to reporters unborn when it happened. Where many other papers died unlamented, the *News Chronicle* was, and still is, perceived to have had something special in the quality and radical commitment of its writers. Among them, recruited shortly before the October execution, was James Cameron, who became the most distinguished foreign correspondent of his generation. In a letter to a local west London paper two weeks after the papers were closed, Cameron expressed anguish about the future of independent, quality papers.

> If the *News Chronicle* could not survive, with its extraordinary advantages of tradition, and loyalty, and talent, who can, outside the great chain-stores of the trade? . . . The newspaper

with the most admirable free-thinking radical tradition withered on the bough precisely at the moment when the nation was ripe to appreciate these Liberal qualities. Its greatest opportunities opened out before it and it surrendered because there was nothing at the top but timidity, conventionality and emptiness. In its closing days, the *News Chronicle* was a potential warhorse ridden by grocers. And thus it died, and great numbers of the most gifted, loyal, frustrated, trained, perceptive and heartbroken men and women are now without a job while the grocers survive.

Cameron was indulging in poetic licence about the nation being ready to appreciate Liberalism: one by-election success in Devon and a few seats won amid the Conservative landslide of 1959 scarcely heralded a new dawn and for many years the jibe would be that all the Liberal party's MPs could go to Westminster in one taxi. But Fleet Street's finest could hardly resist a cause so close to home. Cadbury was assailed on all sides, not only from the journalistic establishment, which might have been expected, but in Parliament, where he was attacked by Jeremy Thorpe for allegedly hanging on to valuable assets such as the Bouverie Street building and the franchise for Tyne-Tees Television, won as a newspaper publisher.

The first allegation was completely untrue, says the family today, and there was only a 'share' in the TV consortium, along with a small publishing interest. Laurence's worst ordeal was to be savaged in a television interview in which he was ambushed by hostile questions very different from those rehearsed in the run-through beforehand. Always a shy man, even with his family, he did not know how to handle a harsh media spotlight and the TV debacle affected him deeply. The whole affair, observes his son Dominic Cadbury, was 'not well managed – it would be done better now'.

The brothers still feel that their father was unfairly pilloried: as Adrian points out, how many public companies (as the *Daily News* was) would turn over the entire sale price to compensate the staff? (Only one shareholder raised an objection.) But the affair is still capable of rousing old Fleet Street hackles: in late 1998 the columnist Paul Johnson launched an attack on Cadbury in the *Spectator*, an adversary of the Cadbury family since the 1900s, reviving an old canard about how Laurence used to sack his editors, sidling up to them in the lavatory and hissing: 'There's an envelope for you in the office.'

Laurence's sons found him a difficult man to read, but they think the public attacks wounded him quite deeply. More devastating personal trials, however, were in store for him. His younger daughter Anthea, born in 1936, was married in 1959 to Lindsay Turner, a former marketing trainee at Bournville and keen amateur actor who had left Cadbury's to make film commercials. His firm, Anglo-Scottish Pictures Ltd., won the Grand Prix at the international advertising film festival in Cannes in 1963 with a commercial made for Schweppes, which would soon join its fortunes with Cadburys.

The Turners lived in London's fashionable Montagu Square and had two young children. On the last day of February 1964 they were both killed when a Britannia of British Eagle Airways, carrying seventy-five winter-sports holidaymakers from London, flew into the summit of a mountain in heavy snow on the approach to Innsbruck airport. There were no survivors. Two directors of another famous family firm, the brothers Keith and Robin Bamford of J. C. Bamford, the digger manufacturer, were also killed.

After this second tragedy, the close-knit family rallied round and Anthea's orphaned children, four-year-old Catherine and two-year-old Duncan, were taken into their aunt Veronica Wootten's family and brought up with her three children. The Woottens had to buy a larger house to cope with the virtual doubling of their young family and life was chaotic for a while. (Catherine eventually went into film advertising like her father while Duncan became a civil engineer.) Adrian, already married and with three children, was soon to become chairman of the company and in a position to realise his plans for modernising its structure. Dominic, who was twenty-four, had just joined the firm after taking an MBA at California's Stanford University after Cambridge. In the early 1960s this was still unusual for a British graduate, and very rare indeed in the ranks of Britain's dynastic firms. It would undoubtedly equip him better to lead the multinational Cadbury Schweppes than if he had followed the more conventional route of going straight from university into the business.

Dominic's interest in business was sparked while he was still at Eton by discussions with Laurence during one holiday outing about the economics of the newspaper business, though it seems to have been more a case of pleasure in establishing a new relationship with the reserved Laurence than anything else. 'I was number five in my family and wasn't close to my father: we didn't have a lot in common,' he says now. The papers were sold while he was still at Cambridge, so that side of the business was never a career option.

After Stanford, where he had focused on sales and marketing, Dominic started in the Bournville sales office at the end of 1964, going through a formal interview first, and in 1965 went to work in Cadbury's South African subsidiary, based at Port Elizabeth in the Eastern Cape. After two years he took over the full marketing and sales responsibilities in South Africa and also met his future wife Sally, a radiographer, He was not to return to Britain until 1969, when the Cadbury Schweppes merger, creating a combined turnover of £222m, was complete. But he had already had a taste of the change to the business. Before the merger he had reported to his cousin Brandon at Bournville, a board director with responsibilities for all the overseas companies. Now his boss in the field was Basil Collins, overseas managing director for Schweppes and the most capable manager in the Schweppes stable; he was later to become chief executive of Cadbury Schweppes.

Meanwhile Jocelyn, the youngest of Laurence's brood, had just left Eton when Anthea died. Six years younger than Dominic, Jocelyn had a more solitary childhood than the others, and devoted much of his time to making working models in the basement workshop at The Davids, as Laurence and Julian had before him. He did well at school and like all the male Cadburys was good at sports, including their favourite rowing and skiing. Already, however, he was showing recurring signs of serious depression, consistently under-valuing his abilities to a point where he became unable to finish his education at Eton. He came home and decided to join an overland geographical expedition to India that was being organised to show poor and disabled people in the subcontinent how handicaps could be overcome by determination and enterprise. It was led by a wheelchair-bound polio victim, Arthur Tarnowski, and Jocelyn, among other tasks, compiled a photographic record of the journey. He also acquired a deep attachment to India, learned Hindi, studied yoga and read widely on Indian art and culture.

Jocelyn's route into the family firm was more circuitous than usual. In 1965 he went up to Trinity, Cambridge, the family college, and read economics for a year before switching to a more congenial subject, social anthropology. He rowed for Trinity in a successful year, but the black dog of depression returned and, as at Eton, he broke off his studies for a while, returning for a fourth year and eventually completing his degree. He then joined Joseph Lucas, the motor and aerospace engineers in Birmingham, specialising in industrial relations, and Lucas gave him time to take a business studies diploma at Manchester Business School. He became a personnel officer at the Lucas Battery Company but found the work insufficiently stretching and in 1974 applied to the now-merged Cadbury Schweppes. He started work as a shift manager in the plant manufacturing Crunchie bars at Somerdale, on the old Fry premises, and in 1976 was appointed back to Bournville, first to the personnel division and then to take charge of the chocolate production lines.

He was about to become project manager for the modernisation programme at Bournville when a long-nurtured ambition to get into politics suddenly came to fruition. He had been active in the left-leaning Conservative Bow Group in Birmingham while working at Lucas, and had unsuccessfully fought the Northfield constituency in 1974 against Labour's Ray Carter. When Prime Minister James Callaghan unexpectedly called the May 1979 general election following the infamous 'winter of discontent', Jocelyn was chosen to fight the seat again. It looked an uphill struggle since Carter was now a junior minister and a popular local MP. A massive 15 per cent swing would be needed: Northfield had never returned a Conservative MP and the polls gave Jocelyn no chance. But the electoral tide against Labour was sweeping across Britain and Jocelyn won by 204 votes.

It was an extraordinary achievement for the scion of a wealthy merchant dynasty to win a solid Labour industrial seat, even by one of the narrowest margins of the election, and should have been enough to banish Jocelyn's personal demons for good. Instead, political triumph was soon to lead to a third family tragedy for the Cadburys. Jocelyn was always on the left of the party and out of sympathy with extreme Thatcherism. The unremitting application of monetarist theory in the early 1980s savaged manufacturing in the West Midlands and Jocelyn was one of the so-called 'Blue Chips', a group of Tory backbenchers who continually pressed for an easing of the policy.

In 1981, Jocelyn had his foot on the first rung of the junior ministerial ladder, becoming parliamentary private secretary to Norman Lamont at the department of industry. He did not expect to hold his seat at the next election, and as the recession bit deeply into manufacturing found it hard to defend the government in his constituency. On 31 July 1982 he took a shotgun out into the grounds of his parents' house, The Davids, which he had used as his home and constituency base, put the barrel in his mouth and pulled the trigger. He was thirty-six.

The inquest provided no answers to his many admirers and friends, except that he had catastrophically lost confidence in himself. Only his mother, Joyce, who had patiently talked him through so many dark depressions from schooldays on and had thought, on the final night of his life, that she had brought him out of it again, can have realised the full desperate background to what seemed a senseless loss of grace and talent.

There were many poignant tributes from constituents such as Paula Greaves, who ran a network of social clubs for lonely people. 'Jocelyn Cadbury MP shone like a beacon in this dark and callous world,' she wrote. 'A good man is gone and we shall not forget him, for he was one of the few in high places that really cared for his people.' Few MPs, church leaders or other establishment figures had bothered with her humble cause, but Jocelyn had come to the Northfield club and spent an evening handing out cards and inviting members to contact him when help was needed.

Adrian, who was seventeen years older than the baby of the family, wrote sadly for the private family record:

Jocelyn was determined to do everything to the highest possible standard and drove himself far too hard. I had always known how dedicated he was, but I had not appreciated the full extent of his meticulousness until I went through his papers. He had, for example, tackled the most abstruse economic textbooks and made notes on their content to ensure that he understood the background to some of the issues about which he was speaking or writing . . . The mental and physical toll which he took of himself through his dedication to his work proved in the end unbearable. The tragedy remains that Jocelyn thought so much less of himself than we all did of him.

Laurence Cadbury was now ninety-three, and did not long survive his youngest child. He died in November that year, in many ways the most gifted and cultivated of all the Bournville Cadburys, and yet the one most dogged by misfortune. By the time of his death Cadbury Schweppes was a global confectionery and soft drinks giant with more than half its sales overseas. It was run by Adrian – who had been knighted in 1977, the second Cadbury to accept such an honour – and Dominic as chairman and chief executive respectively, a unique family double act in the world of multinationals.

The Schweppes bid for Cadbury had come out of the blue in 1968, amid a flurry of takeover and merger activity in the food sector. It offered a neater fit than many others in the field and indeed has survived better than most mergers from that time, such as Rank Hovis McDougall. Soft drinks and sweets made ready partners, but the real attraction was that each owned a food business that formed a natural half to the other and together could make a sizeable impact on the market. If there was any residual opposition among the Cadbury family directors, it reflected the fact that the company seemed to be doing very well on its own. Adrian knew he would have a hard time carrying the board on anything less than a 50-per-cent split. (Cadbury's had more assets than Schweppes, but Schweppes had more profits.)

In 1968 Cadbury's controlled about a quarter of the UK confectionery market. It had diversified into the packaged cake market in 1962, gaining over the years about a five-per-cent market share in the teeth of competition from Lyons, McVitie and Rank Hovis McDougall. Marvel, the instant milk powder, and Smash, the instant mashed potato, had been successful innovations. Managerially, Adrian Cadbury had carried out a quiet revolution at Bournville, described by *The Times* at the time of the merger as 'bold and successful'.

But the threats, as Adrian saw them and persuasively presented them to the board, were clear. The home market for confectionery had reached a plateau, aggressive lower-cost competitors like Mars were threatening Cadbury's position, and the growing power of the supermarkets challenged every supplier. Added to these was the ever-sharpening competition from large international companies in Cadbury's overseas markets, which had traditionally been strongest in the old Empire and Commonwealth countries. Alliance with the right partner could provide the resources to enter new international markets and extend the Cadbury brands geographically, especially into the United States.

Schweppes had been founded in London's Drury Lane district by German-born John Jacob Schweppe in 1792, two years before Richard Tapper Cadbury set up his draper's business in Birmingham. Schweppe co-invented a method of carbonating water to match the natural aeration found in some springs, launching his product spectacularly by winning the refreshment contract for the Great Exhibition of 1851 and selling more than a million bottles at the Crystal Palace in less than six months. In the 1960s Schweppes was famous for its advertising slogans such as 'Schweppervescence', 'How many Schwepping days to Christmas?' and 'Schhh ... you know who', coined when the James Bond secret service thrillers were at the height of their fame. Under the postwar leadership of the shrewd publicist Sir Frederic Hooper, it had employed the humorist Stephen Potter to invent Schweppshire, populated with fantasy figures like Samuel Schwepys, Percy Bysshe Schweppey and Dante Gabriel Rosschweppi. (Would such a literary conceit work in today's less educated world?)

A year before its approach to Cadbury, Schweppes made overtures to

Rowntree with a view to a merger, but the talks came to nothing. At that time Cadbury was also thought a likely bidder for the York chocolate and cocoa firm. Then America's mighty General Foods stepped into the bidding ring for Rowntree, and Schweppes began to look at Cadbury as a partner.

At the end of 1968 Lord Watkinson, the Schweppes chairman, approached Adrian Cadbury with a formal merger proposal. It had a logical attraction: the combined company (turnover of £222m, generating half its sales overseas) would have the resources to enter international markets, the companies complemented one another geographically and the structure would fall neatly into three substantial product divisions – confectionery, drinks and foods. Schweppes' household-name products included Rose's lime juice, Typhoo tea, Kenco coffee and Chivers-Hartley jams. Since the firm produced soft drinks, there was nothing to ruffle the Quaker conscience on alcohol, except for Schweppes' interest in sales of Dubonnet, the French aperitif, but that was a marginal factor. Schweppes was an ideal geographic fit, being strongly established in the US and Continental Europe, as well as having an assured UK base. Both companies, coincidentally, had employed the US management consultants McKinsey to do a thorough re-evaluation, which helped to streamline some of the post-merger restructuring.

Culturally, too, they seemed natural partners: though not Quaker-founded, Schweppes had a similar tradition of social reform and had introduced a profit-sharing scheme for its workers just after World War II, when such a thing was virtually unknown in British business except for the John Lewis Partnership. But in all mergers, however equal or close-fitting the partners, there are cultural battles and turf wars, and usually one partner emerges dominant. Both Adrian and Dominic admit that the merger was massively difficult to manage. 'I didn't realise what a tough job it would be to put two large businesses together,' recalls Adrian. 'Much the most difficult decisions in a merger are those about placing people, because you know one half of the business but not the other. Maybe we didn't envisage some of the practical decisions to be made – that there would be one finance director, one headquarters, one IT system.'

Some twenty years after the merger, old Cadbury hands were still saying you could tell a 'Cadbury man' from a 'Schweppes man', and the Cadbury identity probably predominated, because Cadbury had more management in depth to supply the merged organisation. What Schweppes did contribute was a much sharper financial edge to the business, and the ability to run a lean commercial operation.

'In an operational sense Cadbury itself was going through quite a period of change,' recalls Dominic. 'At least in the first five years of the merger Cadbury didn't come through on the figures as well as Schweppes and there was a feeling in the first year that Cadbury had slightly let the side down. The pressure was to ensure that Cadbury was not the poor relation in this merger. One was conscious of the need to have it firing on all cylinders.'

The terms of the January, 1969 merger valued Cadbury at just under £121m, or 87s. 6d. per Cadbury share. The Cadbury-Fry family trusts became the major shareholders in the new group, with about 25 per cent of the combined equity – they had previously held 50 per cent of Cadbury following its flotation in 1962. The Cadbury share has been greatly diluted in the years since and now amounts to perhaps 2 per cent, as the trusts have diversified their portfolios following the switch out of family ownership. No current family members have ever held substantial individual shareholdings in the business – they were all in the multiplicity of trusts created by the previous generations. George Cadbury had eleven children and they all created trusts in their turn. When the *Sunday Times* began to publish its annual Rich List in 1990, Adrian Cadbury protested that the family's listed wealth of £300m was completely inaccurate and succeeded in getting the Cadburys dropped from the list. At that time some 300 family members had shares through the trusts, so the total value of the holdings was meaningless under the *Sunday Times'* own criteria, which counts 'family' wealth as shared between about six to ten members.

Lord Watkinson became chairman of the merged business and Adrian Cadbury, then forty, became sole deputy chairman and joint managing director with the managing director of Schweppes, James

Barker. This arrangement was never going to prove workable in the long term and when Sir James Barker, as he became, went off to chair the Unigate dairy group, Adrian Cadbury succeeded Watkinson as chairman at the end of 1974.

Adrian worked well with Watkinson: the older man was unlikely to stand in his career path and it was always understood that he would again become chairman when Watkinson retired. But the pressure was on Adrian to fire up the Cadbury cylinders; the hardest task, as ever, being to cut overheads in a company as employee-centred as Cadbury. He agreed a target figure of job reductions with Watkinson, focused mainly on Bournville with its array of non-production support services. But job cuts were totally alien to the Bournville tradition, and Cadbury got a bad press, especially in Birmingham.

Reality now set in with a vengeance. As Adrian recalls:

> There was a sense throughout the business that it was a very major break with the past. We were no longer going to be masters of our own fate. An enormous amount of time was wasted in management with arguments about who had taken over whom. The problem was that negotiations had had to be kept to a very few people, and the Cadbury board was much better informed about its business than some of the Schweppes directors, because they had all been hands-on managing directors.

Four Cadbury family directors left at different stages after the merger. Brandon, who had trained as a solicitor and had joined the firm only in his mid-thirties, after service in World War II, was not happy with the change generally and felt sidelined when his overseas responsibilities went to a Schweppes man. Temperamentally he was not well suited to the cut-and-thrust of multinational business: he said he would 'see the merger through' and then took early retirement at fifty-six and enrolled at the Birmingham Polytechnic on a new course for probation officers. He became fully qualified in September 1971 and went on to work full-time in the service for the next eight years, and for three years after that on a part-time basis. Charles Cadbury, Paul's son who had been by-passed for chairman in 1965 in favour of Adrian, left to run a housing association, while Michael and John Cadbury, born in 1915 and 1905 respectively, left at normal retirement age.

Five years after the merger, the Cadbury performance shot ahead and over the first decade as a whole, it was the Cadbury business that was perceived as stronger than Schweppes, which had failed to spot recent marketing developments in the soft drinks industry and was under challenge from new competitors, including the pharmaceutical company Beecham, makers of Lucozade. By the time Dominic Cadbury, who had joined the board in 1974 to run the foods business, was appointed chief executive in 1983 to succeed his old Schweppes boss Basil Collins and to form a Cadbury fraternal duopoly at the top of the company, the merger was a mature fourteen years old and turf rivalries had faded.

Adrian Cadbury was not a member of the committee which appointed his brother, but Dominic knew of no opposition from the Schweppes side.

> Our relationship had always been extremely close and strong, and I think one reason the board committee selected me was because they saw me as the person who could most easily work with and make the best use of Adrian. Where you have an internal chairman – today, more come from outside – that relationship with the chief executive is so important.

Over the thirty years since the merger, and particularly under the leadership of Dominic Cadbury first as chief executive, then as chairman, the business has changed radically in emphasis. The turning point was the £1.6bn acquisition in 1995 of US brands Dr Pepper (third biggest after Coke and Pepsi) and Seven Up. This strengthened its share of the US soft drinks market, the world's largest, to 17 per cent, though still well behind Coca Cola at 42 per cent and Pepsi at 31 per cent. The food businesses – ironically the main rationale for putting the companies together in the first place, but less important as the business became more global – were jettisoned, leaving two business streams, confectionery and beverages.

In December 1998 Cadbury Schweppes sold the majority of its beverage brands that were bottled and distributed outside the US, mainland Europe and Australia to the Coca Cola company for £800m. The reason was that these represented only three per cent of the market in the world outside the US, whereas inside the US Cadbury Schweppes enjoyed a 15-per-cent share of the huge American fizzy drinks market, mainly on the back of the popular Dr. Pepper brand. Their drinks markets outside the US were fragmented, and though profitable, were fraught with distribution problems. The deal gave them a substantial cash mountain and strengthened the balance sheet for future acquisitions or organic development.

What Cadbury Schweppes did was to sell the least profitable third of its drinks business at 20 times the trading profit, and the City saw it as a smart move at the time. However, questions have since been raised as to whether the strategy is working in terms of the promised push into more lucrative markets.

At the time of the deal, CEO John Sunderland said the firm saw greater opportunities in confectionery than in drinks, which seemed to signal Cadbury Schweppes going back to its roots for future growth. The *Financial Times* commented that it was 'the end of an attempt to conquer the world for British soft drinks.'

Confectionery is still managed on a global basis from Bournville and the Birmingham plant still delivers between 40 and 50 per cent of the group's confectionery profits, but the increasingly dominant beverages business is run from the US, which leads some to believe that Cadbury Schweppes is becoming a US company. Not so, says Dominic; it is still 75 per cent owned in the UK and only 20 per cent in the US, 'but once we decided to focus on confectionery and drinks, it was predictable that the US presence would become greater'. A third of all the soft drinks consumed in the world are drunk in the US, so it is hardly surprising that Cadbury Schweppes' US operation is highly devolved. Its chief, John Brock, comes to Britain twice a year, once for the annual planning review and once for a long-term planning session. There is no central strategic function except for acquisitions and investment, both business streams being responsible for their own strategy.

The 1990s saw the group's trading profits jump from £360m in 1991 to £642m in 1998, with soft drinks generating roughly 55 per cent of those profits to confectionery's 45 per cent. Worldwide, Cadbury Schweppes has 4 per cent of a highly fragmented confectionery market, ranking third after Nestlé and Mars with 8 and 7 per cent respectively. Hershey just pips Cadbury Schweppes' share, but its market is mainly in the US. Cadbury is the clear chocolate leader in the UK, with a third of the market compared to a quarter for Mars and between 20 and 23 per cent for Nestlé.

April 1997 marked another major turning point within the group, with a thoroughgoing shakeout and revamp of management and performance incentive schemes. About 150 managers were moved, promoted, or departed. A US management consultancy called Marakon was hired to analyse the strengths and weaknesses of the organisation, and a new management philosophy, Managing for Value, was proclaimed, along with a booklet on what was now required in the 'competencies and behaviours' of executives. Bold new targets were publicly adopted, including doubling shareholder value over the next five years and achieving double-digit growth in earnings per share while also generating £150m in free cashflow each year. The CEO since 1996 has been John Sunderland, a Cadbury Schweppes veteran whose career spans both main streams of the business and four different countries including the US.

In the public eye, and also among its employees, Cadbury Schweppes still has a strongly ethical reputation which must owe a great deal to the persistence of the Quaker legacy. Soon after he became chairman of the merged company, Adrian Cadbury distilled what he saw as the guiding values of the business into an eight-paragraph leaflet called 'The Character of the Company'. It was an early version of what are now fashionably called mission statements and it expressed Adrian's belief that while the company could not depend on its history to carry it forward, it could build on the best of its inheritance.

The characteristics he set out as essential to success were grouped under eight headings: competitive ability, clear objectives, taking advantage of change, simple organisation, committed people, openness, responsibility to all those with a stake in its success (stakeholders, as they would now be called) – that is, shareholders, employees, customers, suppliers, government and society – and quality. Under the last heading he quoted an early Cadbury statement of aims: 'Our policy for the future as in the past will be: first, the best possible quality – nothing is too good for the public.'

'But quality applies to people and relationships, as well as to our working lives,' he continued. 'We should set high standards and expect to be judged by them. The quality we aim for in all our dealings is that of integrity . . . it must be consistently applied to everything which bears the company's name.' In conclusion, he wrote: ' The character of this company is collectively in our hands. We have inherited its reputation and standing and it is for us to advance them.'

Sir Dominic Cadbury, chairman of Cadbury Schweppes since 1993, has broken with the family's Quaker inheritance and is a confirmed Anglican. One is not automatically born into the Society of Friends: joining has to be a conscious decision. He thinks that the Quaker values have survived to the extent that Cadbury Schweppes has a culture which reflects 'the values put in place and developed over all those years from the idea of Bournville'.

> It's about things like openness, fairness, integrity, honesty, straight dealing. I don't know how far they are Quaker values any longer, but the strong value system put in place then is a strength in the culture of the company, and you don't have to write it up on the wall. Perhaps we don't write it up often enough, perhaps we take things too much for granted, but one of the great benefits of having a continuity like this is that you inherit all these principles and you don't have to think of them for yourself.
>
> We are seen to be a very community-friendly company, wherever Cadbury Schweppes has expanded or invested. You see those relationships emerging very early on in establishing

a site, say in Russia or Poland. People in the company don't have to invent it, or make a case for it. It is part of the way we do business.

The emphasis on training and education that has run through the company since the invention of Bournville is something other corporations have adopted belatedly in the fashion for 'learning organisations.' For Cadbury's, it was originally a way of providing a continuance of education for employees who were still in their teens, but as Dominic points out, it wasn't a big step from this to introducing professional management development in the 1950s. For him, Uncle Edward's 1912 book on the blueprint for Bournville has been unexpectedly useful in his role in a CBI committee on training.

I'd like to feel that while the business has changed in many ways, the basic value system of the company has not changed. Works councils have changed, trade union structures have changed, we are more focused all the time on performance and on trying to achieve a competitive edge. People move around in jobs and don't work here for their lifetimes. All those factors apply everywhere, but I like to think that the fundamental values of the company have been maintained in terms of the way we do business and the relationships we have both internally and externally. I think this company is admired for the right things.

The lingering Quaker association in the public mind can have disadvantages. 'If people want to criticise us, they say you're not a Quaker company any more.' The most potentially contentious area here, he admits, is Cadbury Schweppes' participation in Camelot, the highly profitable consortium that runs the National Lottery. There are parallels with George Cadbury and the controversy over his decision to continue a betting column in the *Star*. Both decisions were taken for hard commercial reasons – sales of lottery tickets take place cheek by jowl with confectionery displays and have obvious customer overlaps, and there was also a competitive desire to stop Mars from getting in. But Dominic says, laughing: 'As chairman, I've only ever had two letters of criticism about the lottery, and both were from [Quaker] members of my family.'

Dominic will probably be the last of the family to run the multinational that includes the confectionery business founded by his great-grandfather John Cadbury. There are only two other Cadburys working in the company: Adrian's second son Matthew, born in 1959, who is a project director in confectionery based in Bournville but spends most of his time overseeing developments abroad, and Andrew, Michael's son, in his mid-fifties, who is sales manager in Exeter. Sometimes Dominic reflects that when he retires it will be the end of an era, but it does not seem strange to him to have only three Cadburys still in the business.

'There has never been pressure that members of the family are expected to work in the firm, and that's always been one of the attractions of this family,' he says. 'I think there is a feeling of belonging in this family, and a pride in it, but also a freedom about it. We all do a lot of different things.' Benedict Cadbury, Adrian's elder son, worked in United Biscuits for a time and now runs his own small business, making energy-saving lamps. Dominic's three daughters are all in professions – medicine, banking, public relations. The rest of the extensive network of cousins are involved in a wide variety of occupations, from farming to sculpting, teaching to engineering. Many are in food-related businesses, but not connected with Cadbury Schweppes.

The impulse to voluntary service is still strong – 'public spiritedness runs through the family', says Dominic – especially in Birmingham. Cadburys can always be relied upon to take an active part in committees to improve civic amenities, as they have been doing for five generations. In the 1940s Paul Cadbury sat on all seven of the Birmingham city committees set up to plan for postwar reconstruction of the bombed city. As early as 1941 one of these committees commissioned a book called *When We Build Again*, with visionary plans for reconstructing the bombed city. Unfortunately the ring roads which had been part of a Birmingham redevelopment dream since the First World War (they figure in a 1915 book on town planning by George Cadbury Jr.) turned out in practice to cut off neighbourhoods from each other, severing the arteries of community life. Paul Cadbury, who was a friend of H.J. Manzoni, the city engineer responsible for planning the postwar roads scheme and Spaghetti Junction, lived to see the sacrifice of Birmingham to road traffic and though sometimes called 'the father of the ring road' by admiring city worthies, did not relish the accolade.

If not close in their geographic distribution, except for a cluster in the West Midlands, the Cadburys remain very family-oriented and prone to large gatherings of the clan at seasonal festivals – there is always a Boxing Day picnic – and family celebrations such as golden weddings. The indefatigable Sir Adrian is the maestro of these occasions, marshalling the invitations to Winds Point in the Malvern Hills, which is managed by resident housekeepers and administered through the George Cadbury Trust. For all its rambling charm, Winds Point was never a vast house and now only sleeps about seven, so numerous Cadbury cousins, aunts and uncles have to be accommodated in nearby hotels in Malvern. Cadbury Christmas-card lists are enormous: Sir Adrian and his wife send out about 250 to family members alone, and John Crosfield, a twinkly octogenarian, counts thirty-nine Cadbury cousins, Adrian and Dominic among them.

Crosfield, who compiled a vast, complex family history as a retirement project, is described by Adrian as the most innovative of all George Cadbury's grandchildren. His father Bertram, who married George's daughter Eleanor, partnered Eleanor's brother Henry when he was unwillingly pitched into managing the newspaper business, and managed to make the papers profitable for a time. After World War II John founded Crosfield Electronics, to which he contributed a number of inventions, among them a machine for note-sorting which was used by the Bank of England. He sold the company to De La Rue in the late 1970s, but it has since become a subsidiary of a Japanese-American combine. Crosfield, whose wife was raised in the United States, celebrated the private printing of his family history in 1985 with a gathering of the American Cadburys, descendants of John Cadbury's brother Joel, at a New York hotel. Around 160 of them turned up, the majority from the Philadelphia area, where Joel Cadbury had founded the second US branch of the family in the eighteenth century.

Except for Laurence, George Cadbury's children in the business had all died by the time of the Cadbury Schweppes merger. Edward died in 1948, Dorothy in 1950, Henry in 1952, George in 1954, Barrow in 1958, and Bertie in 1967. Bertie was knighted in 1957 and, unusually for the Cadbury family, lived in some style with homes in three counties and a twin-screw yacht moored at Lymington. He had two sons, one of whom died tragically at twenty-one, sleepwalking out of a window at his Cambridge college. The other, Peter, became a flamboyant businessman who rescued Keith Prowse, the theatre booking agency, and founded Westward Television. Three times married, he could be regarded as the black sheep of the family, having figured more in the tabloids than any other Cadbury. A coincidental connection with the Sainsbury family occurred when he sold his Hampshire estate at Preston Candover, near Micheldever, to Sir John Sainsbury, who subsequently took his title as a life peer from the village. In an attempt to make the place look less plutocratic, Sainsbury had the helicopter pad removed and planted a screen of trees.

The chocolate side of the family remains true to its modest Quaker character, living in unpretentious houses and driving unpretentious cars, devoting generous time to good works in and around Birmingham. Their roots are still firmly planted in the West Midlands. 'I wouldn't live anywhere else,' says Sir Adrian.

Many of the family remain Quakers, including Adrian, who describes himself as a 'non-attending' Friend. One elderly aunt still uses the 'plain speech' of thee and thou when addressing members of the family. Michael Cadbury, Adrian's cousin, who died in 1999, walked to Meeting every Sunday from his home on the edge of Bournville despite being well over eighty.

Adrian Cadbury epitomises the family's ethos of plain living and high public service. His wife Susan describes him as 'frugal, even austere' in his habits. He takes cold baths and always flies economy unless a pressing business schedule dictates otherwise. He abhors waste of any kind, including time, and is driven to fill every minute usefully. He keeps a running list of things to do on his desk at home, but deals with them so expeditiously that there are never more than six items outstanding. He has, in his wife's words, 'a high sense of duty' which keeps him on a treadmill of public commitments that he keeps telling his family will slow down but never does. Like his great-uncle Richard and grandfather George, he is extraordinarily punctilious about correspondence, replying to letters within two days.

In personality and demeanour, Chaucer's phrase 'a verray parfit gentil knight' might have been coined for Adrian Cadbury. A tall man with a donnish stoop and a modest, almost diffident charm, he is widely admired in the business community for his willingness to give his time and experience to scores of committees and causes, to draft forewords and write contributions to business books. Any fees go to a designated Cadbury charity such as the Runnymede Trust, which fosters better race relations. Cadbury employees around the world continue to keep in touch with him and his wife, adding to the deluge of Christmas cards.

The brothers are very different in lifestyle – Dominic is the model of a modern multinational chief, with houses in fashionable parts of London and the home counties, and has no taste for austerity – but they exchange their itineraries and contact numbers whenever they are moving around the world, and enjoy intellectual sparring when they meet, sparking ideas off each other. There is a patently close bond and mutual admiration between them.

Adrian Cadbury was an appropriate choice by John Major's government in 1991 to chair the Committee on Financial Aspects of Corporate Governance, now known as the Cadbury Committee. This was set up under the wing of the London Stock Exchange in the wake of several corporate financial scandals including Polly Peck and the Bank of Credit and Commerce International (BCCI), and it formulated far-reaching recommendations on the proper conduct of the board, its responsibilities and directors' remuneration. Since 1992 the guidelines have been enshrined in a Code of Best Practice, endorsed by the Stock Exchange and widely adopted among UK companies, at least publicly. Son-of-Cadbury committees chaired by Sir Richard Greenbury, then chairman of Marks and Spencer, and Sir Ronald Hampel, then chairman of ICI, have taken the work forward, though Greenbury found that his committee, which concentrated on directors' pay, thrust him unpleasantly into the media spotlight and he vowed he would never take on anything like it again.

Seven years on from the Cadbury Committee and pushing seventy, Sir Adrian still travels the world lecturing and chairing seminars on corporate governance, which he sometimes feels has taken over his life. In 1999 he was trying to wind this down and concentrate on causes closer to home, including chairing a new Birmingham-based charity called the Aston Reinvestment Trust (ART). Described as 'a social reinvestment fund for Birmingham', the purpose of ART is to provide investment capital for projects that could regenerate deprived areas of Birmingham but which are not likely to be regarded as 'bankable' by the high-street clearers, who have fewer and fewer branches in poor urban districts anyway. It is designed as a community bank for both saving and borrowing, including a property loans service. 'Funds invested in ART will be put to good use over and over again, as loans are paid off,' says Sir Adrian.

In its appeal to individuals as well as organisations to contribute to 'the making of a better world', the idea is typical of the community self-help and social idealism that made the Cadburys and other Quaker business dynasties so remarkable a part of British industrial history.

PART TWO

THE LEWISES:

PIONEERS OF PARTNERSHIP

CHAPTER 5:

A MAN OF GRANITE

As IN MOST English counties, the landscape in Somerset changes as you move through it from one compass point to another. The rolling pastures around Shepton Mallet, an ancient grey-stone cattle market town on the southern slopes of the Mendip Hills, are quite different from the steep-sided lanes of south Somerset or the sweeping wooded landscape to the north-west, on the edge of Exmoor. Until municipal vandals tore the heart out of the old town in the 1960s to build a mundane shopping centre, Shepton Mallet had changed little since a cabinet-maker called John Lewis plied his craft in the 1830s in Town Street, a steep, picturesque thoroughfare of narrow three-storey Georgian houses running down to the ornate Market Cross, lined at street level with cluttered shopfronts; drapers, bootmakers, bakers, butchers. In the early nineteenth century the town was still suffering from the collapse of its once-prosperous woollen industry. Its population had slumped in forty years from 10,000 to 4,000, but it could boast two substantial family businesses – still based locally in the 1990s – in C.&J. Clark, the Quaker-owned boot- and shoe-makers, and Showerings, the cider-makers.

The Lewis family had been established as shopkeepers and craftsmen in Shepton Mallet since the 1660s. Originally they must have come across the Severn from Wales in search of a better living, like thousands of other Welsh families who ended up in Somerset, and the Welsh genes remained strong. John Lewis's fifth child, also called John, who was to found one of London's leading department stores, was described by his son, John Spedan Lewis, as 'Welsh through and through', though he spoke with a strong Somerset accent all his long life. For forty years after he left Shepton, he frequently revisited the town and childhood haunts such as the little stream nearby where he used to catch minnows.

By the time their fifth child was born, at 3.15 a.m. on 24 February 1836, to John Lewis and his wife, the former Elizabeth Speed, the cabinet-maker had done well for himself and his family. The birth took place at their home on Cowl Street, then the main road leading out of Shepton Mallet and a desirable address. Cowl Street boasted a historic building in the so-called Monmouth House, where the Duke of Monmouth took refuge in the Civil War. Unbelievably, it was razed to the ground by the 1960s developers who also destroyed half of Town Street, and was replaced by a standard-issue housing estate known as Hillsmead.

Young John was orphaned at seven and he and his four sisters (one had died in infancy) were brought up by an unmarried aunt, Ann Speed. The unique middle name he bestowed on his own son, Spedan, and eventually on his Gothic mansion in Hampstead, Spedan Tower, was invented in tribute to this aunt, and one of the five John Lewis Partnership company yachts, among several benefits offered to all employees or 'partners', is also named *Ann Speed*. John attended Shepton Mallet Grammar School and at fourteen was apprenticed to a linen draper called Joseph Tasker six miles away in High Street, Wells. Like most apprentices, who were often relatives of the shopkeeper, he would probably have slept on the premises: living-in arrangements suited the employer, who could save on the boy's wages by offering free accommodation; it also, with good employers, meant that the apprentice got decent meals as well as somewhere to sleep.

From Wells he moved at eighteen to another draper's, Nicholls in Bridgwater, where he learned a great deal from the two owner-manager brothers, including a crafty dictum he passed on to his son: 'The art of pricing is to get profit where the public will not see it.' While working in Bridgwater he resolved to have a shop of his own and, after a short, unhappy interval in Liverpool, he set off for London in 1856, aged twenty, borrowing a sovereign for the journey. In the bowels of the John Lewis Partnership archives at Stevenage lies a battered and dented locked metal box with a central handle which is treated with some reverence as the one in which young John brought his possessions to London.

Here he got a job as a salesman at Peter Robinson's store in Oxford Circus, in the heart of the newly fashionable West End. Shopping as a middle-class pastime was on the rise in Oxford Street and Nash's recently constructed Regent Street, both now illuminated by bright gas lighting and thus safer for women after dark. The old shop windows with their small panes were being replaced by plate glass, allowing attractive displays of goods behind them, and shops were open six days a week from 8 a.m. to 8 p.m., later in the summer months. The only day off for shop employees was Sunday, and in the bigger shops the living-in system persisted, with the young sales assistants sleeping in dormitories of six to sixteen people, often two to a bed. Many shops forbade their employees to go out except on Sundays, when they had to find their own food: in cold weather, some would be forced to seek shelter and somewhere to rest in churches, or even on gravestones. Assistants could be fined threepence for gossiping, bringing a newspaper into the shop or 'lounging about in an unbusinesslike manner'. Many shops set sales targets for their employees, threatening dire consequences if they were not reached. Both men and women were dismissed or expected to leave if they had the temerity to get married and thus distract themselves from the business of selling.

It was a gruelling, joyless life, harsher even than that of H. G. Wells's Kipps, and one may well wonder why anyone put up with it except to learn the secrets of the trade, or because the alternative was sheer poverty on the streets. Only the young could tolerate it and most drifted into other work as they got older. Not many would have the ambition or be able to save enough from their meagre earnings to set up on their own, although London would soon provide role models to inspire young apprentices with dreams of fame and fortune in the shopkeeper's trade.

Young Lewis arrived in London a year after William Whiteley, who would become a business rival much envied by Lewis for his greater wealth. When Whiteley was sensationally shot dead in his office in the last week of the January sales in 1907 by a man who claimed to be his unacknowledged son, he left a fortune of £1,452,825. Lewis, who had a personal account at Whiteley's, was 'bitterly mortified' by this and other wills left by rivals. Lewis did make a substantial amount of money over his lifetime – nearly £1 million in all – but when he died at ninety-two in 1928 he left only £84,661 in the bank. His legacy was tied up in his stores.

Wandering around the capital to spy out the competition, Lewis and Whiteley would have found a variety of drapers but as yet no proper department stores. The nearest equivalents were the bazaars such as the Soho Bazaar in Soho Square, which had a series of stalls selling millinery, lace, gloves and jewellery, or the Pantechnicon in Motcomb Street, Belgravia, which sold a strange mixture of carriages, furniture, household goods, carpets, wine and toys. Other similar establishments could be found in Baker Street and the Gray's Inn Road.

Otherwise, shopping was dominated by drapers. There were five in the City, the grandest being George Hitchcock and Sons of St Paul's Churchyard, silk mercer, linen draper and haberdasher with the largest plate-glass windows in town. In Tottenham Court Road, then London's principal shopping thoroughfare, was Shoolbred's, founded in 1820 as a linen and woollen draper and silk mercer catering for the aristocratic residents of Bloomsbury. Close by was Maple's furniture store, founded in 1842, and the older Heal's, set up in 1810, which specialised then, as now, in bedding. Walking west down the newly-laid out New Oxford Street, which had replaced the disreputable old thieves' rookery of St Giles, one would have encountered an upholsterer, Jackson's, and a linen merchant, Williams and Sowerby. In Oxford Street proper, still lined by houses with single shops in them, came more drapers: Peter Robinson, occupying four houses, Williams and Hatton, Marshall and Snelgrove, founded in 1837 and spread over six houses, and Debenham and Pooley, of Wigmore Street. The last two would evolve in the next century into full-blown fashionable department stores.

Regent Street, some thirty years after its rebuilding by John Nash, was the glory of the West End with its wide roadway and elegant pedimented frontages. In 1859 the social commentator Augustus Sala called it 'the most fashionable street in the world', a place of 'fancy watchmakers, haberdashers, and photographers; fancy stationers, fancy hosiers and fancy staymakers; music shops, shawl shops, jewellers, French glove shops, perfumery and point lace shops, confectioners and milliners'. The two biggest emporia were Swan and Edgar, silk mercer and linen draper founded in 1812 at the Regent Circus end (as Piccadilly Circus was then known), and Jay's Mourning Warehouse at the Oxford Street end, founded in 1838. (Victorian bereavements required full mourning wardrobes for women, and there was enough trade to keep a major West End store busy.) In between these two was Dickins, Smith and Stevens, founded in 1803, the forerunner of Dickins and Jones. Over in the still relatively countrified Kensington and Knightsbridge were the draper John Barker, founded in 1840, and Ponting Brothers, while Harrods, founded in 1849, was still a modest grocery store. There was plenty of scope for an enterprising retailer to provide a greater range of products and services under one roof, and William Whiteley was the first to do it.

While John Lewis was working his way up to the position of buyer of silks and woollens at Peter Robinson, and by his own account looking enviously at the costermongers in the streets 'with barrows of their own', Whiteley boldly opened his first shop in Westbourne Grove, Bayswater. A quiet suburban road lined with cottages and gardens, it had such a poor record for trading that among local shopkeepers it was known as Bankruptcy Avenue. All that was to change, however, with the opening of London's first underground railway, the Metropolitan Line, in 1863, running steam trains on a cut-and-cover track between Paddington Station and Farringdon on the edge of the City. Whiteley, a shrewd operator in everything except his private life, was quick to capitalise on the coming of the Underground by opening a bigger shop, which soon developed into London's first real department store, guaranteeing lower prices than in Oxford Street and boasting of being 'the Universal Provider', able to furnish 'anything from a pin to an elephant' – a boast later adopted by Harrods.

A year later, in 1864, John Lewis rejected the opportunity of a partnership in Peter Robinson and with money borrowed from his unmarried sisters, set up as a draper and haberdasher in a small leasehold shop, a former tobacconist's, at 132 Oxford Street, on the north side four houses west of Holles Street, more or less where John Lewis is today. The neighbouring shop, which he would eventually take over, belonged to a fruiterer who had the sole franchise in London to sell bananas and used to hang great green bunches of them in his basement to ripen. Other businesses nearby included a brushmaker, a dentist, a goldsmith, a shoemaker, and a bookseller.

In those days a shop in Oxford Street could be rented for as little as £1 a week and if a shop-owner was well enough known to the City wholesale houses – which a Peter Robinson buyer would be – he could secure up to six months' credit for the purchase of stock. Even so, Lewis found the experience 'hard and dreary', as he told his son, and doubted that he could ever bring himself to go through it again. His first day's takings were only 16s. 4d. (82p) and over the first six months he lost money. Then he boldly invested in a job lot of silks and the display attracted interest. An elderly customer of his from Peter Robinson's, whose husband had made a fortune in wholesale drapery and who had encouraged Lewis to take the plunge on his own, came in and remarked approvingly of the crowded shop: 'You are doing what my husband did – buying cheap and selling cheap.'

Years later, Lewis was to tell his sons that that conversation was a turning-point: the trading policy he evolved was based on paying low prices for cash and passing the benefit on to the customers, on honest prices, good value and the widest possible range of merchandise. You could not better John Lewis for the choice of colours and qualities he carried in silks and woollens, sewing threads, ribbons, laces and other trimmings. His policy of honest dealing was also a novelty in an age when merchants were apt to cheat their customers with short measures and adulterated foodstuffs. It was quite common for shopkeepers to display fine quality goods in their windows and sell inferior look-alikes inside. On one famous occasion, a man accompanying his wife to the store unwisely suggested to John Lewis that the goods on show in his windows were better than those on sale. Lewis seized him by his coat collar and bundled him out of the shop: the story went the rounds of fashionable London and Lewis's trade boomed. Even the thrown-out customer and his wife returned on several buying expeditions.

In 1928 John Spedan Lewis recalled how astonished he had been to hear his father put 'assortment' (variety and range) above even value in his trading principles, but he had grown to understand that

> it is good business to give the public the service of having constantly actually ready for them articles that they do require, but only rarely. He [John Lewis] realised that if you are asked two or three times a year for a particular shade of some plain ribbon or braid and a large body of customers come in time to know that you will go to the trouble and expense of keeping that thing constantly in stock, they will come to you whenever they want that or anything else that is exceptional, and you will get the rest of their business as well.

A quarter-century later in the 1950s he was still hammering the theme in a memo to the managing director of Peter Jones: 'Assortment is vitally important. Strive never to let a customer come into your shop to buy something that ought to be there and is not. Ceaseless diligence in contriving to have actually in stock what in theory you are stocking on that particular day is crucially important to a solid trade . . .' He did, however, criticise his father for not making sure, as the business grew, that his buyers followed his own principles: often, Spedan observed, buyers did not provide the range of goods they should have done for the budgets they were allowed.

Spedan became a far bolder and more innovative shopkeeper than his father – or, indeed, than any since – but he was always quoting admiringly from the old man's business philosophy. In 1943, in one of the 39,346 memoranda he poured out to his staff between 1916 and 1955, he wrote to his director of trading that the fundamental factors in his father's success were:

> Pay cash, take great pains to find the best sources of supply and to get the very lowest price. Carry extremely complete assortments, keep working expenses as low as ever you can and be satisfied with whatever net profit you find that you can get without ever being dearer than your competitors and being as a general rule cheaper.

Unlike his rival Whiteley in the western suburbs, whose shop had ten departments within four years of opening and thirty by the turn of the century, John Lewis was content to build his business slowly, diversifying cautiously from dress fabrics by the yard into ready-made clothes for women and children and fashion accessories such as hats, gloves and shoes, and from furnishing fabrics into furniture, china, glass and ironmongery. In 1869/70, after five years in business, his sales reached £25,000 a year and by 1879/80 they had risen to about £70,000.

It was a good time to enter the retailing trade: steam shipping was opening up new overseas sources of raw materials, trade barriers were coming down and new manufacturing processes meant goods could be produced at lower cost. Railways, becoming more efficient as the century advanced, brought these manufactures to the capital quickly and cheaply. Above all, from about 1870 onwards, there was a huge expansion of the professional and middle classes and of the aspiring middle class, like the clerks satirised in George and Weedon Grossmith's Mr Pooter. Although there were huge pockets of poverty in the inner-city slums, such as London's East End, where the population traded only among themselves, buying second- or third-hand clothes and never venturing 'up West' to the glittering shops, there was much more money about for more people, and they were ready to spend it.

John Lewis's little shop soon became so cramped that to gain less than an inch for wall fixtures, plaster was scraped off the walls. Then he acquired the banana-seller's shop and threw the two into one, gradually leasing more houses: first on Holles Street and then, between 1878 and

1892, on Oxford Street to fill the gap between his first shop and the Holles Street corner. In 1895, he rebuilt the individual houses to make an entirely new shop with retail showrooms on three floors, lifts, a restaurant and staff dining rooms. The business now employed 150, mostly women, and 100 young single women were provided with hostel accommodation in nearby Weymouth Street.

Lewis was in many ways typical of what a century later we think of as the hard Victorian employer. For forty-two years, from the day he started the business until he took his elder son Spedan into partnership in 1906, he ran the firm as an absolute ruler, providing minimal comforts in his hostels, giving his employees little information and concentrating only on those areas of retailing that he understood – the drapery business. He flatly refused to advertise and believed customers would buy from what they saw in the shop windows, so he crammed as much variety as he could into them. Whiteley, by contrast, was constantly expanding the number of his store's departments and activities – by 1875 he had added an estate agency, a cleaning and dyeing service, house decoration, banking and provisions to the original mix of drapery and furnishings. Unlike Lewis, he had a flair for publicity and in May 1876 placed an article in the New York *Graphic* which depicted a prosperous expatriate returning to England travel weary and without a home to go to.

> All he has to do is to go to Whiteley. He can take a bath, have his hair cut, and be rigged out in fashionable garments . . . Then, without leaving the place, he can in a few hours be set up . . . in a handsomely furnished house with servants, equipages and everything handy about him, and to make him perfectly comfortable Mr Whiteley will take his money on a deposit account, give him a cheque book and pay him five per cent interest besides. If he wishes to build a house, Mr Whiteley will build it for him. If he rents one and wishes it repaired, furnished and decorated, Mr Whiteley will do that also . . . Mr Whiteley will bury you, if you like, and erect a monument to you. In a word, Mr Whiteley will take charge

of you from the cradle to the grave, and give you your meals as you go along – if you can pay for it.

Other competitors were springing up, closer to the West End. The Army and Navy Stores opened in Victoria in 1871 and Gamages' great sandstone emporium in Holborn in 1878. Lewis ploughed on, resentful of his more flamboyant peers but apparently unaware that he was leaving great stretches of the business slumbering. Whiteley had by this time bought a mansion in Melbury Road, Kensington, where in 1882 he entertained the defeated King Cetewayo of the Zulus, and a farm at Finchley which supplied his new and bigger store in Queen's Road, Bayswater. When Spedan came into the business in the 1900s he saw his father as having got himself into the position of the captain of a big but under-engined ship 'and with those engines much under-fuelled'. He saw that the staff were thoroughly demotivated and great areas of floor space under-used where they were not completely neglected. His father seemed unaware of it and was extremely out of touch with what was happening outside his own business, except to grumble constantly about the fortunes other department store owners were making.

Lewis spent a gruelling twenty years' bachelor existence building up his business, which according to his eldest son warped his attitude to money and fuelled an obsession with financial security that stemmed from the poverty of his early years. He seemed to have few interests outside the drapery trade except in acquiring property, which he did with obsessive zeal. Whenever he had a surplus of cash in the accounts, instead of investing it in improving the store premises or staff accommodation, as his son would have done, he put it into property, scanning the advertisements in the newspapers and cutting out and filing interesting-sounding purchases. He would often put in a bid for a property without seeing it. By the time of his death in 1928 he had over 100 shop and residential investments. The list, recorded in a thick red leather-bound ledger, ranged all over London – Pimlico, Belgravia, Notting Hill Gate, Bloomsbury, Balham, Hyde Park, Fulham, Eltham, Great Portland Street, Hammersmith, Maida Vale, Portobello Road, Regent Street and Regent's Park. He owned nine different houses in

Norland Square, Holland Park, between numbers 18 and 35. He also bought properties in Brighton and a shop in Weston-super-Mare for one of his sisters. He could drive a shrewd bargain: the square, high-chimneyed mansion on the edge of Hampstead Heath with four acres of ground which he bought in 1886 for £5,500 and named Spedan Tower had a 970-year lease at a fixed ground rent of £70 a year: in July 1916 he bought the freehold for £1,800.

Spedan Tower was bought to celebrate his late-flowering marriage in 1884 to Eliza Baker, a schoolmistress from a West Country drapery family. He had met her father, Mills Baker, when both men were on solitary holidays in the Scottish Highlands which included a cruise through the Caledonian Canal, and in due course got to know the family. Eliza's brothers found it hard to believe that Lewis could be making what he claimed from such a small shop, but when one of them was on a business trip to London and made a detour to observe the shop for himself, he was impressed by the constant stream of customers.

Lewis was forty-eight and Eliza eighteen years his junior. Although she was no intellectual and rarely read a book, she had been one of the first students at Girton, the Cambridge college for women founded in 1869, and was a lasting influence on her sons, whom she taught at home before they went to their preparatory school. Spedan's restless intellect and social conscience came from the Baker, not the Lewis genes. Although a kindly man in his own household, Lewis must have been an intensely irritating husband, regarding holidays, novel-reading and piano-playing – which Eliza loved – as a waste of time, and ridiculing her Christian faith. Lewis was a dyed-in-the-wool agnostic. Eliza Lewis was not able to have the boys, Spedan and Oswald, baptised until they were in their teens, and then she had to resort to strategems and deceptions to have the ceremony performed at a church some miles from their home.

The family holidays Eliza organised at lodgings in Norfolk or Kent seaside resorts were another bone of contention: except for visits to his sister at Weston-super-Mare, Lewis regarded these as an unnecessary interference with business, and when they went to Ramsgate or Margate he would escape back to London several times by paddle steamer. At

Cromer, he hit on another way of profiting from the holiday by persuading Eliza to collect large flints from the beach and smuggle them into their boarding house under her cloak. These were then transported back to Hampstead where Lewis made rockeries in the gardens of Spedan Tower. He was now a man of substance, making his daily journey to Oxford Street from the airy heights of Hampstead by carriage and pair – in those days it took an average of only twenty minutes, even by horse-drawn transport – and later in an enormous Rolls Royce Silver Ghost with brass lamps, made with specially wide bodywork to take three people sitting abreast in the back seat. By the time of his death he owned two.

By the 1890s, when the new John Lewis shop was built, the department store had well and truly arrived in London, and over the next twenty years would enjoy a heyday as a place of leisure and entertainment, rather as shopping malls have become in the 1990s. The man who did most to create this atmosphere was Gordon Selfridge, the American midwesterner who had learned his trade at Marshall Field of Chicago, America's first department store. Selfridge's Ionic-pillared temple of commerce in Oxford Street opened in 1909 amid such public relations coups as exhibiting the oil-stained canvas monoplane in which Louis Blériot had just flown the Channel. Its policy was to give people 'the freedom of the stores' – freedom to browse around and even handle the goods on sale without being pressured to buy. Selfridge's windows, unlike John Lewis's, emphasised a few products of special quality rather than attempting to put everything on view.

Department stores provided enormous employment in late nineteenth-century and early twentieth-century London: in the 1880s, Whiteley's was the largest, with 2,000 staff. Harrods, Barker's, Shoolbred's and a few others employed between 500 and 1,000, while Debenham's, Marshall and Snelgrove and Jones Brothers of Holloway could boast 500 each. As the buildings were enlarged to provide restaurants, tea rooms and the novelty of lifts and escalators, as well as expanding workrooms, accounts departments and transport sections for delivery vans, so employment soared. By 1900 there were at least a dozen department stores employing 1,000 people, and by 1914, Harrods and

Whiteley's employed 6,000 and 4,000 respectively.

In the first decade of the new century some department store owners were attracting as much public interest as their stores. Whiteley, never popular among his employees, was detested by the local shopkeepers whom he ruthlessly put out of business, and his store had suffered several spectacular fires from arson attacks. When he was murdered, there was enormous public pressure for a reprieve for his killer, Horace Rayner, who was defended at his trial by the eminent barrister Henry Curtis-Bennett. Rayner did escape execution and only served twelve years in prison. But the Universal Provider lived up to his self-styled title even after death with unexpected largesse: £1 million of his estate was willed to a trust to provide and maintain 'Whiteley Homes for the Aged Poor'.

This remains a handsome legacy in Whiteley Village, a community of redbrick and white stone cottages set in wooded parkland in one of the richest parts of Surrey's stockbroker belt, the Mole Valley between Merstham and Weybridge. No longer restricted to 'the poor of Paddington' in their sixties, as Whiteley's will directed, the homes are let out to pensioners of limited means at the discretion of the trustees. The will also provided £5,000 for Christmas gifts for poor families in Paddington, and another £5,000 for prizes to encourage sports such as cricket, football, rowing and swimming among young people living within a five-mile radius of the Whiteley store.

Selfridge, always the showman, was rarely out of the popular papers from the moment he arrived in London. He rented a castle in the New Forest for weekends, bought a steam yacht, invited nephews and nieces of King George V and Queen Mary to watch the Coronation procession of June 1911 from the store's main balcony – the only store-owner along the route who had thought of it – toyed with the idea of buying *The Times* newspaper and became a fixture on the West End theatre and nightclub circuit, often accompanied by his mother after his wife died in 1918. Long before his expensive liaison in the 1920s with a couple of cabaret stars, the Dolly Sisters – he frequently appeared with one on each arm – he was the butt of music-hall songs and sketches. But he was also a genuine innovator, the first store-owner to introduce a staff council and tirelessly energetic in personally monitoring the details of trading. Customers used to see him write notes on his stiff starched cuffs as he made his daily tours, and if anyone personified the mantra 'retail is detail', later adopted by Sir John Sainsbury, it was Gordon Selfridge. Spedan Lewis would have the same obsessive hands-on approach, expressed in his case through tens of thousands of notes and memoranda which required the services of three secretaries to take his dictation in relays, often through the bathroom door while he was shaving.

John Lewis, by contrast, was far from being a household name. Few of his customers would have recognised the dour, frock-coated figure with the white spade beard. The nearest he came to capturing the headlines was in 1903 when he was jailed for three weeks for contempt of court after a six-year running battle with his landlords, the Portland Estate, owned by Lord Howard de Walden. After rebuilding the corner set of houses on Oxford and Holles Streets, in 1897 he acquired another property, Cavendish Buildings, which he set about connecting to 16 and 17 Holles Street in order to extend the depth of his new store. The trustees of the Howard de Walden estate grew alarmed at the spread of commerce towards the fashionable town houses of Cavendish Square, to which Holles Street led, and in 1901 they obtained a court injunction to restrain Lewis's activities. This he ignored, partly out of resentment at the whole leasehold system which always ended up benefiting the landlord, whatever improvements the tenant made.

There followed a labyrinthine battle of wills between old Lewis, now approaching seventy, and the young heir to the estate. When de Walden came of age he gave Lewis permission to build the connecting wing and to use the Holles Street houses for trade, with the stipulation that they should not look like shops, but like the private houses they were before. Lewis was instructed to put back the fireplaces that he had ripped out and replaced with central heating. He flatly refused to comply, claiming that the trustees had approved the original plan and that he did not see why, for a rent of £20,000 a year, he should not do as he wished with the property. This refusal constituted contempt of court, carrying a penalty of imprisonment.

It was announced in the press that the arrest would take place at 2 p.m. on 17 June 1903, and a large crowd of well-wishers turned up at the shop to watch the white-haired Lewis shake the hand of the sheriff's officer, call 'Goodbye all' to his assembled staff and drive off in his own carriage for the trip to Brixton Prison, followed by sympathetic choruses of 'For he's a jolly good fellow'. This, as his son Spedan later pointed out, was at a time when middle-class suffragettes had not yet made the imprisonment of respectable people commonplace.

> My father arrived at Brixton in his own carriage and pair and for most of his life told with chuckles how, when the prison authorities inquired his religion and he replied none, the Governor answered, 'Oh, we call that Church of England.' For three weeks my father sat in Brixton Prison reading Freeman's *Norman Conquest* and sustaining life on salmon and green peas and similar viands that my much distressed mother was allowed to cause to be sent in to him.

He purged his contempt by signing an undertaking to comply with the court's order, but the row rumbled on for years. During his absence in Brixton prison, the landlords had started to reinstate the fireplaces, but found it could not easily be done. Banned from overtly trading, Lewis put up notices on the boarded-up windows denouncing 'the unjust operations of the law'. He also posted notices on the pavement, inviting passers-by to consider the two houses as a 'monument of iniquity'. Another notice accused 'the young Baron' (Howard de Walden) of 'pulling the wires for the imprisonment of his old tenant'. Eventually, in 1911, the estate sued him for libel in the High Court of Justice, claiming damages. The celebrated F.E. Smith, who defended Lewis, expected damages to cost £3,000. Instead, the jury awarded the derisory one farthing. *The Times* observed tartly that the case could easily have been avoided 'by the exercise of a little common sense and moderation'.

The old man's obstinacy was a byword among his friends: after the court case the Liberal cabinet minister John Burns, strolling with an acquaintance in the London streets, described him as 'a difficult man,

John Lewis, very difficult. Not like that stone there, which is Portland stone and wears away in our London fog. Some day we'll stop that fog, as we'll stop the Thames from smelling. But he's like those setts out there – granite, Aberdeen granite. Horses' hooves won't wear that away.'

He grew increasingly eccentric about private obsessions. At the outbreak of the First World War he put up public notices denouncing the compulsory vaccination of recruits for Kitchener's Army, even managing to obtain a meeting with the prime minister, Herbert Asquith, who, in his career at the Bar had represented Lewis in at least one of his prolific lawsuits. Asquith received Lewis in his private room at 10 Downing Street on 16 June 1915, at a critical time in the war when the U-boat offensive was sinking British merchantmen (the Cunard liner *Lusitania* had been sunk five weeks earlier with the loss of 1,200 lives) and the Gallipoli campaign was foundering in bloody disaster. He listened politely as Lewis harangued him about 'the medical priests' who were bent on 'poisoning wholesale', and promised to consider the matter, but the inoculations continued.

Lewis was now over seventy, and in spite of investing his surplus cash in other property, he had still not expanded beyond the single shop in Oxford Street, though he longed to have a branch. The John Lewis store had become a successful London institution – a 'good old shop', as customers called it, remaining faithful in spite of the showy lures of Whiteley's and Harrods. In 1906, just after his elder son Spedan had been given a quarter-partnership in the business to mark his coming-of-age, Lewis walked across London from Oxford Street to Sloane Square with £20,000 in banknotes in his pocket and bought the ailing Peter Jones store, whose eponymous founder had recently died. The move was to usher in a business revolution.

CHAPTER 6:

SPREAD A LITTLE HAPPINESS

JOHN SPEDAN LEWIS, born on 22 September 1885, grew up thinking his father 'a superman, virtually infallible in matters of business'. With his brother Oswald, two years younger, he had a comfortable but narrow upbringing within the family circle. Since their father hated holidays and was only dragged to the seaside under duress, the boys seldom left the big grey mansion on Hampstead Heath except to visit the aunt in Weston-super-Mare for whom John Lewis had bought a shop.

John junior, nicknamed Speedy in the family, was a serious child, not much given to jokes. Even in school plays at his preparatory school in Hampstead, Heddon Court, he took sombre roles. A contemporary who recalled him playing Death in the *Alcestis* at the age of thirteen or fourteen said he was 'very impressive and monumental . . . a tall, bony figure with a rather dictatorial manner'. He won a Queen's Scholarship to Westminster School, where he was a day pupil and where one of his fags was Adrian Boult, later the distinguished conductor. Undoubtedly because of his mother's influence, he developed into a thinker with a social conscience and at nineteen, when he elected to join the family business rather than go to Oxford, his education was already a great deal deeper and wider than that of his father, who had been apprenticed at fourteen and had rarely thought of anything since but silks and ribbons and what they could be bought and sold for. He was given no office of his own, merely a desk in the counting-house at John Lewis: his father told him that his place was 'about the business'. Spedan compensated by devising a kind of mobile filing system of information, notes written so small that he could keep them in his pockets.

Around this time, he experienced a sudden vision of the 'extreme happiness' that could come to those who renounced great wealth entirely. The vision came to him, prosaically enough, on the top of a horse-omnibus as it turned out of the Haymarket into Trafalgar Square and became caught in a traffic jam.

> I can remember very vividly the warm glow that ran through me as for a moment I saw something of the satisfaction of those who ... renounce – and do not afterwards regret renouncing – great wealth and choose a life of extreme material simplicity, such a life as in those days, about 1907, would have cost three or four pounds a week.

But almost at once, he decided that he would not have the capacity for such a dramatic personal sacrifice.

Spedan's young manhood coincided with a tidal wave of change in British society and politics. In 1904 John Lewis senior had been elected a Liberal councillor on the London County Council – perhaps surprisingly, given his authoritarian style as an employer – and was re-elected two years later. The year 1906, when Spedan turned twenty-one and was given his quarter-share in the business, was the high summer of Liberal power in England, when the government containing Asquith, Churchill and Lloyd George was taking office and the infant Labour party, headed by Keir Hardie, made its parliamentary début with thirty seats.

In his two years 'about the business', Spedan had made many shrewd observations. His father, he now realised, was far from the superman he appeared to his family at Hampstead. Although Spedan always admired his business policy of value, assortment and absolute honesty, he now saw the limitations of his father's horizons. He consistently failed to maximise revenue from the store, which was generating profits only on the ground floor and part of the first floor; all the rest was trading at a loss. There was a mass of outdated stock and a ludicrous waste of floor space: the third floor was simply used as a stockroom. Two other huge rooms in the basement were completely empty except for some pieces of timber.

Wages were low, old John's management dictatorial and decisions arbitrary. Illness invariably meant the sick person's pay was stopped for the duration of his or her absence. There were no pension arrangements for long-serving employees, no leisure amenities for the staff, and the catering and housekeeping were inadequate for those who lived in the hostel. The business, as Spedan would later judge, was 'no more than a second-rate success achieved in a first-rate opportunity'. This was perhaps all the more surprising since the elder Lewis was forever carping at the wealth-creating success of a contemporary like Whiteley, yet failed to draw the obvious lessons from Whiteley's greater entrepreneurship and ability to anticipate shopping trends.

Lewis usually had the right ideas in theory, as his son readily admitted, but in practice things were very different. He always said he was willing to pay enough to get the right person for a given job, but when it came to the point, he resisted paying more than the minimum. He constantly advocated 'praise in public and blame in private', but in practice, Spedan wrote, 'he blamed in public at the top of his voice and hardly ever praised at all'. He often warned that the most common cause of failure in business was omitting to keep accurate accounts and to pay constant attention to them. But when the young, underpaid auditor came in with the books each year, old John would lock them up without looking at them and start talking about the land laws or some other hobbyhorse. The head of his post order department and the head of his counting house robbed him chronically for years: one was jailed for eighteen months and the other absconded to New Zealand.

Even with all this wastage and inefficiency, the store was so successful among its loyal customers, who could not find such variety or value anywhere else, that John Lewis was able to accumulate a substantial fortune, and presumably he thought this sufficient reason not to change anything. But as Spedan noted later, it mattered to the staff that the store was not operating at full throttle; they knew it could do better but they had no incentive to perform well.

Spedan's critical views hardened considerably when, on his twenty-first birthday, he was given £50,000 – a quarter of the capital of the business – and a partnership that carried a quarter of the profits after 5 per cent had been paid on the capital. The same privileges were given to Oswald when he came of age in 1908. Around this time Spedan got his first look at the accounts of the business and discovered with a shock that he, his father and his brother were together drawing £10,000 a year in interest and a further £16,000 in profit, which was as much as the entire staff was being paid.

Outside the three owner-partners, only four people were earning more than £5 a week or £250 a year, and not many were earning over thirty shillings a week. There was no sales commission except on a few premium articles. Shopwalkers got about £100 a year and buyers were recruited internally, and therefore cheaply, on five-year contracts at £100 a year rising to £150 in the fifth year, with the employer able to terminate the contract at three months' notice. Buyers had responsibility for spending large sums of money on stock and their employment contracts forbade them to take their knowledge to any competitor within a radius of three miles. When a buyer was headhunted by Whiteley's, John Lewis took William Whiteley to court over it. The radius agreement was upheld in court and the buyer had to return to Lewis's. He died in his fifties after a career that saw him create the best silk department in London, but he never earned more than £1000 a year and told Spedan he reckoned himself to be 'the worst paid man in the trade'.

Spedan was surprised that, despite his father's close-fistedness, many employees chose to stay with John Lewis for years, but screwing wages down as shops grew larger was common enough among store owners of the time, and it was leading to a lower quality of employee. By the late 1900s it had become a saying in the trade that while drapers used to get the farmer's son, now they only got the farm labourer's son. Given that the staff as a whole were earning no more than a bare living, with nothing left over for enjoyment or saving for retirement, Spedan found it shocking that his father should spend money like water on his frequent forays into litigation, and that he should be disposing of surplus cash by investing in property around London – at a far lower rate of return than he deluded himself he was getting – instead of ploughing it back into the business.

The truth was that his father for many years had been accumulating more money than he knew what to do with, and where this had not been wasted in failed litigation it had gone into investments that barely paid their way. If the elder Lewis had put his surplus cash into the business he would have been less rich in capital but drawn not a penny less in income, while 'the real money-making machine, that was the supremely important consideration, would have been much sounder and stronger', Spedan wrote in *Partnership For All,* the testament of his philosophy published in 1948. On the one hand Spedan perceived an owner with over 100 separate properties that he never saw and cared less about, and with an income so large that he was constantly buying more property to reduce the surplus, and on the other a staff so meagrely paid and insecure in their posts that they were 'far less happy than they perfectly well could have been, a happiness that would have increased very greatly both the soundness of the business and the real happiness of my father's own life'.

Spedan understood the driving force behind his father's miserly ways: that the poverty of his orphaned childhood in Somerset had obsessed him with the need to surround himself with wealth and to pass on that security to his children (he determined to have two sons and no more than two: the second son, said Spedan wryly, was simply an insurance policy against the risk that he might lose one). This 'over-developed impulse to make money' got in the way, Spedan believed, of the other side of his nature, which had real sympathy with the poor and under-privileged. He was certainly a committed radical in politics and professed egalitarian beliefs, although in the family it was said that what he really believed in was 'the divine right of employers'.

All this combined to form a powerful belief in Spedan that the essence of good management was a contented workforce. When he came to issue what we would now call a mission statement about the unique partnership concept that he introduced to British business, it ran: 'The supreme purpose of the John Lewis Partnership is simply the happiness of its members.' He also came to feel that a business was 'a living thing with rights of its own', whose earnings should be used with care to increase its efficiency, 'exactly as a good farmer feels a duty to maintain and develop the fertility of the land that he farms and to leave it in better, rather than worse, heart than when it came into his hands'.

Spedan's instincts that there must be a better way of managing the business might have taken longer to formulate as a strategy had he not suffered a riding accident in May 1909. He was thrown from his horse while riding through Regent's Park on the way from Hampstead to the Oxford Street store, and one lung was badly injured. He had to have two operations and was away from work for nearly two years, during which time he bought a farm at Harrow in Middlesex, where he lived by himself and brooded about the future of the business he was to inherit and how its wealth could be distributed more fairly.

By October 1910, two or three weeks after his twenty-fifth birthday, he was recovering in a nursing home from the second operation and formulating a set of ideas for employee ownership. (The two operations carried such an uncertain prognosis that Spedan was rated C3 for military service, which kept him out of the coming war.) The business would first be made into a limited liability company and each year would distribute non-voting shares to the employees in proportion to their pay so that they could sell them or keep them. They had to be non-voting shares to prevent outsiders from gaining control if shares were sold in sufficient numbers. Whether kept or sold, their holders would benefit from the firm's profits. Dividends to the owners from its capital should be restricted to 'a moderate fixed interest' and the remuneration of its principal manager or managers be limited to 'a handsome professional income such as an able, hard-working man might hope to make in the law or medicine or architecture'.

When his recovery was complete and he was back in Oxford Street, Spedan plucked up the courage to broach the plan to his father. Lewis senior already considered his son irresponsibly extravagant because he went to the opera once a week, but he was little disposed to encourage him even when he devoted time to new ideas for the business. This latest brainwave struck him as unrealistic and completely unworkable from the owner's point of view. 'Who do you suppose,' he demanded with his countryman's turn of phrase, 'would bear the carking cares of business for such a miserable remuneration as they would get from such a scheme as this?'

Spedan felt too emotional about it to argue, so he let the matter drop.

There was no common ground to be had. Both men were convinced of their arguments, and Spedan was unable to try any of his ideas out at Oxford Street, with the exception of setting up committees 'for Communication between the Rank and File and the Principal Management'. He also managed, when he was twenty-three, to buy sixty-three acres around the Harrow farm to be used as playing fields for the staff. He let his father think that the purchase price of £7,100 came out of his own money, although in fact he obtained a bank loan to do it; old John classed sport along with holidays and novel-reading as a waste of time and would never have countenanced spending the firm's money on such a venture.

In the meantime Spedan had many misgivings about staying in the business while his father controlled it. About once a year the pair had a major row, which would last two or three days before Eliza made peace. Spedan told his mother that whatever the 'worry and vexation', he would 'stick it until I am thirty', but if his father had not retired or was near retirement by then, he would quit. 'Another ten years of it would be too much for anybody. By the end of it there would be nothing left of them.' In the event, old John never retired formally, and Spedan was forty-four before his father's death released him into control of the business. But just before the First World War broke out he finally got his chance to manage part of it as he wanted.

Peter Jones's dire performance had not responded to Lewis's ownership, and in 1913 the Chelsea store was on the verge of collapse. In January 1914, Lewis suddenly invited his son to take over the day-to-day direction of Peter Jones as chairman, and gave him a controlling interest in the shares. But with typical miserliness, he insisted that Spedan should continue to work a full day at the Oxford Street store, only leaving for Sloane Square after 5 p.m. Since Spedan was living at Grove Farm in Harrow, this meant an extremely long and exhausting business day: night after night, he wrote, he got home about 9 p.m., 'so tired that my voice was nearly gone'. Nevertheless, he was delighted at being given a free hand at last to take a grip on the management – they had been 'spending a guinea to make a sovereign', as he said – and to try out some of his new ideas.

Spedan's first action was to shorten the working day by an hour and to start a system of 'pool' commission by department to act as a sales incentive. He then set up a series of staff committees elaborating on that at Oxford Street, through which elected representatives of the rank-and-file committees were able to meet the chairman regularly, without their managers being present, and to discuss anything they wanted with him – a distant forerunner of the 'town meeting' system that was hailed as a breakthrough for industrial democracy when America's General Electric instituted it in the 1980s.

These innovations produced a gratifying response; after six months, sales had grown by 12 per cent. Yet doubts persisted among some of the buyers, and particularly in the elderly senior partner of the accountants who audited the Peter Jones books, that a failing business could be regenerated by these methods. The doubts were relayed to John Lewis, who was already alarmed by the experiment and not impressed by its early results. He told Eliza that Spedan had no conception of the difficulty of reviving a failing business. He gave his son an ultimatum: give up his theories or return the controlling equity interest in Peter Jones.

When Spedan refused to budge, his father warned that if he did not comply, his quarter-partnership at John Lewis would be terminated. Spedan now took a calculated risk in challenging his father head-on, a bold decision given the nature of their relationship. He agreed to give up the John Lewis quarter-share in exchange for the rest of his father's interest in Peter Jones. Old John's response was to ask his younger son Oswald, with whom he had fallen out six years before, to return to the firm as Spedan's replacement in Oxford Street.

All his advisers, from his mother to the auditors, pressed Spedan not to give up his share in one of the soundest retailing businesses in London for a controlling interest in a store with a doubtful future. The Midland Bank branch adjoining Peter Jones refused to take the store's account if he went ahead. Against all this powerful opposition, Spedan forged on, reckoning that if the worst came to the worst and the business was liquidated, he would lose £35,000 but he was still single and could take the risk. One of the first things he did when he gained full control was to have the brass frontage of Peter Jones cleaned and polished. His father had regarded such niceties as a waste of money and, not wishing to draw more criticism than he needed, Spedan had let the metal go uncleaned for a year, though he thought it a great mistake, since Peter Jones was 'on Belgravia's back door step and should be its village shop'.

Working much of the time at home to give his managers a sense of freedom from supervision, he improved the wages and the catering, and separated the management of sales and buying, which greatly improved budgetary control. His biggest expenditure was on the staff accommodation above the store, which the founder of Peter Jones had formed by putting together a number of Victorian redbrick houses. Spedan thought the accommodation 'wretchedly uncomfortable' and a considerable fire-risk. The houses had not been linked by passageways, and the upper floors in each were served by a single wooden staircase. All this was changed under Spedan's direction. Corridors were driven through the party walls and hot and cold running water installed in the bedrooms. The staff now also had the luxury of plenty of bathrooms. In the great influenza epidemic of 1918, a local doctor who had known the old building commented that the Peter Jones staff had been remarkably immune, which he attributed to their hygienic conditions. By the end of the First World War, turnover at the store had increased five times to £500,000 and by 1920 a yearly loss of £8,000 had been converted to a profit of £20,000.

In fact Peter Jones, almost alone among London drapery stores, found its takings increased during the war years, and it seems likely that Spedan's reforms had something to do with this, because other stores were suffering a substantial loss of business. The wet winter of 1914 was the first setback, with rainfall two-and-a-half times higher than the average. After a year of war, Libertys of Regent Street declared less than half the previous year's profits; Swan and Edgar two-thirds. Whiteley's cut its dividend from 7 to 5 per cent and Harrods recorded a £20,000 lower profit. At Peter Jones, Spedan Lewis said with satisfaction, sales had not fallen off at all; in fact, they were the highest for eight years.

Although he remained at odds with his father over so many fundamental aspects of staff management, Spedan adhered firmly to some key John Lewis principles of trading: for example, never to hold sales with bought-in goods, only genuine clearances of surplus or old stock. Like his father, he also distrusted the value of advertising, saying 'you may hit the public on the right nerve or you may not'. At a shareholders' meeting in April 1914, a Mr Stevens asked the new chairman why Peter Jones held no sales while other stores were packing customers in at these events. 'There seems to be no life in this place,' the shareholder complained.

Spedan retorted:

> My father has traded in Oxford Street for fifty years and has never had a sale yet. I hope to trade there for another fifty years and I shall never have a sale. I thoroughly disbelieve in sales. They served, no doubt, a useful purpose at one time and they may serve a useful purpose in the suburbs now. But the public has been had in every possible way through these sales, and the public that we want to cultivate – the sensible public that appreciates good value and comes back to the same business and is not caught with chaff – that public is increasingly suspicious of the sales. My father has an overwhelmingly strong opinion that sales are a mistake for building up a sound permanent business and I entirely agree with that opinion . . .

He then proceeded to give his views on advertising, and when the same shareholder persisted: 'Why not have a good sale and advertise that way?' Spedan simply ignored the speaker, asking around the room, 'Are there any other questions?'

In 1915 Oswald Lewis, who had graduated in law from Oxford and become a member of Middle Temple, though he never practised as a barrister, was invalided out of the Westminster Dragoons and returned to John Lewis in Oxford Street where he had worked in the counting house between school and university, and during vacations from Oxford. He was to spend just over ten years with the family business as a young man, but his heart was in politics – like his father, he served as a London County Councillor, though as a Conservative, not a Liberal – and in 1926 he left the firm for a career as a Tory MP. He represented Colchester in Essex from 1929 to 1945, never rising out of the back benches but serving on numerous committees, the meat and potatoes of Westminster parliamentary life. In 1951 he returned to John Lewis for the third and last time as the partnership's director of financial operations until he retired in 1963.

Oswald Lewis never had the driving ambition of his brother, but he seems to have been an engaging personality, who comes across in those leisurely years before the Great War as a young man-about-town fond of nights out in the West End and forever aggravating his father by some sloppiness or other. Letters from him to Spedan in the year 1907, when he was turning twenty, have a Bertie Woosterish tone.

> Dear Spedan
> Joys of life!
> Dad's make [sic] another oration about my handwriting. He now says that if I cannot satisfy his wishes in this respect I cannot come back to the business after my holiday.
> No heat displayed on either side, on the contrary we remain on the best of terms. As Carson [a colleague in the store] remarked: 'If this is the sort of thing that Mr Lewis says about the people with whom he is on the best of terms, what does he say about those with whom he is on bad terms?'
> Yr loving brother Oswald
> Cheer ho! Girls!

Again in the summer of 1907 he writes: 'You'd have smiled to see me curled up in the corner of a motor-bus with an opera hat over one eye bowling along the Edgeware [sic] Road at 4 a.m. last Friday! . . .' and tells of his father bawling out an employee over the phone. 'You should have heard him blackguarding Harry on the phone this morning, he might have been 27 instead of 72!'

Oswald has left a vivid picture of what it was like to work in a pre-1914 department store, with frock-coated shopwalkers – one to each department, though the important silks department had three – signing bills and running the department in the absence of the buyer. One of Gordon Selfridge's many innovations, startling to the old-school London shopkeeper, was to demonstrate that the shopwalker was a redundant figure. Women employees at John Lewis all dressed in black; long woollen dresses if they were working in the storerooms, silk if dealing with customers in the showrooms. The dresses had to have high collars held up by wire supports, a considerable discomfort to those with less than swan-like necks, who would keep their collars tucked inside. As one contemporary remembered, 'when the alarm went round that old John Lewis was coming through the departments there was a frenzied pulling up of collars'.

The buyers were godlike creatures who carried themselves with dignity and were expected to wear top hats – even, as one complained, on a visit to silk manufacturers in Switzerland. He said a top hat did not seem to go well with the mountains. When Oswald decided to wear a stylish morning tailcoat instead of the customary frock coat he was made to feel frivolous. Male employees predominated; John Lewis thought no woman could fold lengths of silk properly. (He was a mass of prejudices, disliking blonde or auburn hair in women and educated accents in his sales staff, which he seemed to think would intimidate some of the customers: he himself spoke with a Somerset burr all his life.)

At the close of business each day, Oswald recalled in an article for the firm's journal in 1964:

> an elderly man used to put the day's takings into a large black
> bag with which he then walked to Oxford Circus, took a bus
> to Trafalgar Square and then walked down the Strand to

Coutts' Bank who then handled our business. He did this at the same time every day, so that to anyone interested it was quite obvious what he was doing, and yet no one thought it at all a rash proceeding. I should not care to do that job today.

In those days we used horse transport for our delivery service, and for this purpose we had a small fleet of two-wheeled carts drawn by horses of which we were justifiably proud. We used to buy them under the hammer at Tattersalls or Aldridges. Their quality was such that when war broke out they were all commandeered and by a strange chance were allotted as chargers to the Yeomanry Regiment [the Westminster Dragoons] in which I had for some years held a commission. So that I had the double coincidence of walking about in my old school [Westminster] playing fields in Vincent Square examining the chargers that had a few days before been drawing the carts of my old firm.

By the end of the war Spedan had clarified the details of what he called 'a far-reaching experiment in industrial democracy'. In essence, as his wife was to write to a male cousin, it was 'to limit the earnings of capital to a reasonable reward and divide the rest among the workers'. Its foundation stone was the concept of 'Fairer Shares', the title of a second book he would write expounding his philosophy in the 1950s. The sharing concept was to be threefold – 'sharing of gain, sharing of knowledge and sharing of power'. This meant more than share ownership; it involved a fundamental reallocation of rewards and responsibilities, with management still retaining the right to manage but being wholly accountable to employees. Access to information about the company was to be a right of every partner, and the John Lewis *Gazette*, started in 1918, has always acted as a conduit for debate, sometimes acrimonious, in which managers could be challenged and required to reply.

Spedan maintained that his concept owed nothing to early social pioneers such as Robert Owen but was 'a gradual, natural growth from practical efforts to solve the problem of one particular business'. Years later, he would express it in rather grander philosophical terms, comparing the concept to the Benedictine foundations of the Middle Ages, which 'tamed the wilderness which still possessed much of Europe, giving their members both something to live for and something to live by. Communities of co-operating producers – or partnerships – give their members the duty and the opportunity of taming the social wilderness of modern times.'

In all his writings, Spedan never fully explained why he had chosen to distribute the wealth of his business to those who worked for him. He was at pains, however, to dismiss any idea of a religious motive ('I do nothing in that way'), or an 'appetite for social distinction'. Writing in an early issue of the *Gazette*, he said of those who sought deeper significance in his actions:

> It does not occur to them that there may be people who will devote themselves to the invention of a new system of business for its own sake, exactly as a man may devote himself to scientific research or to writing a book or to painting a picture, simply for the sake of doing the thing and not for any consequential reward at all.

Spedan once said that his work on the Partnership vision was really 'a new form of political career' – indeed, in his early twenties he turned down a number of invitations to stand for Parliament, including a tempting approach from the whips of the then Liberal government. He had no financial motive for remaining in the business world: his father was in favour of him taking up politics and quitting the business – presumably taking his threatening ideas with him – and Spedan was in no doubt that he would still inherit a substantial part of his father's fortune if he went to Westminster. But the vision of what he wanted to do in business was too strong, and for over forty years he continued to think out and develop his ideas for the Partnership experiment, which he confidently expected would be the spearhead of a new movement in British industry. Looking back on those forty years, he wrote: 'A society should aim at dealing with its members like a sensible, well-to-do, good-hearted British family. This implies a blend of constitutional monarchy, equality before the law, freedom of speech and majority voting.' Perhaps he saw his career as accomplishing in reality what politicians could only talk about in abstracts.

> The British are natural team-workers, quite exceptionally gifted with ability to trust each other and to give and take, to make not merely easy but really quite difficult concessions. In politics we have invented a system of self-government that has been taken as an example all over the world, and in the co-operative society of consumers we have achieved another invention of which the same is true.

Just after the Oxford Street store was bombed out in September 1940 he said that if the Partnership had not been organised as it was, he doubted whether the business could have stood the strain of being so heavily damaged. The set of ideas behind it, he explained, was really very simple.

> Capital should have a moderate fixed interest with a reasonable but never unlimited reward for taking a risk. All further earnings should go to all workers alike from top to bottom. Thus the whole of the true profit of the business would be ploughed back into its own efficiency and there should be all possible care to ensure that the efficiency is as great as may be.
>
> If a business is expanding and needs working capital, the workers should take their profits in stock instead of cash. The stock should be their permanent property to sell whenever they choose. It should be entitled to a moderate fixed cumulative dividend and no more, and it should have no votes so long as its dividends are paid punctually or so long as there is a certain dividend reserve fund . . . For my own part I have not the slightest doubt that the great part of the business of the world will come to be done in this way . . .

More than thirty-five years after his death, only a handful of companies in Britain has followed the example of the John Lewis Partnership. Profit-sharing schemes abound, and industry is full of hollow talk about staff 'empowerment' and participation, but Spedan Lewis's revolutionary ideas of 1910, enshrined in the company constitution as settlements in trust in 1929 and 1950, evidently look as threatening to the owners of family firms at the end of the twentieth century as they appeared to old John Lewis with his 'carking cares of business'.

In 1918, it was all fresh and new. The first issue of the *Gazette*, on 16 March that year, began the revolutionary idea of publishing weekly sales and profit figures. It also contained a letter addressed 'To My Fellow-Employees of Peter Jones Ltd.' and signed 'J. Spedan Lewis', in which he set out his plan to share with them the government and profits of the business. A month later, at the annual general meeting, Spedan announced his intention to introduce a profit-sharing scheme. He told the Peter Jones shareholders:

> Believe me, in the next twenty or thirty years if you want a really sound industrial concern you will have to admit your employees to a far larger share of the total earnings than before. The days when a lot of shareholders could stay home doing nothing and take a very large proportion of the earnings of a business are well over.

Later that year Spedan gave the employees a third week's paid holiday, unheard-of in the retail trade of that time, and began to recruit university graduates, both men and women. He was convinced that business would never be properly efficient until it could attract the same kind of well-qualified candidate as the learned professions: eighty years on, the fact that as a whole it still fails to do so is yet another testimony to his extraordinary foresight. One of the women graduates was Sarah Beatrice Hunter, the daughter of an architect and a graduate of Somerville College, Oxford, who joined the buying department in 1922 because of sympathy with the aims of the new partnership. She married

Spedan Lewis a year later. Another was the young Amy Johnson, newly graduated from Sheffield University in 1925, a fact which she was careful to emphasise in her application. Five years later she would be making her pioneer solo flight to Australia and embarking on a record-breaking career and international fame, but in the mid-1920s she recorded that while looking for hostel accommodation as an employee of Peter Jones, one landlady advised her 'not to tell the other girls that I worked in a shop, because they were rather snobbish and wouldn't have anything to do with shop girls'. In the store itself, Amy Johnson seems to have enjoyed the work and the atmosphere, despite a flash of snobbishness herself. 'In spite of being tired, I've never felt miserable or unhappy. Everyone is so extraordinarily nice. I think shop girls in a good class of shop are among the nicest working girls there are. All I know in Peter Jones are nice – though of course not the kind one makes intimate friends of.'

Spedan constantly thought about ways of improving efficiency and was a devotee of the Philadelphia engineer Frederick W. Taylor's 'scientific management', then sweeping US industry. In 1919 he suggested to the finance director of Peter Jones that calendars could be used in all departments to show at a glance those activities that were routine, those which arose only occasionally, and by what date materials were to be delivered. This, he added, would also enable people's work to be covered by others in case of illness. But he admitted that he had 'a terrible time' in dealing with Peter Jones's finances. His ideas of financial management had been formed in a business with 'a great superfluity of ready money' and in which a good half of the turnover was in cash, while most John Lewis account customers paid by the month. At Peter Jones, he had started a policy of encouraging credit sales, which raised the turnover enormously but damaged the cash flow because a full 80 per cent of sales were now on credit. The cost of renovating the delapidated staff quarters absorbed nearly all his spare funds. 'I began to discover that making a profit is not necessarily to be paying your way.'

By the end of the war there was an urgent need for working capital. Spedan was forced to sell his farm at Harrow and move into a flat. With the farm went the playing fields, which distressed him deeply. He had thought of them as a sort of fairyland and for years afterwards he used to dream that he had got the property back and was walking around it looking at new buildings and thinking how they could be cleared away or changed back to the old standards. Shortly before his death, old John told Spedan how sorry he had been that he had had to sell, and that he would gladly have lent him the money.

'He had obviously forgotten utterly, and I did not try to recall to his mind, that I had almost gone down on my knees to him to do that very thing,' Spedan wrote bitterly in 1948.

> The Partnership now has some hundreds of acres of very lovely country club on the Thames at Cookham and is starting others in Liverpool and Sheffield and in Hampshire, but nothing will make up for the loss of those sixty acres adjoining, as they did, two railway stations [South Harrow and Sudbury Hill] by which the ground could be reached in twenty minutes from Marylebone on the Great Central Railway and forty-five minutes from Sloane Square on the Metropolitan and District. So far as I was concerned, the loss of those playing-fields was in some ways the most painful of all the many sorrows that my father's temperament, aggravated and warped as it had been by the hard conditions of his early life, made for us both.

He used some of the proceeds of £20,000 from the sale of Grove Farm to replace the loss of the sports grounds by acquiring smaller club premises in Teddington. In 1920 Peter Jones' profits for the first time exceeded £20,000, and Spedan was able to distribute the first 'Partnership benefit.' First, however, he had to obtain the formal consent of the outside shareholders in April to change the Articles of Association and allow profit-sharing to begin.

It was not a happy meeting. Some shareholders had come in order to oppose it on the grounds that it was unfair to them, while others criticised the 'unwarrantably uncompromising tone' of Spedan Lewis's communications about the scheme. He apologised, launched into an eloquent defence of the plan and set out his own financial interest. He held £35,000 of debentures and almost all the £60,000 (nominal) ordinary shares, but not many of the £60,000 (nominal) preference shares, whose cumulative dividend of 5.5 per cent was far in arrears. It was proposed that these arrears should be foregone in return for a permanent increase of 2 per cent in the rate of the preference dividend and a reduction in the rights of the ordinary shares so that the profit would go to the employees. He won an easy majority on a show of hands.

The next issue of the *Gazette* featured the first use of the words 'Partnership' and 'Partner', which were soon in common use throughout the firm. At the same time, Spedan said that the profit-sharing scheme would be called 'Partnership Benefit' to differentiate his system, where the workers would share the whole of the profit among themselves, from schemes where profits were shared between workers and owners. Employees were given 'Share Promises', handsome printed documents with an orange stamp telling the holder how many shares he or she would receive in due course, together with a cumulative yearly dividend of 7½ per cent, payable twice yearly. If for any reason shares could not be provided, the promises were to be redeemed for cash. In the first ten years of the Partnership's existence, from 1920 to 1930, these benefits ran at about 20 per cent a year, or ten weeks' extra pay over a full year. In the early 1950s the chief accountant worked out that between Spedan taking over Peter Jones in January 1914 and January 1951, Partnership members had received in all more than £3.25m over their regular pay.

In his memoirs *Partnership For All*, Spedan recalled how moved he had been to learn that one of the shop girls, convinced at last that the promissory documents really represented money, exclaimed: 'But I have got thirty of them. Fancy me worth thirty pounds!' and burst into tears. The share promises were finally redeemed in 1929 by a special share issue worth just under £77,000 when the John Lewis Partnership was floated on the Stock Exchange.

Ironically, just as the Peter Jones workers were benefiting from Spedan's revolution, over in the parent store on Oxford Street the employees were going on strike for the first and only time in the company's history. It started in April 1920, precipitated by resentment at the knowledge that the firm had done well during the wartime boom but that pay levels remained low. At the outbreak of war in 1914, John Lewis had announced that he would make good any differences between the military pay of staff who were called up and their peacetime earnings. But by the end of the war, pay in the retail trade generally had fallen badly behind that of other occupations and the Shop Assistants' Union, formed in 1891, was fighting for a fixed minimum wage and an improvement in working conditions. At John Lewis in 1920, a salesman of twenty-one with three years' experience was still getting only £2.15s. a week, and out of that he was expected to pay ten shillings for meals and another ten shillings for lodging if he lived in.

Reacting against old John Lewis's increasingly authoritarian conduct of the business, 400 of the 500 staff agreed to join strike action. Although Lewis, along with thirteen other store-owners, had agreed to raise pay rates to the minimum approved by the new Grocery Wages Board, this was still felt to be too low for central London. Some strikers wanted a rise of 50 per cent. They also demanded easier working conditions; to be able to leave the shop during their lunch break; to be given an elected committee to control the living-in arrangements; and to be allowed to join a trade union. This last was complete anathema to the eighty-four-year-old owner, who considered that the 'vapourings of the accursed Trade Unionists' were to blame for the whole thing, especially for sending young girls out in the streets on picket duty while the strike leader, 'this scoundrel, lies in bed at six o'clock in the morning'. In a communication addressed 'To our young men and maidens', Lewis noted that 'no small number' of women employees had remained working at the store 'from girlhood to advanced age'. The 'accursed Trade Unionists' were out 'to lead idle lives at your expense by drawing from you money that might be saved for better purposes . . .'

The strike was planned to coincide with a big silk sale on 26 April. Lewis took immediate action. He closed all the other departments on the day of the sale, transferred the non-strikers to the silks counters, which he took over in person, and was sold out by 4 p.m. As the weeks went by, Lewis refused to be interviewed except to growl, when asked whether he would reinstate the strikers' jobs, 'If I see them on their hands and knees I shall not take them back.' The women and girls on strike were told to quit their hostel accommodation.

The strike was followed with fascination by the press and other department store employees, and there was considerable public sympathy for those taking part. The *Daily Sketch* carried animated photographs of 'London's happy shop-girl strikers', contrasted with the glowering, white-bearded figure of old John in his Homburg hat and overcoat going home after work with a wrapped roll of silk under his arm. Telegrams of support came from former John Lewis employees all over the world, and donations totalling nearly £2,500 poured in. The staff of Harrods and the Army and Navy Stores both sent £300, the wholesale textile houses £250, the dressmakers £150. Even Queen Mary instructed that money from her should be regularly put in the strikers' collection boxes in Oxford Street.

Well-wishers sent theatre tickets, music-hall artists gave concerts for the strikers' benefit, they were entertained in private homes, at restaurants and at seaside boarding-houses, and cars were put at their disposal for outings. Offers of accommodation for the dislodged women employees came from all sections of society. The National Union of Railwaymen and the Vehicle Workers' Union instructed their members not to handle goods destined for John Lewis. Every day the 400 strikers marched round the store building, through Cavendish Square and across Oxford Street into Hanover Square, holding up the traffic as the crowds of shoppers cheered.

On 5 May Lewis complained in his diary: 'The Press still lean to the Strikers,' and on 11 May he noted that Oswald was 'depressed by the picketing outside my premises.' Oswald was told to distribute a £50 bonus to each of the men remaining loyal and £20 to the senior women, 'with which they were much pleased'. On 2 June the strikers gave in, while defiantly declaring 'We retire in the firm belief in the justice of our cause, and decide that no one shall return to work for John Lewis.' He had already replaced them in any case. 'The world around him may have altered,' wrote the London *Evening News* in an editorial, 'but Mr Lewis remains fixed and unalterable.'

Lewis may have reacted like a harsh Victorian employer, but by now he had changed his mind about Spedan's experiment in Sloane Square. Soon after the strike the pair were reconciled and the old man was telling his wife: 'That place is a credit to the boy – a very great credit.' In 1923 he invited Spedan to rejoin him in partnership at Oxford Street, on the understanding that he could continue to run Peter Jones separately. Three years later, when the General Strike brought large sections of British commerce to a halt, Peter Jones continued to function: the store sent out notices to its account customers that the staff's wages would continue to be paid so long as funds were available, and that account customers could help this by paying as soon as they could. Customers actually queued to do so. (Twice in the Second World War when pay rates had to be cut, the Partnership issued a pledge that the money would be made good when circumstances made it possible.)

Spedan had for some time been pondering over his father's wish to have a statement of the store's policy placed on public view in the stores. He thought he could improve on the old man's version: 'John Lewis and Company, founded in 1864 to supply the public with good value for ready money.' In the summer of 1921 he began to formulate the pledge for which the John Lewis stores remain famous. A memorandum that year to a manager at Peter Jones ran:

> My other main rule, to which there must never be any exception without my express consent, is that, profit or no profit, we must never be undersold ... if I did stock [an article on which a competitive price meant inadequate profit] I certainly should not ask for it any more than the lowest price at which the customer can obtain it elsewhere ... I should certainly never let myself be under-sold by any shop of standing within two miles of these premises.

The slogan 'Never Knowingly Undersold' was introduced in April 1926 with a memorandum from Spedan to all buyers at Oxford Street, and copied to Oswald Lewis. Paragraph six ran: 'The policy that you are to follow henceforward is this: Never knowingly be undersold without my consent in writing. If you break this rule to any serious extent I am sure to hear of it before very long and carelessness in this respect is a thing of which I take a very grave view.' From time to time senior managers would protest that the pledge was unworkable, but Spedan always maintained that the psychological effect was so valuable, both on customers and staff, that it should be kept going whatever the difficulties. At one stage when price competition became particularly fierce it was qualified from 'any shop in London' to 'anyone whose premises are so near that the cost of journeying to them would be negligible in time, trouble and money'. Today, the policy has so proved itself that no such qualifications are made – it has even been extended to purchases made abroad – and many other retailers offer to refund or even pay more if a customer finds a similar article cheaper elsewhere.

As John Lewis entered his nineties with no sign of retiring from active participation in the business, relations between father and son had reached a kind of wary equilibrium. Spedan remained in awe of his father's volatile temper until the old man died, as did the rest of the staff at John Lewis and Peter Jones. 'When old John came down from Hampstead in his top hat and tails we had to watch out – somebody was for the chop,' as one pensioner recalled in the 1980s. 'If he was wearing his old green muffler, all was well.' Another pensioner, interviewed for the *Gazette* in the 1950s, remembered how, before old John acquired his Rolls Royce Silver Ghost, he would drive to the store every Sunday in his carriage and pair, and rattle every door-handle in the building to assure himself that it was locked, despite the fact that there was a watchman on duty. As late as 1926, two years before he died, he still had the power to cause his son, then aged forty-one, to fret about him coming to lunch at Oxford Street. A memorandum dated 25 October that year and marked 'Confidential' went to the restaurant manager, with detailed instructions on his father's faddish eating habits and how he should be kept happy.

His father, Spedan wrote, was likely to order soup or coffee and a large number of a particular biscuit, 'a large, thin, square water-biscuit', which the restaurant should be sure to have 'in first-rate condition'.

He has an extreme dislike of any biscuits that bear any name other than that of Huntley and Palmer. The other day he came to lunch and you sent him some biscuits that seemed to me to be very inferior in themselves and that were, in fact, not Huntley and Palmer's . . . Please to keep always also a jar of the very best French dried plums that can be got anywhere, and never to be without Parmesan cheese. My Father will sometimes lunch off beans sprinkled with this cheese when he cannot be induced to eat anything else. I do not think that he will come at all often [to the restaurant] but, of course, we ought to be most careful that there is nothing to fret him when he does come.

For the same reason, never let the waitress who is waiting upon his table have so much to do that she is in the least likely ever to keep him waiting or to keep anyone waiting at any of the adjacent tables. My Father is extremely fidgety upon this point. Delays on the other side of the room . . . will not catch his eye, but there must be no delays in his own immediate neighbourhood.

Never come near his table yourself unless he sends for you. His temperament is now naturally querulous and it is, therefore, better that he should be given the least possible opportunity to begin talking to anyone about anything. He likes your lady superintendent: he might or might not like you and it will be better, therefore, that . . . she rather than you shall catch his eye.

In the same year, Spedan was fretting to his advertising manager: 'I am anxious that my Father shall not become aware that we are spending even a little money in advertising. For this reason I want to avoid all the papers that he is especially likely to see' – and he went on to list *The Times, Sunday Times, Daily Chronicle, Evening Standard* and *Daily Mirror* among others. Many perfectly valid business practices introduced by Spedan, such as buyers' sales targets and how far departmental figures differed above or below that of the previous half-year, had to be kept from old John – indeed, he seemed to feel that the less old John knew about anything, the quieter life would be. In April 1926 the manager of the counting house was asked to get a copy of the figures showing differences of sales and stock at Peter Jones and to post them on consecutive afternoons in the buyers' dining room at Oxford Street, but not before 3 p.m. and to take them down at close of business so that 'we shall run the least possible risk that my Father will go into the dining-room and see them himself.'

Later that year Spedan was worrying that reports of how he was managing the stores would get into the *Drapers Record*, a paper regularly read by the old man. He asked an intermediary to get in touch with the editor and persuade him that any suggestion that Spedan was running the business differently from his father's ideas would be 'deeply distressing to him'.

On 19 September 1928, in his ninety-third year, old John died at Spedan Tower. Control of a business worth over £1 million, with two famous stores in central London, now passed absolutely to Spedan, who had already acquired his brother's quarter-partnership by mutual agreement. Decades later, two women employees then living in the Weymouth Street hostel recalled how Spedan's taking over meant immediate improvement in their living conditions. There were rugs beside their beds and an evening meal laid out on tables when they returned from work. 'We'd had to go and collect it ourselves before, and it made all the difference in the world to find it ready waiting for us.'

Spedan's first move was to buy the neighbouring store to the east, T. J. Harries and Co., which had a short frontage on Holles Street and a long one on Oxford Street, the prime display area. John Lewis had always had most of its frontage on Holles Street and, thanks to old John's belief in the pre-eminence of piece goods, the shop windows it did have on Oxford Street were filled with lengths of fabric, despite the fact that these sales were now losing ground to ready-made fashion garments. The former Harries premises were immediately turned over to fashion and accessories, though John Lewis as a store continued to prosper out of dress fabrics as other stores contracted their business in that area: it remained *the* place to shop in London for dressmaking materials, a reputation it maintains today.

Spedan floated the business on the stock market as John Lewis and Co., raising over £1.5m. in preference shares. He was now free to put his Partnership plan into full action. The John Lewis Partnership was formed in 1929 with a capital of £312,000, and the first 'settlement in trust' was drawn up, selling to the employees the right to all present and future income from his property in Peter Jones and John Lewis. This was a necessary legal mechanism to entrench the new distribution of profits, whereby they would be taxed on numerous lower incomes instead of one high income as before.

Spedan was advised that the two businesses could be sold at two to three hours' notice for more than £1m in cash. This became the valuation for the sale of the John Lewis Partnership to its employees, and by taking the price chiefly in a mixture of deferred bonds and deferred ordinary shares, the repayment period for the workers was spread over more than thirty years. Both Spedan and Beatrice renounced their directors' fees and other remunerations. 'If my wife and I had chosen to sell out,' Spedan wrote many years later, 'we should have had a seven-figure fortune that, invested in sound securities, would have produced an income of upwards of £40,000 a year.' He admitted that such a prospect would have had attractions, without any of the strains of running a business and while they were still in their early forties and able to enjoy moneyed leisure. But remembering his moment of truth on the Trafalgar Square omnibus, he was sure that the alternative course had brought more satisfaction in the end.

Introducing the new era, Spedan wrote:

> The Partnership's supreme purpose is to secure the fairest possible sharing by all its members of the advantages of ownership – gain, knowledge and power; that is to say, their happiness in the broad sense of that word so far as happiness depends upon gainful occupation. No one partnership can hope to suit everyone and the John Lewis Partnership does not attempt to do so. It is intended only for those who to be

really happy need to feel they are giving good service to the general community and whom its characters and methods suit well enough in all other ways.

He was later to sum it up more succinctly in one of his many memorable aphorisms: 'Partnership is justice. Better than justice, it is kindness.'

Chapter 7:

'The Good Captain

of a Well-Run Ship'

'MY FATHER REACHED the age of ninety-two and never retired,' wrote Spedan, a touch bitterly, in his testament, *Partnership For All*, published in 1948. 'That exceptional chance crippled for upwards of fifteen years this partnership's development. Ten years later, the approach and advent of this war crippled it again for upwards of seven years, to say nothing of all that we lost, and are losing still, by our special bad luck in being so heavily bombed.' But for those two circumstances, he felt the experiment would have made much further progress. If his father had retired at seventy-five, the age subsequently laid down by the Partnership, Spedan would have had full control of both businesses as early as 1911, and he was in no doubt that both financially and in its social development, the Partnership would have been much better off.

The 1929 settlement in trust was only an interim measure. Spedan was still worried that he had not worked out a way to preserve the Partnership against control passing to an outsider, or from being wound up and its assets distributed. Since his riding accident and the serious chest operations that followed, which offered no reliable assurance for his future health, Spedan had been haunted by mortality and the fear he would die before the Partnership was properly secured for its members. Although all dividends from his shareholding now passed to the trust, he continued to retain practical control through the retention of ordinary shares until the second settlement in trust was drawn up in 1950. At that stage, all his remaining shares and the control that went with them passed to the trustees, and Spedan finally renounced the power to wind the Partnership up: henceforth its future lay in the hands of the chairman, his deputy and three partners elected by the central council.

For the shop workers and managers in John Lewis and Peter Jones, the scheme quickly showed results. In 1929 it produced bonuses of some £75,000 over and above the ordinary earnings of the partners, as they were now officially known. This was in addition to heavy investment in a sickness benefit scheme and holiday facilities, including a riverside country house called Odney, capable of sleeping nearly 100 people, at Cookham on the Thames. The atmosphere in that first year of the Partnership was full of optimism and pride. There was a new relaxation in the air. The male assistants still wore striped trousers and frock coats, with stiff white collars, but women could now shed their Victorian black for the new house colour of green, in dresses of their choice. There were tennis and boating weekends at Cookham and 'a marvellous country house-party atmosphere', recalled one manager of the time. The Partnership had its own music society with a conductor, Charles Groves, who later became a distinguished conductor with the BBC and music director of the English National Opera. It also boasted a soccer team which in the spring of 1929 played and beat the team of Peter Robinson, the old-established fashion store on Oxford Circus. The stores were becoming fashionable and newsworthy: Gracie Fields, then Britain's biggest popular singing star, caused a stir when she was seen shopping at John Lewis, and in June of 1929 a Peter Jones removals van was spotted outside 10 Downing Street loading up the possessions of the defeated Conservative prime minister, Stanley Baldwin.

The Partnership's undoubted *esprit de corps*, to which scores of old employees testify, was partly due to the magnetic personality of the Founder, constantly to be seen in different departments each day, but on a practical level it was the profit-sharing that counted. From 1928 to 1970, bonuses were paid in 5 per cent preference shares, negotiable on the stock market; it was only from 1970 that they became wholly paid in cash. Above all was the umbrella of secure employment. In the great depression which followed the stock market collapse of October 1929 and the failure of much of the US banking system, people recruited by Spedan – always, from his retirement day in 1955, known as the Founder – were thankful to be in the Partnership with the safe jobs assured by its constitutional principles. Paul May, an Oxford First in classics who was one of a select group of brilliant graduates brought into retailing by Spedan, was offered a management job in 1932 on a three-year contract rising from £500 to £700 a year, a good professional income at the time. No other retailer then was recruiting the sort of people who might have become high-flying civil servants or academics, and, apart from the pay and prospects, one reason they joined him was the attraction of the Partnership vision.

'His ideas on how business should be organised were very far ahead of their time and, unfortunately, still remain so,' said May in a 1985 book published to mark the centenary of Spedan's birth.

> I think in his own way he was a genius. He was single-minded in devoting every minute to forming the Partnership and giving it a satisfactory commercial base. His imagination and concept of Partnership, his very keen quick brain, his clear understanding of merchandise techniques, his determination, his ability to attract and retain the respect and affection of good brains with his standards I think made failure an impossibility . . .

Spedan thought and wrote a good deal about leadership. He was constantly referring to Napoleon and the attributes of a man 'whose soul is born single, able to be alone, to choose and to command'. But he was realistically aware that a business enterprise could not be sustained on the chance of finding such rare attributes. The Partnership should therefore not depend so much on the genius of a single leader as on the skills of good management. In later years he would say that whoever was at the head of the Partnership need have no more uncommon qualities than 'the good captain of a well-run ship'. In his stores he was a very visible leader, like his father a familiar figure on the shop floor, but unlike some other store owners, his presence was intended more for the benefit of the staff than the customers. Sir Woodman Burbidge, the founder of Harrods, once told the young Spedan that he had his top hats made with especially stiff brims because he spent so much time among customers who liked to be 'recognised and saluted'. Spedan preferred to do less socialising and more active work on the shop floor. If the boss had any spare time, he once suggested, he should help out a junior member of staff with the duller parts of his job.

Spedan in his mid-forties was one of the handsomest men of his generation, with a chiselled face but legs oddly short for his long torso. He was always impeccably groomed and turned out, his hands were immaculately manicured and his hair was cut once a week. But what impressed people who encountered him for the first time was the coiled-up energy and dynamism that swept them along on the wave of his ideas. Sir Bernard Miller, who succeeded the Founder as chairman in 1955, recalled his awed first meeting with Spedan, who used to sit behind a very high desk with only his face and shoulders visible. 'He seemed to be almost on the point of explosion all the time, tremendous force coming out of this very long chin. The absolute dynamism of the man came through.'

Spedan believed in the value of energy almost above that of intellect. 'There is one quality that a trader needs that is not a matter of mere combination of talents individually not rare,' he wrote to one of his financial staff in 1950. 'I mean sheer nervous energy. . . If the Partnership is really to prosper, its leaders need continually to be asking themselves not how can we be more intelligent, but how can we be more effectively energetic.' His own inexhaustible springs of energy and stamina came, he claimed, from his mother's side of the family. A Baker had won the 'crick', the three-mile race at Rugby school. His father, on the other hand, used to get tired very quickly, though his nervous energy was recharged rapidly through sheer effort and the will to work.

Spedan told Miller, an economics graduate who had passed the tough

Civil Service examination and had already been offered a Whitehall place, that he was recruiting from universities to form a team to develop the Partnership. He made the young man feel that here was a businessman concerned with more than just making money; that his ideas were an exciting new manifestation of the sort of thing that had been stirring in the early part of the nineteenth century with the philosophies of Robert Owen and other social pioneers.

Miller and May, and most of the other high-flyers Spedan lured to Oxford Street, were often forced to the point of resignation by the pace at which he drove himself and others as he fine-tuned the Partnership idea and how the business should be run, and by the torrent of memoranda from the Founder that poured out on departmental managers. He could fly into uncontrollable rages, throwing his hat on the floor and jumping on it, or banging his desk so hard that the inkwell bounced up and overturned. But invariably, just when a permanent rift seemed inevitable, he would disarm the harassed executive with a dinner at Prunier's in St James's Street, then London's pre-eminent fish restaurant, or an invitation to the country house he had acquired in Hampshire's Test Valley, Leckford Abbas. 'At times one thought this man must be crazy, but one was swept along,' recalled Miller. 'It was really a tremendous experience.'

Miller later compared Spedan's intellectual style to that of the Conservative maverick Enoch Powell, able to think an argument right through and pursue it to its conclusions whatever the opposition. Miller thought Spedan would have been outstanding in any number of fields. He was widely read with a huge trove of knowledge on all manner of subjects, and was never short of examples to illustrate a point. 'He could find the weak points in anyone else's argument with tremendous accuracy and devastating pungency, which made him a formidable debating opponent,' said Miller. His principal failing lay in the demands he made on individuals for efficiency and avoidance of failure, which sat oddly with his genuine care for people in the mass. Barbara Thomas, editor of the *Gazette* for twenty-three years, wrote in the seventy-fifth-anniversary issue that 'editing in the Founder's day was like going over Niagara Falls in a barrel'.

Several of his protégés, while admiring the almost daily evolution of the Partnership in its founder's brain, thought his incessant urge to experiment often led to a lack of cohesion in the business. His approach to both people and business, said May, had 'a strong element of the naturalist experimenter' (which happened to be one of his hobbies). 'Try anything that looks promising, scrap it if it doesn't work, and now and then pull the plants up to see how the roots are growing.' May believed that, dynamic leader though Spedan was, it was only after his reluctant retirement in 1955 that the Partnership began to work as he had intended it should, both as a social and as a trading organisation. Although the Partnership became Spedan's whole life outside his hobby of natural history, May suggested that he never really understood the difference between running a single shop, as he had managed Peter Jones, and running the group of widely dispersed stores which he built up in the 1930s.

Spedan found it difficult to delegate and thought central management should know everything that happened in the group. He also had an imperfect grasp of finance and taxation, and some of his ideas on remuneration resulted in tax problems for senior partners. He himself did not see his management style as being one of control and command; rather that of a racehorse trainer who succeeds through studying temperament and form and giving the right orders to the stable-men, not by riding the horses at exercise himself. That was not the impression left with his managers and departmental heads, who daily received a stream of memoranda from him, on everything from leadership to keeping a good range of stock.

Innovations and ideas poured from him, transmitted to paper and copied to their recipients by three devoted secretaries who worked all hours – even on Saturdays – and, rather surprisingly, stayed with him for years. He was in the habit of writing immensely long letters of up to eleven single-spaced pages. Both letters and memoranda, which were typed in single space on both sides of the paper, had each paragraph numbered, giving them an even more didactic tone. At home, he kept files on the talks he gave his children, often about birds, plants and the wildlife of the river. New recruits to the company, invited to lunch or dinner at Leckford, were often daunted to find a secretary sitting beside Spedan at the table making notes of what they said in conversation.

A typical Saturday recorded in his diary for 1938 started with three hours of dictation, beginning as he bathed and shaved while a secretary perched outside the bathroom door taking notes. The diaries, also entered by a secretary, record the time spent on everything in his private life, from reading or playing chess with his children to meetings of the British Ornithologists' Union and the Royal Geographical Society; golf games, visits to Covent Garden in winter and Glyndebourne in summer, 'translating French plays with Mrs Lewis', visits to the theatre (mainly revues and light comedies such as Dodie Smith's *Dear Octopus*, about a suffocating family) and to concerts (Sargent, Toscanini at the Queen's Hall). On 12 September 1938 one entry for 8 p.m. to 8.30 p.m. reads: 'Listening to wireless (Hitler's speech).'

In directing the business, his guiding principle was to look after the buying side above all, and he did so personally, engaging the buyers himself and reviewing their progress every six months. Some of the senior buyers became directors of the business and one buyer was paid more than anyone else in the Partnership except for Spedan himself. This concentration on buying was a legacy from his father, who succeeded in spite of his poor talent for sales promotion by having a great assortment of first-quality goods, bought at the cheapest possible cost. Spedan enjoyed philosophising on the psychology of trading and a favourite argument was that if two sales managers had the same amount of silk to sell, a low price or a particularly attractive material would work better than salesmanship in overcoming a customer's resistance. 'The buying side was a splendid machine when he eventually handed it over, unquestionably the best team in the trade,' recalls Max Baker, another of Spedan's bright academics (a First in mathematics at Cambridge) who joined the Partnership in 1934 and became director of trading for the department stores.

Another legacy of his father's was a lifelong belief in attractive window displays over advertising. In 1953 he told his director of selling that Marks and Spencer understood, as he had fifty years earlier, that 'windows are the cheapest form of publicity'. To the managing director of Peter Jones he recommended that the best place to have a competitor was 'absolutely next door . . . The nearer he brings his customers to your windows the greater his risk of losing them if your selection is more pleasing or your value better.' Spedan also paid close attention to the style and tone of the stores, which he thought should send a message about taste and value. A memorandum of 1950 advocates a 'Quakerish elegance', not trying to appear opulent or grand. 'Daintiness and inconspicuous but real good taste cost relatively little and I am sure that they are the best policy for shops that profess to give good value . . . The ignorant newly rich, the real vulgarians, will like gorgeousness. But they are not our true public and I think they never will be.'

In 1933 the Partnership acquired its first properties outside London: Jessop and Son of Nottingham, a venerable establishment founded in 1804 as a haberdashery and millinery shop, and Lance and Lance of Weston-super-Mare, another family-owned business. Buying was centralised in 1928, a factor which Sir Bernard Miller, Spedan's successor as chairman, regarded as the single biggest factor in the Partnership's trading success. Like the Cadburys at Bournville, the Partnership also introduced a free medical service and eventually – though not until 1941 – a pension scheme. For some reason Spedan took a great deal of persuading that a pension scheme would be welcomed by older members of staff and not be regarded as an interference in the way they provided for their retirement. It was an odd attitude, given how well he knew that older members of staff, hired when wages were minimal, would have had scant opportunity to save anything at all for retirement. But he was ready to spend money on opera tickets for the use of partners: each year the partnership bought at least 200 tickets for Glyndebourne, the country-house opera company founded by John Christie in Sussex. Spedan neither asked for nor received any corporate discount, but partners could buy the tickets at reduced prices.

More provincial stores were added in 1934, and then in 1937 the Partnership branched into the food business by acquiring Waitrose, a family-owned (Waite and Rose) provision chain with its head office in Gloucester Road, Kensington. It was not until 1940, however, when the Partnership bought fifteen of Selfridge's lesser stores – six of them in suburban London including Jones Brothers of Holloway, and nine in the provinces – that it became overnight a major national department stores group. Although all fifteen Selfridge stores had been trading poorly and therefore fitted Spedan's belief in acquiring and turning round what he called 'derelicts', the purchase came just in time to spread the Partnership's risks during World War II, when five of its stores were either destroyed or severely damaged by bombing, including the flagship on Oxford Street.

In 1934 Spedan took the decision to rebuild Peter Jones, a five-storey redbrick Victorian building on the west side of Sloane Square, by now somewhat faded although its interior still had a certain grandeur with marble pillars and a richly carpeted walnut staircase with great mirrors at the top. In keeping with the visionary principles of the Partnership, he decided to commission a radical modernist replacement. The resulting glass-and-concrete structure, designed by Slater and Moberly between 1935 and 1937 and constructed by John Lewis's own building subsidiary, was one of the first examples of curved curtain walling, each of its six storeys supported on outspread cantilever arms allowing the maximum amount of light and air to enter the building. From the outside it looked as if nothing supported the continuous horizontal line of windows. A supreme model of form following function, it remains London's most striking department store design; not tied to its period like the former Simpsons of Piccadilly (now Waterstone's), but as fresh and innovative in its sweeping curves as if it had been built yesterday.

The following year, 1935, offered the best opportunity yet for expansion on Oxford Street when the old D. H. Evans department store building next to John Lewis was put up for sale and D. H. Evans moved west along the street. John Lewis now occupied two whole blocks separated by Holles Street, and all fashion items were transferred to the new western building, leaving the eastern block, formerly Harries, to be developed for home furnishings.

Spedan's family life suffered a tragedy during these years of expansion. His son John, the eldest of three children, had just entered his ninth year in 1932 when he contracted meningitis and died in three days. Beatrice was pregnant with their fourth child but the shock caused a miscarriage so severe that she was told she could not conceive again. During the 1920s all three Lewises had made their homes in Hampstead, on the invigorating wooded heights of north-west London. Old John Lewis lived at Spedan Tower, on the edge of the Heath near Kenwood House; Spedan and Beatrice lived in a house called North Hall off Greville Road, where favoured partners invited to play tennis were alarmed to find cages at each end of the court containing live lynxes; and Oswald lived in a rather grander nineteenth-century residence, Beechwood, in Hampstead Lane, set in twelve acres overlooking Hampstead Heath. After Oswald's death in 1966 the house was sold for £200,000 to a property tycoon called John Hines, who sold it in turn for £1.9 million to King Khalid of Saudi Arabia. In 1985, as Middle Eastern money flooded into Hampstead, it changed hands for £8 million, a record at that time, to the Emir of Qatar.

When John Lewis died in 1928, Spedan and his family moved into Spedan Tower, but he also acquired several country houses, all of which were eventually turned over to Partnership use. His own retreat was Leckford Abbas, a rather forbidding grey-stone Jacobean-style manor built in 1901 in the prime fishing country of the Test Valley between Stockbridge and Andover. He actually had his eye on the much grander Longstock House, a creeper-clad, L-shaped nineteenth-century mansion a couple of miles away across the valley, and bought Leckford so as to have a local base from which to pounce when Longstock came on the market – an event for which he had to wait nearly fifteen years before acquiring it in 1945 from the Beddington family. With Leckford Abbas came a stretch of the Test river and the village of Leckford, whose cottages were in poor repair and mostly without a piped water supply.

Spedan saw the village and its surrounding farmland as an opportunity to regenerate another 'derelict', to provide local employment and either form a smaller partnership or add its proceeds to the big partnership. The village was indeed regenerated and the farmland put back into good heart, raising the corn yield from just over three sacks an acre to just under nine, but with the outbreak of war in 1939, over 500 acres of prime farmland were commandeered by the Air Ministry at a rent which meant a £10,000 loss to the John Lewis Partnership, as well as wiping out all the work done on the agricultural yield.

The Lewises were never interested in the social life of the country in the way it was led between the wars, when the squirearchy still left calling-cards with each other, and with newcomers of the right class. In the 1930s, realising that they had not repaid a round of calls from the village gentry, Spedan wrote to all the card-leavers explaining bluntly that he already had an enormous circle of friends within the Partnership and therefore wasn't able to take part in any social events in the county. This rebounded on him after Beatrice's death in 1953, when the county abandoned him to his lonely retirement.

Both Leckford and Longstock are now used as country retreats for partners, though Longstock, which sleeps only sixteen in comfortable elegance, is reserved for senior managers, directors, and guests of the chairman, and for management conferences and seminars. Leckford, where partners and their families can holiday with fishing rights at nominal prices (roughly £10 a day) on one of England's finest trout rivers, sleeps twenty-four and has a heavily panelled interior with somewhat small and dark public rooms. It has a spectacular garden at its back, and two steep grassy hills which were carved by Spedan out of a bigger one and landscaped to his own design. In spring these hills and the valley between are thickly carpeted with wild flowers: Spedan was a gifted garden designer and believed in planting en masse, what he called 'clouds' of snowdrops and daffodils.

The Longstock estate, where Spedan lived from 1945 to 1961, before moving to a smaller house nearby, dates back to Henry VIII, and the present house was built on the site of a much older one. It has sweeping east-facing views over the Test Valley and a spectacular double-height drawing room which also serves as an entrance hall, and is the archetypal English country house retreat, built on two main floors with broad, thickly carpeted corridors and an air of deep but not over-grand comfort. There are still many signs of Spedan's private interests, in the bookshelves filled with books on birds and wildlife and in the stuffed fish hanging in the billiard room. In his day the decoration was drabber, mainly greens and browns; now the walls are warm pastel shades and the atmosphere is both restful and cheering.

In 1935 Spedan, still preoccupied with thoughts of mortality, decided that he would 'die experimentally' to see how the Partnership could run without him. He handed over the job of chief executive to Metford (Mike) Watkins and retired to the life of a country gentleman at Leckford. Three other senior executives, the heads of buying, selling and branch operations, were given autonomy over their sides of the business and told they would report to Watkins, not to Spedan. After a year's trial, Spedan asked the four to draw up their own agreements, with legal advice provided at his expense, to remain with the Partnership for the rest of their working lives until the age of sixty-five. At the suggestion of the then Lord Chancellor, Lord Maugham, whose daughter was married to one of the four, the agreements were indexed against inflation on the prices of 1914. All four executives stuck to their agreements until retirement.

Spedan's hiring tactics were often unusually liberal for the time. When Enid Rosser, one of the first women to be called to the London Bar, joined the Partnership as legal adviser in 1933, she was first taken to lunch with the Lewises at the old Langham Hotel where they kept a permanent suite. After lunch, Spedan walked her round Cavendish Square, talking eloquently of his dreams of common ownership of business as the answer to the country's economic problems. He asked her to help in refining and redrafting the partnership's constitution, offering her complete autonomy, six weeks' holiday a year and her own choice of working hours. 'In other words, I was to be master of my own time, free to come and go as I thought fit, as long as I did my work,' Rosser recalled later. 'This promise was never broken over all the years.' She remained legal adviser until 1955 and worked closely with Spedan on the second trust settlement that irrevocably turned over his last shreds of ownership to the partners.

Enid Rosser, later Enid Locket, described Spedan in her memoirs as a man of many contradictions:

> a curious mixture of determined aggressive forcefulness together with a respect for other people's idiosyncracies and opinions. He could be utterly ruthless but he had the most

beautiful manners. He was completely without a sense of class and loved his home, which was comfortable but not luxurious, bearing in mind the riches which he possessed. He demanded, and got, devoted service from those who formed his innermost circle. His secretaries, three resident, were driven mercilessly but they never left him. He dictated endlessly except when he was asleep. When he was in his bath a secretary frequently took notes from outside.

He could talk endlessly and he once said that he loved the sound of his own voice; and a beautiful voice it was . . . He liked working with women and I very soon learned that, however astonishing his suggestions were, my job was not to dismiss them out of hand but to see if and how they could be made effective . . . To me one of the great charms of working with Spedan was that to every problem you had to apply the same intellectual principles, be it in the purchase of a new business or property, the prosecution of offenders or shoplifters, or a complaint by a customer, if only about a packet of pins. His integrity was absolute, and compromise just to save trouble unthinkable.

Other people in his employment found him hard to like. In the first five years after the Second World War, when jobs were easier to find than in the 1930s, a large number of recruits stayed only a year or so. Maurice Jones, who managed his estates at Leckford and Longstock, testified to his boss's short fuse while supposedly enjoying himself in country pursuits. If he missed a bird while shooting, he was liable to blame it on his chauffeur for wearing a loud checked suit that made the bird swerve. On another occasion, the head water-keeper reported to his colleagues that Mr Lewis had stamped on his rod in rage because a trout slipped the hook.

The Partnership had prepared for war from early in 1937, expanding its branches outside London and organising air raid precautions. Complete copies of sales ledger records were sent into the country for safe keeping, so that when John Lewis in Oxford Street was largely destroyed at the height of the Blitz in September 1940, suppliers' invoices were the only documents lost and they were asked to send replacements. John Lewis was the only department store in central London to suffer a direct hit during the Blitz, though the nearby Bourne and Hollingsworth and D. H. Evans were also badly damaged. At about midnight on 18 September 1940, during a pounding air raid on the West End, an oil bomb struck the recently enlarged and rebuilt main West House, on the site of John Lewis's original little shop of 1864. It was a night of high wind and the resulting fire raged for hours, leaping Holles Street to the East House and continuing to burn for a day and a half. About 200 people, half of them employees of the Partnership, had been sleeping in the basement shelters: they were unharmed, although three firemen were killed in the raid. Nearly £1m worth of stock was destroyed or charred beyond use: fortunately, stock reserves as well as the sales records were being held outside London, and within three weeks, part of the damaged East House was reopened for business.

The Oxford Street store was the largest single shop in the Partnership and had provided the bulk of its pre-war profits. Its partial loss brought a severe challenge to Partnership principles: at the outbreak of war in September 1939, senior partners had agreed to a reduction of 5 per cent in salaries and all those earning more than minimum wage level had been asked to defer some of their pay. More than a fifth of the monthly-paid staff agreed, along with a small percentage of the weekly-paid. By March 1940 these reductions were no longer seen as necessary, but the damage to the Oxford Street flagship forced their reintroduction.

By 1950, a temporary shop had been built on the bombed site, but it would be twenty years from the night of the raid before John Lewis was completely rebuilt. The new store was opened on 17 October 1960 by the Dowager Marchioness of Reading, who among her other public activities was president of the Women's Voluntary Services. This accounted for the unusual gift presented by the managing director of the Partnership – 20,000 terry towelling nappies for refugee babies.

Spedan Lewis had retired in 1955, five years after signing the second trust settlement for the Partnership which irrevocably handed the ownership of the capital in the company to the people who worked in it. In order to do this, because the size was much greater than that of a conventional partnership – and would continue to grow indefinitely – control of the ordinary share capital of John Lewis Partnership Ltd. was transferred to a new company, the John Lewis Partnership Trust Ltd., which had the sole function of acting as a corporate trustee. Spedan became its chairman, and three 'trustees of the constitution' were elected by the Partnership's central council. Spedan remained chairman for the next five years of the original JLP, which administered the stores group, but all his executive powers were henceforth exercised within the constitution of the Partnership.

Unlike the British constitution, that of the John Lewis Partnership is very much written down, in a complex, dry language that covers every detail of the capital structure, the relationship of management and partners, the elected representatives who hold management accountable to the partners, the branch councils and the various bottom-up mechanisms of communication by which any manager or director – or the chairman – can be held to account by an individual partner on any matter within the bounds of legal comment. It begins with a four-point definition of the Partnership's behaviour as good corporate citizen, service-conscious to its customers, straight dealer with its suppliers and as a competitor 'as friendly as may be compatible with the utmost vigour of fair competition'. (In 1999, the constitution was rewritten in more modern style, in time to clarify the debate over the Partnership's future.)

The Partnership is listed on the Stock Exchange for its preference shares, but because of its unusual capital structure cannot issue any equity shares. All it has is its 1929 equity base, a modest £600,000 held by the trust on behalf of the partners. When Pauline Graham, who joined the partnership in the 1960s and worked for it in a variety of managerial positions for ten years, first came across this anomaly, she wrote: 'How long the Partnership can carry its growth on its very slim ordinary share base remains to be seen.' In 1996 she had to admit: 'The Partnership has carried on growing – and handsomely so.'

Its capital structure was designed to make the Partnership immune to takeovers. Spedan did not want there to be any risk of partners' employment being placed in jeopardy. In 1999, when analysts speculated whether the Partnership could be 'demutualised' like a building society, releasing windfalls for its 39,000 partners, hypothetical valuations of the business ranging between £3bn and £4bn were bandied about. This sparked something of an internal revolution in the John Lewis ranks. At a market valuation of £4bn, many partners saw the prospect of up to £100,000 dangled before their eyes.

Could the unthinkable happen? To do so would require a wholesale revision of the trust, not merely the constitution. The current chairman, Sir Stuart Hampson, declared flatly in the *Gazette* in the summer of 1999 that 'the Partnership is not for sale' and dismissed the idea of a referendum of partners on the issue. In theory, the central council, four-fifths of whom are directly elected by the partners in annual secret ballots, and which in turn elects three trustees of the constitution, can remove the chairman if there is sufficient feeling against the way he is doing his job. But the constitution and its governing trust remain a formidable legal obstacle to change (see Chapter 8).

Sir Stuart Hampson once told a financial journalist that the Partnership was 'more communist in practice than the Bolsheviks ever were'. Well, not quite. Worker ownership at JLP does not mean worker control – far from it. It was always laid down that if the business was to succeed and be sustained, the power to make policy and take executive decisions at the highest level 'must be concentrated in the hands of a few people'. Managers are not elected, they are appointed, and paid on a comparable basis to managers in other organisations. Profit-sharing is not distributed on a flat-rate basis either, but as a percentage of salary, so some partners are definitely more equal than others, as a number of disaffected correspondents to the *Gazette* were quick to point out in the acrimonious debate over a sell-off.

Changing the bonus share-outs to a flat rate, says Spedan's nephew Peter Lewis, has been suggested many times over the years but it would be

> extremely difficult, even if one wanted to. Spedan wasn't an egalitarian, he was a great believer in rewarding distinguished performance, he didn't want to level down pay. He wanted

people, if they were really good, to feel they were earning as much as they could get anywhere else. He thought equality was not right. I think he would also say it was playing to the gallery.

Where worker democracy does make itself felt is in the functions of the central council, which elects five directors to the central board – five others, and the deputy chairman, are appointed by the chairman. The central council has quite extensive powers to demand accountability and consultation by the central board; for example on proposals to close a branch or a specialised department with twelve or more partners working in it, or on decisions affecting the Partnership's capital and assets. Beneath the central council is an elected council for each branch. Operational management is decentralised to heads of branches, subject to agreed targets and budgets. But to ensure that devolved power is used in the interests of the partners, the constitution provides for a post peculiar to the John Lewis Partnership – that of registrar. Within each branch, the registrar is the representative of central management but acts as the 'conscience' of the partnership in the branch with an encyclopaedic knowledge of the constitution and a watchful eye on management to see that there is no deviation from Partnership principles. Each local registrar has equal status with the branch director, and the chief registrar is elected to the board by the central council.

When Spedan Lewis invented the role of registrar in the late 1930s, he thought of it as work 'peculiarly suitable for women', though several chief registrars have been male, including the holder of the post in the late 1990s. Lewis also invented the role if not the term of ombudsman in 1944, a decade before the Danish government introduced this public official, and twenty-three years ahead of Britain. Lewis called his creation the partners' counsellor, an elected member of the main board. Any partner has access to the counsellor and his representatives who chair the committees for communication, the Partnership's oldest democratic institution, introduced in 1914. These are elected in each branch and through the counsellor can communicate their views upwards to the chairman.

The final instrument of accountability is the weekly *Gazette*, founded in 1918, which is the principal communication channel and 'noticeboard' for the organisation. Its unique feature is a no-holds-barred correspondence page, in which any partner can anonymously call to account any manager, or even the chairman. All letters, unless libellous or otherwise outside the bounds of legality, must be published within twenty-one days, together with a reply from the senior executive concerned. Pauline Graham, who was a director of buying at the time, was mortified by an anonymous correspondent ('Concerned Partner') who called her to account for breaking the company no-smoking rule in her private office. 'Has the Director of Buying (Fashion Accessories) a dispensation to smoke in her office? If yes, why?' In 1995 one brave soul signed her name to a letter demanding: 'I would like to ask the chairman how he can justify accepting a twelve per cent pay rise.' He did so in 300 words.

The Partnership has a strict code of ethics on the acceptance of gifts or hospitality, and partners have never been slow to question, through the columns of the *Gazette*, why such and such a manager has accepted tickets to Wimbledon or Premiership football from suppliers. In a spate of such correspondence in 1996, one writer, signing himself or herself 'Egalitarian', suggested that directors in receipt of corporate hospitality should give half a day's pay to the Partnership's central committee for claims and retirement. The reply came from the chief registrar, setting out the Partnership's four principles about accepting gifts or hospitality and reiterating that acceptance must always include an element of benefit to the Partnership rather than to the individual partner – an element almost impossible to prove or disprove. 'The main safeguards against abuse in this area are personal integrity and self-discipline – which one hopes these correspondents observe as characteristic of Partnership managers – not the kind of arrangement Egalitarian advocates,' wrote the chief registrar, K. D. Temple.

A certain pious and patronising tone does come across in some of these official replies, and there are many who claim the John Lewis Partnership is no more equal or democratic than any other retailing organisation. The *Gazette*'s correspondence over the possible break-up of the Partnership took the lid off many other grievances, from dismissive treatment by managers to ever longer working hours. But the fact remains that no other retailing organisation even bothers to address employee concerns in such a public manner. Resentments that in other companies might simply multiply on the gossip grapevine do have the opportunity of a very public airing in the *Gazette*, even if some feel that nothing much is done about them. Managers are also openly judged by their departmental results, which are published each week in the *Gazette*, together with percentage changes over the last year of every buying section, every department store and every Waitrose operation group, attached to their managers' names. It is about as transparent and no-hiding-place as you can get in a big company.

Perhaps the concept most ahead of its time that Spedan invented was the importance of sharing knowledge in an organisation as a means of sharing power. That was one driving factor behind the house journal's outspokenness and the committees for communication. 'The sharing of managerial knowledge is indispensable,' Spedan wrote in one of his many flashing insights into the management of the future, 'not only if power is to be shared but also for happiness. A chief problem of large-scale teamwork is to prevent dullness for those whose work requires little skill or even judgment of any kind . . . A sharing of knowledge without a reasonable sharing of power may result in discontent.'

Today, the business sections of bookshops are awash with books about knowledge management, the knowledge economy, and intellectual capital. Yet in practice, very few managers will abandon the ingrained belief that knowledge is power and turf to be jealously guarded and used as a lever of promotion. Even fewer industrialists have the insight and courage to turn their companies into organisations based on a culture of responsibility rather than of power, where knowledge sharing is rewarded rather than penalised by loss of territory. In this, as in so much else, Spedan's road to Damascus on the omnibus in London's Haymarket had turned him into a prophet of remarkable vision.

Despite the fact that he had effectively ended the family business by handing it over to its employees, Spedan had originally hoped that his formidably clever wife, who became deputy chairman, would succeed him as head of the Partnership, but she predeceased him in 1953, aged sixty-three. Spedan then looked to his surviving son Edward Grosvenor (Ted), but Ted stayed only a few months in the firm and displayed no inclination to take on his father's creation. He later trained as a barrister but has lived abroad for many years. Spedan's daughter Jill worked for a while as general editor of the *Gazette*, then left the Partnership. She died in her forties after a long illness.

In 1955 Spedan retired, his departure marked by a huge assembly of some 2,500 partners in Central Hall, Westminster, and the presentation of a cheque for £10,000, with which he set up a trust to study ecology, his great passion. The chairmanship passed to one of the high fliers he had recruited from Oxford, Bernard Miller, but as with so many entrepreneurs who identify with their business, he could not bear to let it go. He wrote endlessly to the *Gazette*, expressing 'extremely bitter regrets' that he had retired and, sometimes anonymously, denigrating his successor. He also vainly tried to persuade the central council to let him return as at least an adviser, which simply had the effect of stirring up hostility against him. Partners wrote to the *Gazette* deploring the Founder's campaign against his successor. 'Let's hear no more of him,' declared one.

In his last years, white-bearded and walking with a stick, he would wander into the Oxford Street store and just stand and stare despairingly, seemingly oblivious to the success of his creation. Two years before he died in 1963, he dispatched a last deranged letter to Miller, accusing him of 'playing the fool with my life's work and breaking my heart'. When his successors sailed out from Beachy Head in a Partnership boat to scatter his ashes, they suffered the ultimate indignity of having the ashes blow back into their faces. Old Spedan was not done yet.

What Spedan objected to in Miller's handling of the Partnership is not clear, because the firm began to prosper mightily in the boomtime Britain led by Harold Macmillan's 'never-had-it-so-good' government. Debenham and Freebody, stretching back to Wigmore Street, had long regarded itself as the Queen of Oxford Street, which in the 1950s and early 1960s was still an elegant street of department stores and speciality fashion shops unrecognisable from the present tacky thoroughfare overrun with short-lease souvenir shops and cheap clothing for the backpack brigade. From the moment the new, sleekly modernistic John Lewis store reopened in 1960, however, Debenham's began to look old-fashioned. From 1959 to 1966 the Partnership stores regularly exceeded, sometimes by 200 per cent, the increase in sales shown by all department stores.

In 1966 Oswald Lewis died at the age of seventy-eight. His son Peter, a barrister of intensely reserved temperament, had been working in the Partnership since 1959. As an undergraduate at Oxford in 1950, he had been asked once by his formidable uncle Spedan whether he was interested in joining the firm. Peter said no, he preferred to do his own thing. Spedan never referred to it again but after a few years of practising law Peter found himself picking up copies of the *Gazette* in his parents' drawing room in Hampstead and in retrospect would like to have joined earlier than he did.

As a boy, Peter had found Spedan intimidating, but looking back he feels sympathy for the old man in his embittered retirement. 'He would have liked a pat on the back instead of being an object of fun or ridicule,' Lewis reflected late in 1998.

> People – the City press and other businessmen – didn't take the Partnership seriously until about 1950. He was a believer in quality and intellect, wherever he found them. Other people thought he was cranky. He made a vast number of mistakes. In his last years, it wasn't that he regretted giving up, but he was unhappy, and there was a quarrel with his successor.

Ironically, it was Miller, whose stewardship Spedan so despised, who changed the business establishment's sceptical view of the partnership by being more accessible and explaining what Spedan had accomplished better than the Founder did himself.

Peter Lewis succeeded Miller as chairman in 1972. At no time did he ever feel he was joining a family business, 'least of all my own'. Technically, of course, it was no longer a family company anyway, but it had also undergone a total culture transformation. When he retired in 1993, Peter Lewis recalled his induction into 'the overwhelming atmosphere of the Partnership itself'. The culture of the organisation, he said,

> had obliterated the notion of family ownership and indeed the concept of the absentee shareholder ... I found the atmosphere from day one the most natural and congenial imaginable, and from that day to this have never, either in decision or discussion, before becoming chairman or after, felt that there was ever any conflict between what I was going to do and what I felt I ought to do.

Inheriting Spedan's blueprint at one remove was daunting enough, but Peter Lewis concentrated with his lawyer's mind on distinguishing between 'the things you mustn't change and modifying those that were no longer sensible because the world's moved on'. Mostly, he found the blueprint stood up well. 'It is still different, like a club,' he says now. 'It isn't for everybody to make it run. You do have to work at it.'

The power of the slogan, Never Knowingly Undersold, was immense, says Lewis – less for its effect on customers than for the responsibility it places on buyers to create value. 'Discipline in the buying – the slogan means you cannot escape it.' He is as reticent about his own time as chairman as about his life generally, proudest of the fact that the councils grew in self-confidence and independence during his term of office, at both central and branch level, and made important gains in terms of what could be discussed, the information that could be shared and the 'sheer enjoyment' people experienced in carrying out that exercise.

'The Partnership had a life and I allowed the flames to burn' is the most he will say. 'The single biggest contribution Spedan made was to make it possible for more people [in the partnership] to be enabled to enjoy business.'

CHAPTER 8:

UTOPIA POSTPONED

SPEDAN LEWIS DIED ON 21 February 1963 in The Burrow, the small house in the grounds of Longstock Park to which he had moved after his wife's death. He was a bitter and disappointed man, not merely because he felt ignored since his retirement, nor because he felt his successor was somehow failing his vision. He had always believed that his invention of a workers' partnership would sweep the business world with its logic, fairness and understanding of human nature. He saw it as more than a great achievement in industrial relations; his work of creating the Partnership, he once said, 'has always seemed to me to be really a new form of political career'. Yet, as his nephew Peter Lewis observed, no one in industry or the City seemed to take it seriously. He was seen as an idealistic crank, and they waited to see his Partnership concept fall apart.

History has written otherwise. Nearly half a century after coming to completion, Spedan's legacy has been visibly more lasting than that of any political career. The John Lewis Partnership is an unqualified commercial success, as witnessed by its steady stream of profits, nearly half of which have been paid out in bonuses over the last twenty years. From January 1980 to January 1999, the bonuses totalled £816.7m out of profits of £1,730.4m over the period, putting an average extra 17 per cent annually in each partner's pay packet. The boom years of 1987 and 1988 racked that percentage up to 24 per cent, while the leanest payout was in 1993 with 8 per cent. With their package of other benefits, including the country clubs, sporting facilities, discounted entertainment and virtually guaranteed employment at a time when the lifetime career is becoming a thing of the past, the John Lewis partners have generally been reckoned among the retail sector's best-rewarded employees. Until windfall fever began to run riot, the Partnership seemed to have achieved, as much as any business organisation could, its founder's aim of happiness for its members.

In spite of its seventy-year track record, though, it remains a virtually one-off experiment for an organisation of its size. Only a handful of smallish companies in the UK have a similar partnership structure, among them the Lancashire-based heater manufacturer Baxi, whose family owner Philip Baxendale handed over his equity to the workforce in 1983, and the Scottish paper maker, Tullis Russell, a sixth-generation family company which became owned by its employees and two trusts in 1994, the year tax breaks were introduced for employee ownership schemes. Why hasn't the John Lewis model been copied on a wider scale, as its founder so confidently prophesied?

The short answer is, of course, profits – and the inheritance imperative. Spedan Lewis remains unique in having inherited a big, profitable business in the heart of London and then voluntarily given it all up in pursuit of a dream of a new and more sustainable way of doing business. 'Not too many owners of businesses want to give them away' is the wry comment of the current chairman, Sir Stuart Hampson. An earlier deputy chairman saw a deeper agenda in the reluctance to adopt Spedan's vision. 'While rich men may give large sums away with varying degrees of publicity,' he said, 'they are almost never willing to give away power, and that in the end is what Spedan did.' Howard Leigh, director of a London brokerage for the sale of private companies, says most owners will have no emotional commitment to sell to their employees if they can get more money – even a marginal amount – somewhere else.

Up to the 1980s the uniqueness of the John Lewis Partnership was perhaps not so surprising. British industry and commerce as a whole remained complacent and resistant to change until the upheavals created by Margaret Thatcher's rampant free market philosophy and severe application of monetarism. In the thirty or forty years that followed the end of World War II, there were few, if any, men of vision and imagination at the head of British companies, whether owned by families or the shareholding public. Hierarchies of many-layered management were the rule until organisations were forced by global competition and economic pressures to dismantle and simplify their structures.

Management versus workers – the adversarial 'them and us' – was the standard pattern for British industry, leading time and again to deadly strikes and eventual failure, as in the UK motor industry monolith British Leyland, or at best to stagnation and loss of competitiveness. The ferocity of two recessions in the early 1980s, the demise of old, inefficient manufacturing industries and the cutting edge of takeover and asset-stripping laid waste the good with the bad. As always, it was the human element that suffered: 'downsizing' was exercised pitilessly in pursuit of short-term profitability to please the City and Wall Street; motivation was destroyed as the dole queues grew. Middle managers, declared Tom Peters, the top US management guru, were 'dead ducks', but his rival on the international business lecture circuit, Gary Hamel, warned of 'corporate anorexia' if companies went blindly ahead axeing overheads without planning how they would handle growth again.

In the midst of all this mayhem, and while the last rites were being pronounced on both sides of the Atlantic on the lifetime career, Spedan Lewis's creation, bound by its constitution, remained true to the Founder's commitment to employing people as long as they wanted to stay with the firm. Now that even Japanese industrial firms are abandoning the lifetime employment philosophy, the John Lewis Partnership stands almost alone in its commitment to the employee. Once partners have completed five years' service, the Partnership undertakes to offer them a job for the rest of their life if they want to stay with the company. The job itself may change and technology replace some processes, but the Partnership does not make people redundant.

If job security contributes to happiness, this is clearly at the heart of

Spedan's mission statement, and Sir Stuart Hampson argues that the principle makes for a good test of management. Speaking at the Royal Society of Arts' forum for ethics in the workplace in 1998, part of the RSA's ongoing study of 'tomorrow's company', Hampson explained:

> If the firm makes a profit it is distributed to the Partners. However, if the only way to make a profit was by making Partners redundant, the firm would hardly be contributing to the happiness of its members . . . One can picture ambitious, highly motivated and creative individuals running portfolio lives, but for the vast majority of people it will be neither practicable nor pleasurable. It is a recipe for anxiety and misery.

Hampson takes the happiness principle so literally that he holds 'happy hours' with his directors, asking them how the business is doing in terms of happiness. 'I am convinced that is the secret of sustainable success,' he says. It's something even a new-age organisation like the much-praised St Luke's advertising agency in London, famous for its employee autonomy and wacky 'bonding' exercises, might balk at putting on paper.

While fashionable business thinking is urging everyone to forget the lifetime career and prepare for a life of constant change and challenge, moving from company to company on short-term projects, Hampson sticks to his belief that the John Lewis way is good for business performance as well as worker motivation. Even though other companies may not have shareholder employees or be committed by a constitution and trust to provide long-term security, he argues that they should weigh the costs of not doing so. Visible commitment and loyalty from the company to its workers, he believes, instil a motivating confidence and free up creative thinking for better performance. If any partner in John Lewis has an idea for improving the efficiency of the business, even if it involves the collapse of their own job, they can bring the idea forward without fear of being made redundant. 'The threat of unemployment is inimical to flexibility; people hold on to what they are doing, instead of moving to what they could do best, what could contribute most to the success of the company,' Hampson told the RSA, adding that the same loyalty and confidence principles extend to the top.

> Senior management cannot simply be mercenaries. Leadership is long-term. Top management is hired, and may, of course, be fired if it does not do a decent job, but directors (and more specifically, chief executives) undertake a commitment. This means, whatever the contract says, that a chief executive cannot simply walk out because a better offer comes along.

This concept, Hampson observes, is being increasingly ignored, even scorned. (One high-profile example was Bill Cockburn, hired from the Post Office to run stationery and bookshop giant W. H. Smith, who then walked out after eighteen months to pick up a more attractive appointment at British Telecom.) Business schools and professional analysts, not to mention headhunting firms, encourage the idea that top executives need to be continually switching companies to enhance their CV and promote their versatility; that, in Hampson's phrase, 'you can't be a shaker unless you are also a mover'.

Yet at the end of the century a new concept of business organisations is gaining ground, and until recently it looked as if Spedan Lewis's original flash of genius was an idea whose time might be about to come. All the talk of 'tomorrow's company' revolves around the idea of stakeholding, in which the interests of employees, customers, suppliers and the wider community are held equal to those of shareholders.

And many of the Partnership's more practical objectives are being adopted in subtle ways by companies of the stature of Shell, British Telecom and British Airports Authority. This, as Hampson says, is Spedan's true legacy. There is growing realisation, for example, that companies can derive solid advantage from the fact that their stakeholders are also writing their computer programs and driving their lorries. It builds in a competitive edge and glues the organisation together in a way no outside consultancy could achieve with a packaged cultural change programme.

It was all the more ironic, therefore, that in the dying months of the century, after carrying its lone beacon of partnership for so long, Spedan Lewis's vision should have been so abruptly jolted by some of the people it was intended most to benefit. At the end of the twentieth century, the nineteenth-century ideal of mutuality, in which business organisations are effectively owned by their members, and which Spedan refined into his own unique model, is heavily under assault by market forces. Building societies which vowed they would never demutualise have been forced to do so against their managements' judgement by weight of democratic voting procedures. Scottish Widows, a venerable life assurance and pensions provider, fell into the £6bn embrace of Lloyds TSB Bank after many denials that it was for sale.

Above all, there were the unreal fortunes that descended like cosmic lottery winnings on the former partners of Goldman Sachs, the Wall Street investment bank that dismantled its mutual structure for a stock market listing. (One of Goldman's forty-six British partners, the economist Gavyn Davies, gained a reported £80m from the share-out.) Deciding to change your partnership status overnight is now demonstrably a very easy way to become a multi-millionaire. As even the London Stock Exchange, fat with the profits of a long bull market, debated whether to seek its own listing, thereby unlocking fortunes for its member firms, nothing seemed impregnable.

The furore within the John Lewis Partnership was sparked in the early summer of 1998 with a speculative article in the *Daily Telegraph*, building on the spate of recent demutualisations – from which some individuals in the Partnership had already benefited – and asking whether the trend could conceivably be extended to the John Lewis trust. Within a year, as more and more mutuals went public or were taken over, releasing a golden shower of cash, the debate was raging at full pelt behind the staid shopfronts and in the staff canteens of the Partnership. Many began redefining Spedan Lewis's goal of happiness as the ability to pay off their debts and mortgages, while letters in the *Gazette* unstoppered a festering dissatisfaction with longer hours of work, low pay, arrogant and poorly trained managers, the perceived privileges of senior partners and a general lack of respect and consultation between management and staff. For these 'revolting peasants', as one termed himself or herself, the annual bonus appeared small compensation. It would take about eighty years, another writer calculated, for the average bonus to add up to a windfall payout. One correspondent, 'Smiler', submitted a bitter joke: 'What is the difference between the John Lewis Partnership and a Third World dictatorship? Answer: one has no belief in democracy, treats its people as second-class citizens who should do as they are told or they will be made to suffer, and the other is a country, not a retail company.'

City investment analysts fuelled the flames by assessing the Partnership's likely market value at £4.2bn, which would in theory (and if equally divided) provide employee windfalls of up to £112,000 if its governing trust could be unravelled. The chairman had already been under regular City questioning as to whether the Partnership could be sold or floated on the stock market, and although Hampson always dismissed the possibility, it was briefly discussed in 1998 at a meeting of the all-powerful central council.

In August 1999, Hampson made an unequivocal commitment that there would be no sell-off under his chairmanship. Writing in the *Gazette* as it carried more pages of letters clamouring for and against the idea of breaking up the Partnership, he clarified the 'myth' that the business belonged to the partners. 'In fact the Partnership is owned "in trust" by the John Lewis Partnership Trust Ltd., the company set up with the sole purpose of carrying out the wishes of Spedan Lewis when he handed over his business.'

Could partners vote for a sell-off by means of a referendum? No, said Hampson.

> Spedan Lewis recognised human instinct and foresaw that in the future some Partners might entertain just the thoughts which are now surfacing. He therefore took great care in the way he set up the Trust to ensure that the gift of his business would be enjoyed by successive generations of Partners and

couldn't be hijacked once he had disappeared from the scene.

So we aren't a mutual. The business isn't ours to sell.

Even if it were possible, he added, it would take both from those who had striven to build the Partnership in the past and from future generations who could no longer benefit as partners. 'At stake here is the ... destruction of Spedan Lewis's vision of an alternative to the conventional company.' As chairman of the trust company, he vowed, 'I would have no hesitation in leading opposition to any action aimed at destroying the Partnership and in contrasting the vision and generosity of Spedan Lewis's bequest with the short-sighted greed of the carpetbaggers who were pushing the matter to these lengths.'

Hampson then moved on to deal with the legal situation. The trust could be altered by resorting to the courts if the aim were to improve the way it operated or to strengthen it along the lines of the Founder's wishes, 'but anyone bent on destruction rather than on improvement would have to go for an Act of Parliament'. This, as the Partnership's director of legal services Terry Neville explained, would have to be promoted as a private bill, a procedure liable to endless delays if so much as a single MP objected to it. Only twelve such bills affecting trusts had been passed into law over the last ten years, said Neville, and none had been so contentious as a proposal to break up the John Lewis Partnership would be. Most had been entirely unopposed.

Trusts, however, do not last indefinitely. By a curiosity of constitutional law, their lifetime is often linked to that of the monarch: in John Lewis's case, the trust comes to an end twenty-one years after the death of the last descendant of King Edward VII to be alive in 1929, the year of the trust's foundation. Those descendants are currently the Queen and her cousin the Earl of Harewood, born in 1926 and 1923 respectively. Prior to the end of that period, Neville concluded, 'a new Trust with similar aims could be devised to follow on, but that is all some distance away'.

Thirty years ago the Partnership was described by the magazine *Management Today* as 'a prime example of the "third-generation" company, founded by one kind of business genius, greatly developed by a different variety of genius, and now in the hands of professional managers'. It might have been a different story if Spedan had been one of a large second-generation family and had to fight for his vision against the desire of the rest to maintain dynastic control, but his brother Oswald had no interest in inheriting the stores; nor, as it turned out, did Spedan's own children. Peter Lewis, Oswald's son, has a son in the Partnership, managing one of the provincial stores in the group. He seems to have been drawn to the business less through family interest than by its culture and sense of common purpose, something he found lacking in his earlier career at Procter and Gamble, the household goods multinational.

If that culture is buckling now, it may have more to do with the fatal virus of complacency in management than with sudden visions of windfall wealth. A recent television documentary about the stores took an often sardonic look at their ponderous bureaucratic ways, yet senior managers were apparently contented with the values that were portrayed. Criticism has been more overt in the wake of the sell-off debate, with press commentators focusing on the dowdy image of Peter Jones, the difficulty customers have in getting advice on products, and the long refusal (until late 1999) to take credit cards, which generate huge volumes of business despite their added cost to the retailer. Yet the Partnership top brass appear serenely convinced that Spedan's big idea is still working as well as ever.

Organisations of such good intent are so rare that it would be sad indeed if Spedan's vision were to founder for short-term gain. His thinking deserved to have a greater influence on the world of business, and might have done so were it not for the fact that his two books of business philosophy, *Partnership For All* and *Fairer Shares*, are among the most unreadable works of the century. He did have a flair for the occasional telling one-liner, though one has to hunt hard for them in the dense thickets of verbiage: 'Only at the risk of loss can you have anyone or anything to love', and 'If you deprive men of freedom to act badly, you may find you have also deprived them of freedom to act well.'

Had he been able to collaborate with the sort of author who has made a business hero out of General Electric's Jack Welch by packaging his sayings and strategies – and sold tens of thousands of books into the bargain – things might have been different. Sadly, Spedan was ahead of his time in this, as he was in his thinking: in the 1950s there was no market for business books, no MBA students writing case studies and a huge, inert lack of interest in how business worked, or could work better. Today, with the advent of the 'knowledge economy' and a growing understanding that a company's assets lie more in its employees' heads than in its plant and equipment, Spedan would have been hailed for pointing out that a partnership structure was the best way to share knowledge for the firm's benefit without individuals feeling they were losing power by the sharing. It was an extraordinary piece of vision for a man born in the last fifteen years of Queen Victoria's reign, and it is still pretty uncommon in practice.

Spedan understood, well before the American human-relations gurus of the 1960s, that a fulfilled working life involved more than earning a decent living, and he understood about team-work, another highly modern concept. In 1954 he wrote an entire chapter in *Fairer Shares* about the sharing of knowledge, which mostly concerned the role played by the Partnership's journal and its other channels of communication such as the committees that linked grassroots workers and management. The chapter begins:

> The sharing of managerial knowledge is indispensable not only if power is to be shared, but also for happiness. A chief problem of large-scale team-work is to prevent dullness for those whose work requires little skill or even judgment of any kind.
>
> Mere curiosity, mere inquisitiveness, mere desire for knowledge for its own sake, is a chief element in the happiness of human life. Its satisfaction may go far to put colour and zest into even the simplest of repetition work . . . The more lively the general understanding of the business and the general awareness of all relevant matters, the tougher will its team-work tend to be against strains of every kind, and the more vigorous and efficient in enterprise . . . Without such

knowledge they cannot feel they have an adequate voice in the management – a proper chance to take, whenever they are so disposed, an appropriate part in it.

No one else in the western business world in 1954, with the exception of the far-sighted Peter Drucker, who was beginning to make his mark as a management thinker in that year, came anywhere near such understanding of the need for communication and openness of information in a business organisation. It is not a bad legacy for an unjustly disappointed man.

PART THREE

THE SAINSBURYS: HIGH STREET MEDICIS

Chapter Nine:

Up By the Bootstraps

Due north from London's bow-shaped street known as Aldwych runs Drury Lane, a name as redolent of theatrical romance to Londoners as Broadway is to New Yorkers. Today there is little romance about it: even the fabled Theatre Royal, always known simply as Drury Lane, presents a blank side to the Lane, its ornate frontage giving on to Bow Street. The first long stretch of the narrow street is a dull parade of nineteenth-century brick tenements interspersed with the odd post-modern office block. Beyond the junction with Long Acre, however, the Lane's character changes, with a cluster of wine bars, restaurants and speciality shops set in flat-fronted Georgian brick buildings.

Of number 173, though, there is no trace left. The mid-Victorian dairy that once stood on the corner of Macklin Street has disappeared and its site is now occupied by a small, featureless glass-and-concrete office block called New London Court. Its street number is 172 and there is nothing between it and number 174, a poky café fronting Macklin Street. The vanished dairy, opened in 1869, was the foundation of one of the greatest fortunes in late-twentieth-century Britain. From that modest brown brick shop with its weighing scales, milk churns and butter block grew the mighty Sainsbury's supermarket and home products group, with sales in 1998 of over £14.5bn. Up to that year, although it had been a public company since 1973, it still boasted a chairman from the founding family, David Sainsbury, who is now a working Labour peer and minister for science.

The Sainsburys' collective family wealth, considerably down from its stock market peak in the early 1990s, was estimated in 1999 by the *Sunday Times* at £3.1bn, of which David's share is just under half. They are among the country's biggest philanthropists, though only a few of their more high-profile benefactions – such as the Sainsbury Wing of the National Gallery in Trafalgar Square, the Sainsbury Arts Centre at Norwich, and generous support of the Royal Opera and Ballet – are known to the public. Like the Cadburys, leading members of the Sainsbury family and their wives have their own charitable trusts. David in particular, a high-profile contributor to Labour party funds, distributes vastly more wealth by stealth through his Gatsby Trust, named after the enigmatic central figure of Scott Fitzgerald's novel *The Great Gatsby*. Privately, even secretively, this trust channels millions each year into causes reflecting its founder's range of interests and sympathies, from disabled children and scientific research to training young engineers for management.

The Sainsburys have come a long way in two generations. Since the 1960s they have climbed Britain's slippery ladder of social class from high street grocers to undisputed grandees, boasting not only a hat-trick of peerages (until the death of the oldest Lord Sainsbury, Alan, in 1998), but also a Garter knighthood, England's most historic order of chivalry and the personal gift of the Queen. The first grocer to reach the highest circles of British society was Sir Thomas Lipton, King Edward VII's yachting and racing friend, but the Sainsburys, while accumulating unprecedented honours as well as one of the biggest fortunes in Britain, have never flaunted their wealth or connections as Lipton did. Indeed, until the 1960s their main claim to fame was having introduced the supermarket revolution into Britain from the United States. Tesco had experimented with self-service in a small way in St Albans before the Second World War, but it was Alan Sainsbury, third generation of the dynasty and a rumbustious, self-confident retailer of flair, who brought the idea over the Atlantic lock, stock and barrel and launched it in the unlikely setting of suburban Croydon in June 1950.

The Sainsburys, like the Cadburys and the Lewises, were a West Country family by origin, and provisioning was in their genes. The forebears of John James Sainsbury, founder of the Drury Lane dairy, appear to have been well established by the late eighteenth century in the Wiltshire parish of Melksham, where Bartholomew Sainsbury, described as a 'victualler', was married to Martha Bruce in 1772. His wife died between 1775 and 1777, soon after the birth of their two children, and Bartholomew remarried, fathering four more children, among them John, born in 1781. John was the first of the family to come to London, setting up as a hatter in Blackfriars on the edge of the City. No further trace of his apprenticeship or trade appear until banns were called for his marriage to Sarah Fletcher on 17 May 1809 at St Clement Danes church in the Strand. Just twelve days later Sarah gave birth to their only child, another John, who grew up to become a framemaker in south London and to father the founder of the Sainsbury grocery business.

John James Sainsbury was born to John Sainsbury and Elizabeth Coombes, the daughter of a Southwark labourer, on 12 June 1844 at 5 Oakley Street, Lambeth, the third of their four children. The youngest, Margaret, died in infancy as so many Victorian children did. (The street was later renamed Baylis Road in honour of Lilian Baylis, founder of the nearby Old Vic Theatre.) They moved house a great deal, as working people did in those days of temporary rented accommodation. In 1846 the family was living in Kinaston Street, Lambeth and five years later the 1851 census listed John Sainsbury, 'composition maker', as head of the household at 7 Short Street in the same borough, together with his wife and their three children: Elizabeth, ten, Eliza Jane, nine, and John, six. The house must have been cramped for space, as it also contained a widow and laundress called Mary Nettleton, fifty-three, and the Rowbotham family – Alice, forty-two, another laundress, registered as head of the family, and her two teenage children, Richard and Alice.

By the time of the 1861 census, the Sainsburys had moved yet again within Lambeth, to 12 Belvedere Road. John Sainsbury, now fifty-one, was listed as a 'composition ornament maker' and described as 'blind in one eye'. His wife Elizabeth's occupation was entered as 'needlewoman' and their unmarried daughters, aged twenty and nineteen, who lived at home, shared the same trade as their mother. A carpenter aged thirty-one named William Streetland from Devon, his wife and two daughters also lived in the house. John James was now fifteen and had already been living away from home for a year, having gone to work at fourteen, a typical apprentice age. He worked for a grocer in the New Cut, near the recently constructed Waterloo Station, a street crowded with market stalls selling all kinds of food on open display. Henry Mayhew, the chronicler of Victorian working-class London, described the weekend scene in the New Cut:

> The street traders are to be seen in the greatest numbers at the London street markets on a Saturday night. Here, and in the shops immediately adjoining, the working classes generally purchase their Sunday's dinner; and after pay-time on Saturday night, or early on Sunday morning, the crowd in the New Cut is almost impassable.

Most food in working-class urban areas was still bought in open markets and from street pedlars under far from hygienic conditions. The first Adulteration of Foods Act was passed in 1860 after articles in the medical journal the *Lancet* drew attention to the health risks at the lower end of the trade. Tougher measures followed in the 1870s and by the late 1880s most local councils had appointed food inspectors to enforce the law. The 1860s saw another huge advance in public health with the construction of London's first modern sewerage system under the supervision of Joseph Bazalgette, engineer to the Metropolitan Board of Works.

Whether young John James was consciously reverting to the Wiltshire family trade or not, the grocery business was a good one to be in as incomes rose after the Industrial Revolution and people were able to spend more on food and enjoy cheap imported luxuries such as tea, sugar, bacon, cheese and tobacco. There was an enormous new market for food in the booming towns and cities as the number of mouths to feed multiplied by the year. The population of England, Scotland and Wales had doubled between 1800 and 1851 from ten million to over twenty million, and doubled again over the next sixty years to forty million in 1911. Well over a tenth of Britons lived in London, whose population also doubled between 1801 and 1851, from 1.1 million to 2.6 million. By 1891 it was 4.2m and by 1911 7.5 million. At the start of the nineteenth century there was no town outside London with a population over 100,000 and only five with more than 50,000 – Liverpool, Manchester, Birmingham, Leeds and Bristol. By 1821 the first three were all over 100,000.

Grocers were the largest category of shopkeepers in all towns outside London in 1851, serving the growing middle class, the tradesmen and skilled workmen from proper shops lit by gas. High-class grocers in mid-century were stocking a sophisticated array of spices such as mace, cinnamon, nutmeg, cloves, ginger, different grades of pepper, mustard, chillies and curry powder. Dried and foreign fruit included plums, figs, dates, raisins, oranges and lemons, along with almonds, chestnuts and Brazil nuts. Some, dealing in what were called Italian goods, stocked vermicelli, macaroni, tapioca, sago and gelatine. There were ready-packaged or bottled condiments that would be familiar to the modern shopper, such as Lea and Perrins' Worcestershire sauce. Grocers would also normally carry household staples like lamp oil, linseed oil, candles, starch, blacklead for fire grates, brushes and blacking such as the young Charles Dickens packed in the factory.

It was more than just a retailing trade, with many craft skills involved. Until mid-century, grocers and provision merchants were usually involved in some processing of the goods they sold. They blended tea, mixed herbs and spices, cured bacon, cut and ground sugar, roasted and ground coffee. After 1850 the business started to divide between retailers and wholesalers and retailing became more aggressively competitive on prices. The aim was for rapid turnover on low margins, using trade-offs between retailer and wholesaler – quick payments in return for good discounts. 'Thanks to these organisations and to other representatives of the new race of retailers,' wrote the retailing historian J. B. Jefferys, 'commodities such as butter, eggs, tea and bacon ceased to be special luxuries on the working-class table and could be, and were, purchased by the working class cheaply, easily and regularly.'

Young Sainsbury later moved on to work for two oil and colour merchants; first Henry Jeans of Green's End, Woolwich and secondly George Gillett at 57 Strutton Ground, off what is now Victoria Street in Westminster. Such merchants had originally dealt in colours, paints and the oils for mixing them but now held a wide range of household necessities – soap and candles, starch, matches, firewood, brushes, lamps, beeswax, soda, lamp-black and ironmongery, grocery staples like sauces, pickles and jams and basic patent medicines such as Glauber's salts. They were mostly to be found in working-class districts and dealt in the sort of measures poor people wanted – a ha'p'orth of this and that.

In Strutton Ground, the apprentice grocer met Mary Ann Staples, a strong, capable girl who was working at Tom Haile's dairy in the same street. She was the daughter of a prospering dairyman with several branches in Somers Town, north London, and had a good practical knowledge of the business. The couple married on 20 April 1869, when John James was twenty-five and Mary Ann twenty. They were already renting the five-storey premises for their planned dairy at 173 Drury Lane and had established that they would be able to make enough money to marry on.

Mary Ann may have brought a small dowry, but Sainsbury family lore suggests that they set up on £100 of his savings, and it was certainly possible at this time for an ambitious young man to start a grocery business on his own savings, or (outside London) on a loan from the farmers who supplied him. A Book of Trades, published in 1837, suggested that a grocer could set up in business on £400–600 or even less, particularly if he sold for cash only. As much as 50 per cent of any retail business at that time was on credit, and bad debts were an endemic problem in the grocery trade, often totalling a third of accounts receivable. A grocer in Salisbury called William Hillier, who set up on £100 saved out of his salary, always required his customers to pay 'ready money' for their first few orders.

Retail food trading was predominantly a family business, depending for its growth on the number of sons who could eventually be expected to manage branches, and in the beginning, the newly married Sainsburys also had the modest ambition of a branch for each son born to them. A grocer called John Shillingford had fourteen children and opened a new branch to mark each birth. Family members were expected to work hard and long, because much of the trading in poorer areas would take place after working hours finished, and shops stayed open until their competitors closed for the night. As the retailing historian Peter Mathias put it, 'in the crucial early stages of growth these individual tradesmen pulled themselves up by their own bootstraps'.

Drury Lane at this time offered a typical mix of food businesses: bakers, greengrocers, butchers, grocers, three other dairies, a tripe-seller, an egg seller, a fishmonger and at least one cowkeeper. This was how most Londoners had bought their milk for generations, from cows tethered in dirty backyards or open pails on the street – inevitably contaminated and usually diluted with pump water (giving rise to the nickname for a street pump, 'the cow with the iron tail'). In 1865 there were 40,000 cows in London and even as late as 1888 records showed 732 licensed cow sheds in the capital. But in the 1860s and 1870s there were epidemics of cattle disease which wiped out large numbers of the city's cows. At the same time, the cheap and rapid transport provided by the railways enabled fresh milk to be delivered to the dairies from as far away as Devon. The old unhygienic ways were rapidly becoming history.

Drury Lane was a poor but respectable street, though it bordered an area of worse poverty and vice which many blamed on the playhouses nearby. Number 173 was owned by a clergyman, the Revd T. H. B. Baker, who had let it to a tradesman – either a butcher or a greengrocer – called Thomas Skivens. He in turn seems to have sublet the shop to Sainsbury, who finally bought the leasehold in 1874. For the first three months of their tenancy, John James was still under contract to Gillett the oil merchant and continued to work a full day there while Mary Ann ran the dairy. Afterwards, he would go over to the Drury Lane premises to help her scrub the counters and clean the scales and weights ready for the next day's trading.

From the start, the Sainsburys determined that their trading policy would be governed by value, quality and cleanliness. Value was essential to attract and keep customers in that penurious district, but quality and hygiene were rare and novel. To begin with, most of their trade was in butter, eggs and milk, and Mary Ann prided herself on selling 'the best butter in London'. Demand for milk in particular was rising in the 1860s as excise duties fell on imported products and tea, once an exotic luxury, began to supplant ale as the everyday drink of the working Briton. Tea consumption rose from 1.8 pounds a head in 1850 to 3.8 pounds a head in 1870, and sugar consumption rose with it, from 24.8 pounds a head to 47.2 pounds a head over the same period.

It was the burgeoning tea trade that drove some of the fastest expansion among grocery stores in the last quarter of the nineteenth century. Lipton's, owned almost outright by its founder, was the most famous example. Its rival, the International Tea Company, had nearly 100 branches by 1885 and over 200 just five years later. The Home and Colonial Stores, founded in 1885, reached 200 branches in ten years and by 1900 had more than 400. Its first chairman and the driver of its growth was an unlikely grocery boss; William Capel Slaughter, who had married into the business. He was a leading partner in the City law firm Slaughter and May, still a well-known name in the legal profession.

The Sainsburys' dairy prospered. Its owners were both experienced in the food trade, had a forward-looking business plan and could have served as models for Samuel Smiles's best-selling book of 1859, *Self Help*, which preached that success in life was a matter of work, order, thrift and self-discipline. By 1873 the family had done well enough to move to a more salubrious district in north-west London, employing a manager to run 173 Drury Lane. (The shop was to remain an old-fashioned branch of Sainsbury's until November 1958, shortly before the corner site was demolished for redevelopment. It was replaced by a Sainsbury self-service store across the street at numbers 24 and 25, which finally closed in 1973.)

They exchanged the Drury Lane house which they had shared with three other families, and where their first three children had been born over the shop, for 159 Queen's Crescent, Kentish Town. Here they opened another shop, selling dairy produce and fresh meats, and two more followed within the next three years. Kentish Town was one of the most rapidly expanding parts of London, with rows of new housing springing up to accommodate the growing number of people employed on the railways that ran into the big northern termini of King's Cross, Euston and St Pancras, and the light industries – notably piano manufacturing – that followed.

The Sainsburys' shops, soon to be followed by more branches in similarly expanding suburbs such as Kilburn and Islington, were designed to a consistent pattern. They still had stalls outside in the fashion of market trading, and their windows were open to the street. Inside, they had long marble counters running down each side, shelves along the walls and room in the centre for a woman to push a perambulator down the full length of the shop. Floors, walls and counter fronts were tiled, and the interiors brightly lit by gas, in sharp contrast to the dim grocers' shops of the time. (John James Sainsbury's dying words in 1928 were 'Keep the shops well lit.')

JJ knew the importance of 'location, location, location,' long before that phrase entered the language of estate agents. He always chose the centre of a row rather than a corner position, because if the business did well, it might then be possible to expand the selling space by acquiring shops on either side. He believed in buying freehold rather than renting, which is still broadly the policy of the group today, although its sites are now a mixture of freehold and leasehold. Sainsbury's location philosophy underwent a revolutionary change a century later with the switch from town-centre to edge-of-town supermarkets, but is now beginning to reverse, following its chief rival, Tesco, with a return to town-centre neighbourhood stores.

If the Sainsbury business was doing so well in 1874, it makes the sad fate of John James's grandmother all the more mysterious. Sarah Sainsbury, née Fletcher, widow of the hatter John Sainsbury, met her end that year aged eighty-six in that bleakest of all Victorian institutions, the parish workhouse. Her husband had died in 1850 of asthma or bronchitis, aged sixty-nine, apparently leaving no will, and the following year's census revealed that his widow, then sixty-five, was a pauper on the parish of Southwark. Ten years later she was apparently employed as 'an army clothing worker', living at 22 Bear Lane, Christ Church,

Southwark, but just before Christmas 1873 she was admitted to the workhouse at Newington, St Saviour's and a year later, on 29 November 1874, she died of 'senile exhaustion' in the workhouse at St Peter, Walworth.

The harsh system in Victorian England for dealing with 'paupers' had been enshrined in the Poor Law Amendment Act of 1834, under which the whole of England and Wales was divided into groups or 'unions' of parishes, in each of which an elected board of guardians administered 'poor relief' (similar to the overseers of the poor in which the Cadburys served in Birmingham). Previously, each parish had been responsible for its own poor relief under a statute of 1601. Under the 1834 law, a workhouse was provided for each union to house those destitute enough to be receiving relief. Outside relief was also distributed to the poor in their own homes if they had them – food, clothing, fuel and small amounts of money.

Life in the workhouses was hard and intended to be so, to dissuade anyone thought to be reluctant to seek work. In London, the boards were required to provide labour yards for the unemployed inmates, where they broke up stones to be used for metalling the roads, and were paid at trade union rates. Upon entering the workhouse, families were split up into male and female wards, separated by sex and age, with another ward for children under the age of seven. Family members were allowed to meet daily but had to separate at night, though a few married couples might be allowed to share a room at the discretion of the guardians. Eventually, many workhouses evolved into hospitals and orphanages, the hospitals being mainly for the aged, infirm or mentally ill.

Workhouses were already infamous by the end of the nineteenth century, when there were over 2,000 of them. Their death rate was appalling. Jonas Hanway, a philanthropist and social reformer of the time (and incidentally, the first man to carry an umbrella), believed that any children under three years old were unlikely to live more than a month or so. He said: 'Parish officers never intend that parish infants should live.' After visiting a Norfolk workhouse in 1781, Parson Woodforde wrote in his diary: 'About 380 Poor in it now, but they don't look either healthy or cheerful, a great Number die there, 27 have died since Christmas last.' Dickens portrayed the workhouse diet in *Oliver Twist* as 'three meals of thin gruel a day, with an onion twice a week, and half a roll on Sundays'.

The 1834 Act was intended to draw a distinction between those who were genuinely unable to work and those who chose not to, but more often than not the inmates were all lumped together, both the 'respectable' poor and the near-criminals. It seems unlikely that John James would have knowingly left his grandmother to die in such a place, even if his own family was cramped for living conditions, but if he did not know of her deteriorating state over many years it does not say much for the extended family values supposed to be typical of Victorian England before the age of the social worker.

John James and Mary Ann were to have a round dozen children in all, six sons and six daughters, ensuring plenty of successors for the business – and in due course, all of the sons worked for Sainsbury's in some capacity. The first child, Mary Ann, named for JJ's mother-in-law as well as for his wife, was born on 29 December 1869 but died at the age of five months of dysentery and convulsions. One in six babies at the time did not reach their first birthday. The young mother was advised not to have any more children, but the second child, John Benjamin, was already on the way. He was born over the Drury Lane shop on 8 January 1871 and was baptised at St Giles-in-the-Fields on 5 February. From childhood John Benjamin liked to help his mother in the dairy, wearing a small white apron and serving customers with eggs. For this he earned pocket money of one shilling and sixpence a week. Later, he helped his father with deliveries from a one-horse van, joining the business full-time as soon as he left school. The rest of the large family arrived at fairly regular intervals during the 1870s and 1880s: George on 12 October 1872; Alice on 7 February 1876; Frank on 11 August 1877; Louise on 31 December 1878; Arthur on 13 April 1880; Lilian on 30 July 1882; Alfred on 7 March 1884; Elsie on 29 April 1885; Dorothy Maud on 15 July 1889 and Paul James on 5 December 1890.

These were years of enormous change, when the modern world was being invented around the lives of ordinary Londoners struggling to pay for food, clothes and a roof over their heads; years when Alexander Graham Bell and Thomas Edison were inventing the telephone, the phonograph and the electric light bulb, when London got its first telephone exchange and the Factory and Workshop Act of 1878 finally regulated hours and conditions of employment, abolishing for ever the degrading spectacle of children being sent up chimneys and down coal mines. In the arts – not a world known to John James and Mary Ann Sainsbury, though their descendants would become modern Medicis – the Impressionists were changing painting; Ibsen was changing drama and George Eliot and Thomas Hardy were changing the novel.

Scientific advances were everywhere, including the food business; in 1874 the pressure-cooking method was introduced for canning food (tinned salmon, meat and fruit made their first appearance in London grocers six years later); in 1877, the introduction of refrigerated steamships brought the first frozen meat from Argentina to France and in 1879, a year marked for most Britons by the Zulu Wars, the slaughter of British troops at Isandhlwana and the heroic defence of Rorke's Drift, Australian frozen meat went on sale for the first time in London, a landmark event in the food trade. Nine years later, in 1888, the first refrigerated railway truck came into operation. The distribution and availability of fresh food was being transformed in the last years of Victoria's reign.

At the start of the 1880s, John James began taking over provision shops that had been run by his in-laws, the Staples. He acquired a cheesemonger in Stepney from his brother-in-law Edward Staples, another Staples branch at Hoxton and a third that had been his father-in-law's original shop at 87 Chalcot Street, St Pancras. The family, who could already afford the services of a maid, though there wasn't room for her to live in at Queen's Crescent, moved up again in the world, buying a house in fashionable Highgate in 1886.

With six branches JJ was now able to make economies of scale in securing the maximum discounts from his suppliers. This principle was taken further in a sort of pact among provision merchants with small chains of shops in London, who were frequently related – directly or by marriage – or had known each other for years. They bought premises from each other, gave each other first refusal when selling, agreed not to set up in competition in the same area and combined for bulk buying. Sainsbury's acquisition of 48 Chapel Street, Islington, one of north London's busiest market streets, was done through the pact, bought from a man called Deacock who had worked with Mary Ann's first employer, Tom Haile. By 1890, the arrangement covered up to eighty members, providing substantial buying clout and opportunities to expand into new trading areas: for the Sainsburys, well into John Benjamin's time as head of the firm, it meant the ability to acquire sites in good shopping areas outside their usual orbit, including the Midlands.

In the whole of Britain's retail food trade in the 1870s there were only around six multiples (defined as a chain with ten or more branches) with 108 shops between them. The first large-scale food retailing in the UK dated back to the 1840s when the Rochdale Pioneers opened the first shop in the Co-operative movement, which paid back any trading surplus to its members as dividends. By 1880 there were over 900 Co-ops with 500,000 members, turning over more than £10m a year. The wholesale arm of the movement, the Co-operative Wholesale Societies (CWS), ran the manufacturing and purchasing side, and by the 1900s were owning tea plantations and chartering ships as well as manufacturing all kinds of groceries from preserves to soap. Co-ops were mainly located in the industrial north and Scotland, whereas the new multiples centred on London and the south.

Between the 1890s and the First World War multiples expanded rapidly, not only in food but also in clothing, chemists such as Boots, newsagents (W. H. Smith), footwear chains like Freeman Hardy and Willis, butchers like Eastmans, tobacconists and confectioners. By 1914 there were sixteen firms with over 200 branches and seven with over 500. The first grocery firm to have more than ten retail branches was the London firm of Walton, Hassell and Port, with thirty branches.

Among JJ's fellow provision merchants were the Greig brothers, David and John, whose shops would become familiar on British high streets in the heyday of the family multiple. It was the Greig chain, according to Sainsbury's own corporate history, that finally broke the cosy no-competition arrangement in the 1930s, when Greig's put up billboards advertising their arrival in districts where they had not yet acquired a site. Young Alan Sainsbury, son of John Benjamin, was dispatched by his father to tell Ross Greig that under these circumstances Sainsbury's would no longer observe the unwritten pact. 'I'll drive you into the ground' was Greig's furious response – but it was his chain that disappeared under the tide of supermarkets unleashed by Alan Sainsbury in the 1950s.

The growth of branches and the ability to buy advantageously in bulk meant that Sainsbury needed a warehouse where supplies could be received, stored and dispatched out to the shops. The firm's first depot was in Allcroft Road, Kentish Town, near the three Queen's Crescent shops. It stored butter, cheese and eggs – unrefrigerated – and also had stoves for smoking bacon. This was to become the first Sainsbury 'brand' – a term, the firm's archivist suggests, possibly originating from the mark of a hot iron on the bacon rind.

The year 1882, when the depot opened, also marked Sainsbury's first major foray into the residential towns around London that would soon become part of its prosperous suburban sprawl. JJ bought a new shop at 6 (later renumbered 9/11) London Road, Croydon, the fastest growing town on London's outskirts and a thriving railway junction with no fewer than eleven stations through which around 400 trains ran daily to and from the capital. Sainsbury's shop was strategically situated opposite West Croydon station, and later that year, JJ decided to invest in making it a showcase for the business. He personally chose the green and brown patterned tiles for the interior, and the rest was elaborately fitted out in teak, mahogany and stained glass. The counters were made of marble slabs, elegant and easy to keep clean. Above the arched plate-glass windows, the legend 'Daily Arrivals of Pure Butter' was carved into marbled granite, with the name J. Sainsbury picked out in gilded letters.

The whole appearance of the shop, with its bentwood chairs for customers, was designed to persuade well-off local matrons that they no longer needed to travel to the West End to patronise smart provision merchants like Fortnum and Mason, and the range of produce reflected this move upmarket, offering cooked and fresh meats, poultry and game, French as well as English country butters, imported cheeses, York, Cumberland and Irish hams and such exotic delicacies as Egyptian quail, ortolans and larks.

Sainsbury's was no longer a chain of neighbourhood dairies in shabby north and east London streets but a purveyor, as it boasted on the windows, of 'high class provisions', and, like all high-class provision merchants, it offered a full delivery service to its new middle-class clientele in the leafy roads of Croydon. Ironically, it was to be this branch that Alan Sainsbury converted to Britain's first self-service supermarket in 1950, to the fury of some of its grander customers.

The immediate success of the Croydon venture led to copies being 'rolled out', as modern management jargon would term it, elsewhere in the rising middle-class suburbs – more shops in Croydon itself, specialising in game and poultry or pork butchery (manufacturing Sainsbury's own sausages), and further branches in Lewisham, Balham and Brondesbury. John James Sainsbury had hit on a marketing truth of the food business that would take some of his competitors two generations or more to comprehend – that luxury products create their own markets and command higher profit margins than basic foods. A century on, it would be JJ's great-grandsons who applied this understanding to supermarket selling, transforming it from the 'pile it high, sell it cheap' philosophy of Jack Cohen, founder of the Tesco chain, to Fortnum-style provisions for the masses.

These early model shops provided a far greater range of European produce than the supermarkets of the 1990s with all the advantages of long-haul air transport. Balham, for example, offered not only new-laid English eggs but eggs from Austria, Italy, Denmark, the Netherlands and Brittany. A worker at Balham, quoted in Sainsbury's in-house corporate history, recalled: 'You could tell where an egg came from by the colour of its yolk. The Austrian egg was small, but had a golden yolk which would always maintain its spherical shape. The Italian was a little larger with a fine reddish brick-coloured yolk. Both Dutch and Danish had pale yellow yolks, and eggs from Brittany scintillating globules of rich gold.' Curiously, at this time French eggs had a better reputation for freshness than English ones: the French collection system was less erratic, the eggs were properly graded and packed and often arrived on the English markets within three days of being laid.

By the end of the 1880s, John James had more branches in and around London than could be supplied from his Kentish Town warehouse. His eldest son, John Benjamin, found new premises for a depot in Stamford Street, Blackfriars, at the south end of Blackfriars Bridge. The firm's headquarters are still there, in a handsome Edwardian brick building constructed in 1912 as a cheese warehouse. (David Sainsbury recalls the smell of cheese filtering up to the offices when he first worked in the family firm in the 1960s.)

The original building had been a horse depository and since there was a clause restricting its use to that purpose it looked unlikely to fetch its asking price of £20,000. In the end it went to auction and the Sainsburys secured it for £2,500. Somehow they also managed to circumvent the restrictions on use and converted it to a food warehouse. It was an ideal centre for a depot, within easy reach of Tooley Street, then the centre of the imported provisions trade; of Smithfield, the famed meat market north of the bridge, and of the poultry market at Leadenhall Street in the City banking district. It was also handy for most of the main London goods railheads and occupied a central point in the triangle covered by Sainsbury branches from Walthamstow in the north-east to Croydon in the south.

The opening of the Blackfriars depot in 1891 signalled a dramatic expansion of the business. Over the next twenty-three years, until the outbreak of the First World War, the number of branches would grow from fourteen to 115, most of them trading within the fifteen-mile radius of Blackfriars that could comfortably be served by the two-horse delivery vans. Branches farther out, at Brighton and Eastbourne on the south coast, at Ipswich, Norwich and Colchester in East Anglia, and at Guildford and Watford in the environs of London, were supplied by railway.

Sainsbury shops that survived into the pre-supermarket era – I remember my mother shopping at one in Porchester Road, Bayswater, up to 1951 – still looked like classic Edwardian food emporia. Their distinctive house style was fostered by green and cream frieze tiles manufactured to a special design by Minton Hollins and marble counter tops fronted by teapot-brown tiling. In memory they are frozen in the Christmas season, with feathered game and turkeys hanging head down above counters presided over by white-aproned men who knew how to cut great rounds of cheese with a wire to the precise ounce, and many other arcane arts fascinating to a small child. So popular were they that many pre-1914 and interwar shops survived even into the 1980s: the Rye Lane, Peckham, branch, opened in 1931, was the last counter-service Sainsbury's branch to yield to the supermarket tide, in 1982.

The last decade of the nineteenth century saw a technological revolution in food production, processing and transportation methods which hugely benefited entrepreneurial provision merchants like Sainsbury. Beef and wheat from North America, Argentina and Russia, canned products such as corned beef and condensed milk and new food developments such as margarine (invented in 1869 by the French scientist Mège Mouriés as a cheap butter substitute for the French army in the field) all helped to expand and make more affordable the diet of the British working class, previously restricted, as William Cobbett observed in his travels about rural England, to 'bread, cheese and beer', supplemented by bacon as the most commonly purchased meat.

Bacon was cheaper than beef and, being preserved, kept well in an age without refrigeration. The Prince Regent's claim for the English that 'beef and beer have made us what we are' came from a vantage-point of privilege: most families never tasted beef until the cheaper imported variety arrived. Charles Booth in *Life and Labour of the People* (1892), observed the poor of London's East End subsisting on bread and tea, with margarine spread on the bread 'or jam if there were children, a little bacon and some fried fish. Potatoes are hugely used, greens sometimes and the cheap parts of beef or mutton on occasion.'

At the time Charles Booth was writing, unskilled labourers were earning about twenty-one shillings a week and skilled artisans between thirty and seventy shillings (£1.50–£3.50; multiply by a factor of between 50 and 55 for today's values). Most East End families made do on a total income of between twenty-two and thirty shillings: the poverty line was reckoned to be about twenty-three shillings a week and studies by Booth and Joseph Rowntree showed just under a third of Britons subsisting at this level. Most of their meagre funds were spent on food. In 1900, Rowntree wrote of working-class families with three or four children buying two to three pounds of bacon a week, three to four pounds of meat, four to five pounds of sugar, twenty-five to forty pounds of flour or bread, six to eight ounces of tea and a pound of butter. They bought much less fresh milk and eggs than middle-class families, but condensed milk was a staple.

The growth of cheap food imports had a dramatic impact on the London wholesale markets in Tooley Street and elsewhere. Merchants like Sainsbury began to cut out the middle-man, dealing direct with suppliers and often buying at the wharves as ships unloaded. John James established his own buying agent for butter in Holland to bypass the importers who, he discovered, had been stockpiling to sell at the highest market price, by which time it was no longer fresh. Sainsbury insisted that each case of butter be stamped with its date of production, and personally inspected every delivery as it arrived in his warehouse. A farmer at Witheridge, north Devon, was signed up by Arthur Sainsbury, JJ's fourth son, who looked after the pork buying, and for years supplied Sainsbury's with poultry, pig meat, eggs, butter, rabbits and, later, beef and mutton. JJ subsequently decided to buy his own farm at Little Wratting in Suffolk, and put in his third son Frank as manager.

Frank Sainsbury had not been particularly happy in the family business, which all the sons were expected to join without question, as indeed John Benjamin, George, Arthur, Alfred and the youngest, Paul, all did in turn, though George did not stay in the firm. Alfred, the fifth son, was apprenticed in 1906 to a tea merchant near Tower Bridge to equip him to become Sainsbury's grocery buyer. At twenty-two, when he was ready to begin work at the Blackfriars head office, he received a note from his father that bleakly informed him to 'commence from April 30th . . . Time to be here 8 O'ck. Your half day Thursday.' For a while Frank managed a branch in the Seven Sisters Road, Islington, but his erratic temper and eccentric behaviour – on one occasion cycling into the shop as it was crowded with customers – caused his father to sack him. He had always wanted to be a farmer, and after a trial period working on the farm of a family friend in Suffolk, he was allowed to take on the newly acquired Sainsbury farm in 1902.

Here he came into his own, revolutionising the quality of English eggs by establishing an efficient, regular collection system throughout a network of small farms in East Anglia. The eggs were then tested for defects by 'candling' – holding them up against the light of a candle – before being graded and packed for despatch to London. Sainsbury's reputation for eggs became unrivalled, and the cottage-industry collection methods lasted until well after the Second World War. Joe Barnes, a former board director for retail operations, recalled in the mid-1980s that his first job with the firm was as a young accountant in East Anglia in 1956, checking the leather money pouches worn by Sainsbury's egg collectors as they toured the little farms of the area, picking up a dozen eggs here, half a dozen there, and leaving the money in pots on the farmhouse mantelpieces. Around 1912 Frank expanded into pig production, providing the business with regular supplies of pork for fresh cuts of meat, cooked meat, pies and sausages.

It was not surprising that Frank Sainsbury preferred the life of a farmer to that of a food retailer. It was a hard, slogging life even for managers, though promotion was rapid and smart juniors could quickly learn the skills that would take them from egg-boy to first hand and upwards. Managers were often appointed in their early twenties. But trading hours were long – even worse than in the drapery business in which H. G. Wells chronicled the thankless life of an apprentice in *Kipps*. Staff were at work by 7.30 a.m. every day except Sunday, though on Mondays, when trade was slack, some would get a half-holiday after 2 p.m. Sainsbury's was unusual in giving this benefit and it was not until the Shops Act of 1911 that one day's early closing became the law. On Tuesdays, Wednesdays and Thursdays trading did not end until 9.15 p.m., on Fridays not until 10.45 p.m., when customers had their week's pay in their pockets, and on Saturdays not until midnight. Then there was the scrubbing down of counters and floors to be done, and the takings to be counted: the manager would handle the gold coins himself. It was often 2 a.m. on Sunday before the shop workers could fall into bed, exhausted. Wages for all this were eight to ten shillings a week for a junior.

Late-night trading ended with the First World War and the Defence of the Realm Act, known as DORA, which changed many social customs for the rest of the century – most notably by restricting the hours during which alcohol could be sold in pubs, bars and shops. Sunday trading was a muddle, as it remained until the mid-1990s, with most food products allowed to be sold but others, such as fresh meat, prohibited. It was left to local authorities to fix trading hours in their areas until more general regulation was introduced in 1936.

In 1896 the Sainsburys forged a dynastic link with one of their leading foreign suppliers when John Benjamin, the eldest son, married into the Dutch van den Bergh family. By the 1890s the van den Berghs were market leaders in margarine manufacture over their compatriot rivals the Jurgens. The consumption of margarine, known as 'butterine' in Britain until legislation outlawed this deceptive term in 1887, rose dramatically after 1890 and by 1914 was providing over three-quarters of the trade of the Maypole Dairy. The Maypole grew phenomenally on the business: in 1905 it was opening a new branch every five days and by 1914 had over 800 of them. It was said of the Watson family who ran it that 'if they opened a shop in the middle of Epping Forest they could have sold margarine'.

Margarine was the subject of cut-throat competition among grocers, most of whom had contracts with either van den Bergh's or Jurgen's. The UK was an enormous market for both of the Dutch makers, and they vied with each other to buy into the leading British multiples to establish trading channels. With a refreshing directness about his product, Henri Jurgens told the Royal Society of Arts in 1884 that the English were the only major nation insensitive enough to put margarine on their bread instead of restricting its use to cooking. Margarine, like butter, had been sold from the cask, patted into the required weight by grocery assistants, but in the First World War, when butter prices rose steeply, van den Bergh's introduced a new ready-wrapped brand of margarine called Blue Band, which immediately proved a winner on grounds of hygiene and convenience.

Margarine did not form a particularly large part of Sainsbury's business, which prided itself on supplying 'the best value butter in the world' (similar claims were made by Maypole and other chains), but it was nevertheless a useful connection when the heir John Benjamin, aged twenty-five, married Mabel van den Bergh, whose father Jacob and uncle Henry had opened a London office in 1879. The couple were married on 8 January 1896 at the West London Synagogue near Marble Arch, a synagogue in the reform movement. John Benjamin would have been required to convert to Judaism before the marriage could be solemnised.

There is an odd sensitivity even today about the connection: a van den Bergh cousin says the two families dislike each other and have little contact. Certainly the dynastic connection is virtually ignored in the firm's official history. Apart from one engagement photograph of 'Mr John' and his Dutch fiancée, the book omits any mention of the marriage, while making a point of stating that van den Bergh's never acquired a financial interest in Sainsbury's, although it and Jurgens between them bought up a number of competitors such as Maypole, Lipton's and Home and Colonial. Later these were to form the nucleus of the giant Unilever conglomerate, of which van den Bergh became a founding company.

Mabel van den Bergh's dowry was invested in the firm, and in the five years following the marriage Sainsbury's opened thirty-two new shops. Business was being accelerated by the big new distribution centre at Blackfriars. Between 1890 and 1900 the number of branches trebled to forty-eight, though Sainsbury's was still a tiny chain compared to rivals such as Maypole, which had 200 branches as the new century opened; Lipton's, which had 500 branches; and Home and Colonial, which boasted 400. Lipton's was headed by the flamboyant Sir Thomas (Tommy) Lipton, a crony of Edward VII. He was invariably photographed wearing a yachting cap and underwrote Britain's entry in the America's Cup ocean race year after year with a series of yachts, all called *Shamrock*. Just as the American showman Gordon Selfridge in the department store world was the ultimate contrast to the frugal, workaholic John Lewis, so the Glaswegian Tommy Lipton and the

Londoner John James Sainsbury occupied opposite poles in the grocery trade. But like the hare and the tortoise fable, it would be the unknown Sainsbury whose business long outlived the Lipton name, which now only survives as a label on packets of export tea.

By the outbreak of war in 1914 Sainsbury's still had only 121 branches, mostly in and around London. The growth of the other multiples in the 1900s sparked a public controversy similar to that over the grip of the supermarkets in the 1990s. They were, said critics, driving the small grocer out of business with their aggressive advertising and price cutting. *The Times* complained of their centralised style that they were nearly all run on 'the same impersonal iron routine system . . . the brains being supplied from headquarters with the consignments of goods'. Their chief aim, said their accusers, was to make profits for their shareholders at the expense of the customer. Yet the small independent grocers could not have supplied a fraction of the needs of London's exploding population. And, compared with the anarchy of half a century before. with unhygienic market stalls and contaminated food, centralisation – if customers worried about it at all – must have seemed a small price to pay for the cleanliness, efficiency, consistent standards and convenience of the high street multiples.

The First World War, or the 'Anglo-German War' as it was termed in a Sainsbury poster promising every effort to keep regular customers supplied, affected most retail businesses in the same way; the loss of skilled young male staff to the armed forces and their eventual replacement by women, necessitating new training; restricted hours of work; shortages and higher prices; the appearance of the first banknotes that would soon abolish the gold sovereign for ever, and in some cases, damage by Zeppelin bombing. While old John Lewis complained loudly to the recruiting authorities that his staff was reduced to 'waifs and strays' in the rush to volunteer, John Benjamin Sainsbury, who was by now managing the business for his seventy-year-old father, tried to persuade young managers that their job was as important to Britain as donning khaki and entraining for the Front. Like John Lewis's London stores, Sainsbury's also suffered from the appropriation of horses for the military, which meant that home deliveries had to be curtailed or at some branches suspended altogether.

The food industry had the additional burden of rationing, though this was not imposed until 1917, when Germany declared unrestricted U-boat warfare on merchant shipping, a full two years after sinking Cunard's crack liner *Lusitania* and a number of smaller passenger ships. In the hot summer of 1914, while the public at large was planning its seaside holidays and relying on the diplomats to sort out the little local difficulty in Sarajevo, there were those who worried about Britain's ability to provide enough food for its citizens if Germany imposed an immediate naval blockade. The first supplies to be hit were those of sugar. Sainsbury's managers were told not to let any customer have more than two pounds. Imported butter and bacon also rose in price, but the policy of acquiring its own farms enabled Sainsbury's to stabilise and even reduce some prices in the first months of the war.

Occasionally there was food rioting, when queues that had waited patiently for a delivery of sugar or bacon saw the van arrive and suddenly broke loose. The lack of cheese caused one riot at a Sainsbury's branch in Woodford, Essex, managed by a woman, Ethel Jessop. Another retailer nearby was killed in the crush. When a solitary mounted policeman arrived to find that the shop had only six members of staff, he suggested closing the top half of the door and then stood his horse across it, allowing six customers at a time to crawl in under the horse's belly.

Rationing for butter and margarine was not introduced until the last year of the war, in contrast to 1939–45, when rationing was imposed almost immediately. By the Armistice in November 1918 the weekly ration had been more or less stabilised at eight ounces of sugar, five ounces of butter or margarine, four ounces of jam and two ounces of tea. Fresh meat and bacon were rationed by value rather than weight, and, as in the second war, game and poultry such as hare, rabbit, pheasant, plover, duck and goose were readily available – at a price.

Paul Sainsbury, the youngest son, was twenty-four at the outbreak of war. He served in the army and survived the short life-span of subalterns in 1914–18 to join the firm and work on its building programme. More than 1,000 of the firm's young men enlisted as volunteers before conscription was imposed in 1916. Nearly a third of those aged between twenty and twenty-three never came home. The company's in-house history records that around 500 male employees were killed and 1,000 suffered serious injuries; on average, every one of the 128 Sainsbury branches lost four of its staff.

CHAPTER 10:

THE BATTLE FOR THE HIGH STREET

SAINSBURY'S REMAINED A simple family business until 1922, when it was formalised as a private company, J. Sainsbury Ltd., with a capital of £1.3 million in one million £1 preference shares and 300,000 £1 ordinary shares, all held by family members. The founder, by this time seventy-eight years old, remained chairman, with JB, then fifty-one, and his brothers Arthur and Alfred as board directors. George, the second son, had left the company, but Paul, who had volunteered for war service, joined in 1921 to work on building development and remained with the business until 1938. The first member of the third generation also joined the firm in January 1921 – JB's eldest son Alan. Aged eighteen, he began working with his uncles Arthur and Alfred, buying eggs and dairy products.

On 3 January 1928, John James Sainsbury died at his home in Broadlands Road, Highgate. He was eighty-three. His wife Mary Ann had died six months before, on 9 June 1927, and he had continued attending the office until 2 November that year; the day, as it happened, that Alan Sainsbury's first son, another John and a future chairman of the business, was born. The London *Evening News* remarked of John James that he was 'a man who disliked the limelight so much that he remained almost unknown to the general public throughout his career'. JJ left a fortune of £1,158,615 and was buried in Putney Vale Cemetery in south-west London in a Greek-style mausoleum of white marble with the name Sainsbury carved in capitals over the entrance. John Benjamin was now in full control of the business as chairman, but in essence he had been running the trading side since 1915, when his father took him into partnership.

JB was by all accounts a single-minded man of immense energy and obsessive attention to detail, traits that were to be shared by his son and grandson, Alan and John, along with a notable short fuse that could erupt in terrible displays of wrath. In spite of this somewhat overbearing image, his personal assistant Frederick Salisbury recalled that he had the capacity to inspire 'the most extraordinary team spirit, indeed in his conception it was more of a big family than a team and he was able to impart a sense of absorption amounting almost to adoption'.

JB was always an extremely hands-on chief executive: when he retired, the trade press, while admiring the way he drove Sainsbury's growth, described him as 'an unapologetic dictator' who controlled everything from buying through to counter sales in the branches. He would go into stores and advise managers how to arrange their counters and exactly where to place their scales or bacon slicer. Managers, he laid down, should never become so embroiled in administration that they could not be available to customers when needed. They were expected to manage the paperwork efficiently and not spend unnecessary time on it. He also took a personal hand in choosing sites for new branches, doing his own market research by counting the number of passing shoppers and often taking his family out on weekend drives to look for new locations.

In the 1920s and 1930s London and the 'home counties' grew twice as fast as the rest of the country. New technological industries such as radio, cars and electrical household appliances were booming as the old heavy industries of the Midlands and north sank into decay. 'Metroland', as John Betjeman was to christen it – the garden suburbs springing up at the end of the Underground lines – provided prime sites for Sainsbury with their neat parades of shops and home-owners' aspirations for a better lifestyle than their parents had enjoyed.

Most Sainsbury stores were now divided into six departments – dairy, bacon and ham, poultry and game, cooked meats, fresh meat and groceries. In meat they even outsold well-established butchers like the Dewhurst chain. JB, or 'Mr John' (the old-fashioned family nomenclature had the advantage of distinguishing between the various family members but persisted long after there was only one Sainsbury at Stamford House), was sharp at spotting the coming trends and was a pioneer in developing own-label products just as branded goods were being homogenised in price by the policy of resale price maintenance. By 1938, when JB retired, nearly all Sainsbury groceries were own-brand.

The only area in which JB seemed reluctant to face the future was in the firm's fleet of horse-drawn vans. He loved horses and insisted well into the 1930s that using them instead of motor vans could save the firm a shilling to 1s. 6d. per ton of freight. Sainsbury's only phased out its last horses in 1937. Nearly all branches in the inter-war years offered a delivery service: it was part of the upmarket image and the middle-class housewives of Metroland expected nothing less. Shops would deliver up to four times a day, by errand boy on a bicycle or tricycle for the nearest customers and by van farther out. The ending of home deliveries with the advent of self-service was a severe blow to many older customers: it would take another half-century before fiercely competing giant supermarkets hit on home delivery again as a way of enhancing customer satisfaction.

The face of food retailing was changing after the First World War. The trade was consolidating, with the bigger firms buying up or amalgamating with their smaller competitors. In the thirty years between 1920 and 1950, some forty companies were acquired in this way by the three largest groupings, Home and Colonial, International Tea and Moores Stores. Early, fast-growing chains like the Maypole Dairies found themselves hampered by a huge number of small branches; too small by the 1930s to carry a competitive range of goods. Maypole, along with Lipton, the Meadow Dairy Company and a number of smaller firms, were combined under the Home and Colonial umbrella while continuing to trade under the familiar names.

Whereas before the First World War expansion in the trade had been led by family firms, now it was public companies that set the pace. Nearly all the big firms did some food manufacturing or processing as well as retailing. Shopping habits were changing, too. As the Depression bit and unemployment rose, less money was spent on food, particularly on groceries. Houses and families had both become smaller, and fewer people had the staff for the extensive home baking and big elaborate meals of Edwardian times. There were fewer bulk purchases and more emphasis on small quantities and ready-to-eat foods.

Retailing histories of the period make little mention of Sainsbury, presumably because, although successfully growing and expanding in the new suburbs, it was doing so on a smaller scale and at a less frenetic pace than the bigger high street chains. Yet under JB's direction, the business more than doubled in size between the wars, expanding from 129 branches in 1920 with a turnover of just over £5m, to 255 in 1939 with sales of £12.6m. New branches opened every year, never fewer than three. In 1932, when the Depression was already well under way, there were fourteen. By 1939, Home and Colonial's chain of nearly 800 shops was producing only £9.9m to Sainsbury's £12.6m, while Lipton's 450 stores yielded less than £7m and Maypole Dairies' 977 shops could only muster sales of £9.1m. Sainsbury had proved to have the right strategy, going for larger, more upmarket premises in key south-eastern locations.

Most of its new branches were start-ups, though some were taken over from competitors such as the Thoroughgood shops, bought in 1936. These had been built up by Alfred Banton, who had sold an earlier chain of shops to John James at the turn of the century, and they took Sainsbury into the Midlands area for the first time, although most of the shops outside London were sold later on. The capital was still Sainsbury heartland: as the founder had once commented, 'All the best food comes to London.' The manner of acquiring the nine Thoroughgood shops that were kept by Sainsbury's shows JB in characteristically decisive form. When he bought them, the bailiffs were already in possession of several and JB was preparing to go on holiday with his wife Mabel in three days' time. Taking Frederick Salisbury, his personal assistant, with him, he went briskly round all nine, assessed their prospects as Sainsbury branches, completed the purchase, paid the bailiffs and caught the boat on time. When he got back a few weeks later, the shops had been refurbished, reopened and were trading under the Sainsbury name.

JB also expanded the food preparation side at Stamford House, the big brick headquarters that had been built in 1912–13 on the site of the original horse depository. JB commissioned Sir Owen Williams, the architect of Wembley Stadium and the black glass *Daily Express* building in Fleet Street, to build a new model factory to replace the old kitchens that stood opposite Stamford House. A specialist in concrete slab construction well ahead of his time, Williams worked on the design with James Sainsbury, Arthur's son, who had joined the business in 1926 and was given supervision of the new project. James insisted on quality control laboratories being included so that the food in preparation could be checked and analysed at regular stages. The factory opened in 1936 and was a source of much fascination in the industry. Pigs from Frank Sainsbury's Suffolk farm went in at one end of the production process and were turned into a myriad pork products, with brawn and Bath chaps being made in the basement and sausages ready for despatch within a hour of the carcasses entering the building. Meat pies and freshly baked bread were made on the third floor and some of the herbs used in the sausage and pie manufacture came from John Benjamin's own gardens.

In 1938 JB suffered a minor heart attack and decided to retire at the age of sixty-seven, handing over full control to his sons Alan and Robert as joint general managers although he retained the title of chairman. Surprisingly for a man who had involved himself in every aspect of the business for so long, once he retired he made no attempt to interfere with his sons' management; another example of the extraordinary self-discipline that marked his character. His health was giving him cause for concern and in later life he would suffer intensely from depression, which undoubtedly contributed to his mysterious death. By his retirement, Sainsbury's was a household name in Britain, with a reputation not only for the quality of its products and shops but also for its ability to provide most of a family's food requirements, including fresh meat.

Alan had worked at the sharp end of the business for seventeen years, at one stage serving at the counter of the Boscombe branch on the

Dorset coast, using the alias Mr Allan. Robert was an accountant by training who had joined the firm in 1930 and served as company secretary for seven years. He remains one of the least-known Sainsburys, despite a long career of arts patronage that brought him his knighthood in 1967. An instinctive collector of genius, Robert used to set aside a portion of his yearly allowance to buy art while still an undergraduate at Cambridge and in his first year spent the entire £200 on a Madonna by Henry Moore: it was said to have been the only sale Moore made that year. Later, regularly allocating £1,000 a year for art purchases, he became an early collector of Giacometti and was a patron of Francis Bacon for seven years before the artist sold a single painting. His collection of primitive art, now in the Sainsbury Arts Centre at the University of East Anglia, is said to be one of the finest in the country.

Taking over from JB, whose experience of the business from its beginnings had been unique, all the way from egg-boy at Queen's Crescent, was a formidable challenge for the brothers. They dealt with it by dividing the management responsibilities between them, Alan concentrating on the trading side and Robert on administrative, financial and personnel matters. It was a partnership that worked well for twenty-five years.

The change at the top of Sainsbury's took place as the escalating political and military tension in Europe began to affect the growth and development of all the distributive trades. From the Munich crisis of 1938 until the outbreak of war a year later, government plans were being drawn up for war and its impact on civilian life, with a high priority given to the production and distribution of food. Several leading multiple food traders played a key part in the Board of Trade's Food Defence Plans Department and the subsequent formation of the Ministry of Food on 8 September 1939, five days after the declaration of war.

Alan Sainsbury became chief representative of the multiple grocers on the government's many retail advisory committees, while James Sainsbury was on a government committee devising price structures and recipes for cooked and processed meats. Sainsbury's was better prepared than in the 1914–18 war for staff shortages. Even before Neville

Chamberlain's fateful broadcast to the nation on Sunday, 3 September, hundreds of letters had gone out to former women employees asking them if they would like to be re-engaged. But the mass evacuations from London meant that many fewer women were available than had been hoped, and a concerted recruitment drive was launched, with short training courses being introduced at Blackfriars to bring the newcomers as fast as possible up to Sainsbury service standards.

Reserved occupation status was initially given to grocery managers, butchers and warehousemen aged over thirty, but this age limit was raised to thirty-five in 1941 and in 1942 reserved status was abolished altogether as the demand grew for servicemen. Young single women were also liable for call-up and Sainsbury's had a running battle with the authorities in trying to explain the time that was needed to train up an employee. By 1942, a workforce which had been predominantly made up of young single men had turned into one composed of older men, part-time married women assistants and teenagers under eighteen.

Most of the headquarters staff was evacuated to depots in Hampshire, Essex, Leicestershire and Hertfordshire, leaving only a core of essential people at Stamford House. The distribution system was also decentralised to render it less vulnerable to bombing and to save fuel. The improvised depots included a former garage in Woolmer Green, Hertfordshire, an old maltings in Saffron Walden, Essex, a disused factory in Bramshott, Hampshire, and a site in Fleckney, near Leicester. Blackfriars continued to supply central London branches, and the office staff who remained there often spent their nights fire-watching. The firm had drawn up contingency plans for a German invasion, and staff in the southern and eastern counties each knew exactly where they were to go. Managers had instructions to remove all ledgers, cash books and rationing registration particulars.

The biggest administrative headache for the industry in wartime was rationing. In November 1939 families were instructed to register with a local retailer as a preliminary to the introduction of the ration-book system. Naturally every branch of every multiple wanted as many registrations as possible, without actively being seen to tout for business beyond the discreet notice in the window saying 'Register Here'. It was the ultimate test of customer loyalty, because registration meant that customer was tied to that particular shop for the duration of rationing. Sainsbury's staff were told that the firm's reputation for quality, hygiene and service would bring in registrations without the need even for window notices.

The first foods to be rationed, in January 1940, were butter, bacon and sugar, followed by meat and preserves in March; tea, margarine and cooking fats in July; and cheese the following year. Most commodities were rationed by weight, and the relevant coupons in the ration books had to be painstakingly cancelled or clipped out. Meat was rationed by value, with special coupons. It was an administrative nightmare, especially as some people's entitlements varied, and customers were also required to re-register twice a year. Sainsburys invented the so-called 'points system', later adopted by the Ministry of Food, to share out non-rationed but scarce items such as sausages, cakes and custard powder on an equitable basis.

Business soon began to suffer. It was down by a third by March 1942, and turnover was half its pre-war level. 'Any lower and we could not have survived,' said Robert Sainsbury later. Sainsbury's strategy of locating in London and on high street sites was now working against it as people left the capital when the heavy bombing began, and many of those who remained were unwilling to risk the perils of the blackout by visiting a high street Sainsbury branch if they could get provisions more easily from their local corner shop.

Sainsbury shops suffered over 600 incidents of bomb damage during the war. Stamford House was also bombed. The worst affected was the Marylebone branch in central London, where a direct hit on the shop killed four members of staff on the night of 19 September 1940. Surprisingly, however, the Coventry branch survived the devastation rained on the Midlands city on the night of 14 November 1940, wrecking the famous medieval cathedral and the historic timbered district around it. 'There wasn't a thing broken, not even an egg,' marvelled the relief manager, and he and his staff opened for business next day. In placid East Grinstead in Sussex, the local branch was bombed twice in successive Julys, in 1943 and 1944. The second of these raids was so severe that the shop had to transfer its trading activities to a nearby Wesleyan chapel. After the war 'the shop in a church' became something of a tourist attraction.

Peace in Europe brought no immediate relief in the supply of essential foods or the recruitment of staff. Rationing continued for years, and became even tighter: bread, which had been freely available during the war, was rationed between 1946 and 1948, and the well-worn paper ration books were not finally consigned to history until 1954. The Butler Education Act of 1944 raised the school-leaving age to fifteen from 1947 and later to sixteen, changing the old patterns of youth work and apprenticeships. Shortage of skilled staff, and of manpower generally as returning servicemen and women found better paid jobs elsewhere, was clearly going to change the way food had been sold and delivered before the war. This, together with the great groundswell of social change in Britain that swept away domestic staff for the middle classes, demanded radical new thinking in retailing.

It came across the Atlantic and its name was self-service, which had been around in the US since the First World War. The world's first self-service grocery store was the Piggly Wiggly in Memphis, Tennessee, which opened in 1916. Clarence Saunders, the founder of Piggly Wiggly, took out a patent on self-service food shopping in 1917, but his idea soon outran him. It developed rapidly during the Depression as a way of reducing distribution costs, with customers helping themselves from open packing cases in warehouses and paying on their way out. Then in 1930 Michael J. Cullen opened a huge, no-frills store on the edge of New York offering free parking and bargain food prices. The store was called King Kullen and announced itself as 'the world's greatest price wrecker'. Within four years, Cullen had a chain of fifteen shops. The modern supermarket was born.

In Britain, a few firms had toyed with the idea even before the war, notably Tesco at its St Albans branch and the Co-op, but it was Alan Sainsbury who first perceived that self-service was an idea whose time had come. 'Mr Alan', as he was inevitably known in the firm, was an astute observer of social trends and a supporter of the postwar Labour government's reforming aims that had been led by the Beveridge Report of 1942. That year, indeed, both Sainsbury brothers wrote to *The Times* declaring their support for Beveridge's vision of a welfare safety net guaranteeing state provision of a pension and free health care. Eight years earlier, the brothers had persuaded John Benjamin to start Sainsbury's first pension and sickness insurance scheme. They promoted reform in other ways too within the old patriarchal system inherited from John James, where security of employment depended more or less on an employee's favour with the boss. In 1944 Alan and Robert wrote to all Sainsbury staff serving with the forces, assuring them that if they wished to return to Sainsbury employment after the war, they would receive a proper contract of service with written conditions and a guarantee of some job security.

A small, energetic man with an impish sense of humour, quite unlike his intimidating son John, Alan was always one of the more interesting and lively personalities of the Sainsbury clan, who were not noted as extroverts. He had at first intended to make his career in social service of some kind and drifted into the family business, he once said, 'chiefly because my mother said it would break my father's heart if I didn't'. He had been a Liberal parliamentary candidate in Suffolk in three pre-war general elections (1929, 1931 and 1935) but formally joined the Labour party in its victorious election year of 1945.

He used to reflect ruefully on the political career he might have had if he had won his parliamentary seat in 1929 – he came within 1,100 votes of victory. He was a close friend of Hugh Gaitskell, who became Labour leader after Clement Attlee, and always believed that if Gaitskell had lived and won the 1964 election (he died prematurely in 1963 and was succeeded as party leader by the technocrat Harold Wilson) he would have been offered a government post. In running Sainsbury's, he was far less tradition-bound than his predecessors and always open to new ideas.

In 1949 he got the chance to study the self-service revolution at first hand when John Strachey, minister of food in Attlee's reforming postwar government, asked him to find out what the British food industry, still in the grip of rationing and chronic shortages, could learn from American developments in frozen food. Alan and his father's former personal assistant Fred Salisbury, now a Sainsbury director, toured US cities for a frenetic fortnight and were immediately struck by the possibilities opened up by self-service. The pair visited New York, Buffalo, Chicago, Philadelphia and Boston and for the whole fourteen days 'were never out of American supermarkets', as Alan recalled in his eighties.

> We were both convinced that this was the future for J.S. Firstly, we couldn't visualise a return to the old type of trading. Many of our branches had been physically damaged during the war – some of them destroyed. Also, with rising living standards, no old-fashioned counter shop could offer the customers of the future the range of choice that would be expected with a higher standard of living.

In an interview with the *Observer* newspaper in 1973, Alan put it a different way: 'In the post-war world, you couldn't do Harrods' and Fortnum's job and at the same time supply the mass market at reasonable prices.'

To talk of rising living standards was unusually prescient at a time when food in British shops was at a twentieth-century nadir in choice and quality. Living standards might be a great improvement on the 1930s, when Sainsbury had seen poor housewives trundling from shop to shop in search of threepence cheaper here, twopence there, but the food of the late 1940s was dire. This writer remembers as a child seeing huge notices over butchers' shops, 'Horsemeat. For Human Consumption Only', and being told sharply not on any account to reveal that we were buying it for the cat. Even worse were whale steaks, which were tough and had a disgustingly fishy undertaste. The only plentiful fresh protein I remember was herrings, which we ate rolled in oatmeal and fried, the Scottish way, and which seemed to consist of nothing but bones and gritty grain. Tinned food was little better – the ubiquitous Spam, of course, pink Danish 'luncheon meat', which was deemed a treat, Fray Bentos corned beef occasionally and that dreary South African fish snoek, which like most other tinned fish at the time came doused in tomato sauce.

Somehow in this uniquely dismal era of food shopping, Alan Sainsbury foresaw a future of bursting and varied shelves, coupled with a vision of more mobility as the car-borne society reached Britain. (In 1949 the streets of British cities were almost empty of private cars, and virtually all the national car output was designated for export.) Lastly, Sainsbury reasoned, the UK would follow the US in the fridge and freezer revolution, though in 1950 only one in twenty British households had a refrigerator: by 1973 the figure would be one in seven. All these intuitions convinced Sainsbury that the future lay with self-service, added to the fact that domestic service in middle-class households had shrunk to almost nothing since the war. Madam would most likely have to do her own shopping, and with the disappearance of the errand boy on his bicycle, home deliveries were already a thing of the past.

After sailing home on Cunard's new *Queen Elizabeth* liner, thankful to get some sleep after their exertions in the supermarket aisles, Alan and Fred Salisbury persuaded the board to go for self-service. The store chosen to launch this revolution was the one at 9/11 London Road, Croydon, which offered the largest amount of floor space. It was equipped with new refrigerators, protective counter covers made of Perspex – the transparent plastic developed during the war by ICI to make cockpit covers for Spitfire fighters – and the first shopping trolleys, at that time nothing more than frames on wheels to carry two wire shopping baskets. The choice of the London Road store, although logical, was laden with irony because it had been this very shop that J. J. Sainsbury had hoped would persuade the prosperous suburban matrons of Edwardian Purley, Croydon and Penge that Sainsbury's could match the West End emporia for service, comfort and choice.

Predictably, some of these matrons and their daughters, who still expected home deliveries and a deferential grocer in a white apron, did not take kindly to do-it-yourself shopping. One woman threw a wire basket at Alan Sainsbury as he dropped in for a visit after the opening on 26 June 1950. Another customer, a judge's wife from Purley, swore coarsely at the Sainsbury boss for daring to expect that she should become her own shop assistant.

But the trade press praised the innovation and the public flocked to try it out. Most people were entranced by the freedom to pick and choose from the shelves and no doubt ended up buying far more than they had intended. Very quickly the London Road Sainsbury's was turning over a greater weekly volume of sales than any other food store in Britain. Choice was expanded, gradually, as wartime regulations were lifted – first on jam and preserves at the end of 1948, then on milk, tea, confectionery sugar, eggs, butter, margarine and cheese. The last rationing – on bacon and meat – was not lifted until 3 July 1954, a full nine years after VE Day.

By the end of the 1950s, it was clear that the era of the supermarket was just around the corner, though Sainsbury's initially refused to use the term in their shops, thinking it detracted from the image of family grocer they still favoured. In 1959 the Conservative prime minister Harold Macmillan, often misquoted as telling the electorate that year 'You've never had it so good' (what he actually said was 'Most of our people have never had it so good'), toured the Harlow Sainsbury and described it as 'a very clean and most ingenious way of serving the public and doing business'.

Self-service spread only slowly through the Sainsbury group, but it made a substantial impact on the business. By 1960 the new stores still only formed 10 per cent of the group's total but turnover and profits throughout the chain had quadrupled. (In another ten years, half the stores would be self-service.) Meanwhile competitors watched, still not convinced that the British shopper would take to it. International Stores and Unilever, which through Allied Suppliers now controlled Sainsbury's old rivals Lipton's, Home and Colonial and Maypole Dairies, stuck to their belief that people still wanted personal service. One respected retail trade analyst had opined a year after Sainsbury's launched self-service that it was 'improbable that this class of emporium will ever be introduced into Great Britain' – a prediction on a par with the IBM boss of the 1940s who put the maximum global demand for computers at six.

Thirty years later, Alan Sainsbury reflected:

Success in business, as in war, depends not so much on your own virtue and foresight as on the mistakes of the opposition. They all thought I was totally wrong. Allied Suppliers' chairman said: 'We still have faith in the small shop and still find it very profitable.' So when our first big purpose-built self-service store opened at Lewisham in 1955 – the largest in Europe at that time, with 7,500 square feet of selling space – and they tried to find out how it was going, I'd make out we were having a lot of difficulties.

Dramatic proof that Sainsbury's had indeed broken with past ways of doing things came on 11 November 1958 when the company's original little shop in Drury Lane was closed and replaced by a larger, self-service branch across the street. It was an emotional decision for many Sainsbury veterans – a spokesman described 'painful agonising right through the firm'. The Sainsbury brothers, however, were more pragmatic. Robert commented wryly that most people seemed to think the shop should never be closed, under any circumstances. In fact, the old store had become so crowded at peak times such as Christmas that Alan and Robert feared the floor might give way. Once the new shop opposite had opened – big, bright and uncrowded despite its busy volume of sales – there was no doubt that number 173 had become history.

Sainsbury's pioneered other innovations in the food industry during the apparently slow advance of the self-service business through its chain of shops. Fresh fruit was introduced in 1955, ready-prepared peas and Brussels sprouts followed, 'oven-ready' frozen chicken came in 1958 from the US, and the company stepped up its shift into own-brand products under the Sainsbury label, abandoning earlier attempts called Gay Friar, Crelos and Selsa.

At eighty-five, John Benjamin Sainsbury was still titular chairman of the firm. He had maintained a proper distance from the management since 1938, observing his sons steer the business through the war years and then enthusiastically embrace American supermarket methods. His wife Mabel had died in 1941 and from his flat in London's fashionable Bryanston Square he watched the stores change one by one. At first he heartily disapproved of self-service but, practical businessman that he was, he quickly came to see its advantages, praised the big Lewisham supermarket on its opening in 1955 and was soon demanding to know why all the Sainsbury shops were not being converted more quickly.

In the spring of 1956 JB had an operation for sciatica, from which he made a good recovery, but in May a new source of pain started up in his left leg and he checked into the London Clinic for treatment. On 23 May the nurse attending him left his room for a short while. As she passed a window outside she heard a commotion on the pavement four storeys down and saw a dressing gown that looked like Sainsbury's. She rushed back to his room to find that both of its doors had been blocked from the inside with chairs. The coroner returned a verdict of suicide by multiple injuries sustained in the forty-foot fall from the window of Sainsbury's room.

There seemed no obvious reason for JB to take his own life, although he had been subject to intermittent bouts of depression and a pathologist testified at the inquest to finding an incurable aneurysm. Alan Sainsbury, the eldest son, had found his father on the previous evening 'certainly better [and] . . . not unduly depressed'. Though described in the tabloid press as 'the millionaire grocery king', JB left only a modest estate of £38,847, having taken prudent advantage of the seven-year rule, which, until new inheritance laws were introduced in 1992, meant shareholdings in family businesses had to be made over to the heirs seven years before death to avoid inheritance tax.

As the 1960s began, Sainsbury's was still a tightly run family company. The first partial flotation of shares still lay thirteen years in the future and the board was dominated by family directors with only two outsiders apart from the long-serving Fred Salisbury. Alongside Alan and Robert ('Mr RJ' in Sainsbury parlance) sat James Sainsbury, son of Arthur and cousin to Alan, born in 1909. Two of the fourth generation were already on the board; John Davan ('Mr JD'), Alan's eldest son, born in 1927, and his brother Simon, born in 1930. Timothy, Alan's third son, born in 1932, would join the board in 1962, his political career still a decade away, and David, Robert's only son, would become a director in 1966 aged only twenty-six.

James Sainsbury had been with the family business since he was seventeen, progressing solidly if unspectacularly up through the cheese department, pork products and management of the Blackfriars factory to a directorship in 1941 at the age of thirty-two. During the war, like the other family directors, he had sat on government committees and organisations for co-ordinating food supplies. After 1945 he continued to serve on trade associations and to act as an adviser to government as rationing eased and normal trading in provisions resumed.

Still a bachelor in his forties, few members of his family knew anything of his private life, much of which was spent in the South of France. It was not until his death in 1984, still unmarried, that the great tragedy of his life was revealed when he left virtually all his £18.4m fortune to set up a fund for research into leukaemia in memory of the actress Kay Kendall, who had died of the disease in September 1959 aged only thirty-two. Friends of hers, including the actress Dinah Sheridan, then revealed that some years before Kay Kendall met and married Rex Harrison in 1957, she had been in an intense relationship with James Sainsbury. Close friends had expected them to marry. While working on the set of *Genevieve* in 1953, Dinah Sheridan recalled thirty years later, 'she would talk of no one else but Jim Sainsbury. At that time there was no one in her life but him.' Kay's sister Kim was quoted in Rex Harrison's first biography in 1987 as saying: 'James used to take her out all the time. Kay said that he wanted to marry her and they almost got as far as the altar, but one or other got cold feet before the wedding.'

If this romance between dedicated businessman and highly-strung actress seemed unlikely, it was by no means unique. James (later Lord) Hanson, who built a northern trucking business into a global conglomerate, led a high-flying social life in the 1960s and at one point was engaged to the film star Audrey Hepburn. Nor were the Sainsburys quite the grey business dynasty they appeared, at least on the female side in the 1920s. In 1926 James's older sister Olive had married the fourth Baron Inverclyde, a narcissistic socialite and heir to the Cunard Line millions. Inverclyde had a castle in Scotland, an overbearing mother and a penchant for glamorous actresses despite, so gossip said, an inability to consummate any of his relationships. The marriage was predictably short-lived: in 1928 the baron and Olive were divorced and in a blaze of publicity he married (though again not for long) the popular musical comedy star June Tripp, who was known to the public simply as June. Doris Sainsbury, daughter of Arthur, went on the stage and became a reliable repertory actress, touring the provinces in hits of the day such as *Ambrose Applejohn's Adventure*. Her one London appearance seems to have been in 1923, as one of the 'castle guests' in the musical comedy *Head Over Heels* at the Adelphi Theatre.

Kay Kendall had flashed like a meteor across the film world in her brief life. Tall and strikingly beautiful in that chiselled 1950s style, with an anarchic humour that went with an alarmingly volatile temperament, she captured public and critical attention in *Genevieve*, a comedy hit about the London to Brighton veteran car run during which she stole the show playing the trumpet in a drunken nightclub scene. Although virtually unknown until then, she had been on the stage since the age of twelve, when she ran away from her convent school. The theatre was deep in her genes. Marie Kendall, the Edwardian music-hall star whose great hit song was 'Just Like the Ivy, I'll Cling to You', was her grandmother – she outlived Kay by five years – and her father, Terry, was an all-round variety artist.

Kay met James Sainsbury sometime in the early 1950s, but soon after *Genevieve*'s release in 1953 she starred with Rex Harrison in a stage play ironically entitled *The Constant Husband*. Harrison was much married – at that time to the Austrian-born actress Lilli Palmer – and a notorious womaniser. Kay fell instantly in love with him and they embarked on a passionate affair which Rex, for his part, did not expect to last. But on Kay's side it gathered momentum and she became desperate to marry Rex while he, though becoming more committed than he expected, was still hoping to keep the affair as an extra-marital fling.

The catalyst came, devastatingly, in a routine medical appointment Rex was asked to keep on Kay's behalf in New York while she was rehearsing in Hollywood for the MGM musical *Les Girls*. Her doctor explained that he did not know Kay's family but that she had confided that she wanted to marry Rex and he was concerned that someone close to her should know the truth about her years of intermittent ill-health and the chronic tiredness which had always been attributed to anaemia. In fact, Dr Atchley told Harrison, she was suffering from acute myeloid leukaemia and even with palliative treatment could not hope to live more than three years.

Rex immediately wrote to his wife in Austria where she was on a skiing holiday with one of their sons and asked her to meet him urgently in New York. They saw Dr Atchley together. Lilli Palmer recounted in her 1975 autobiography that the doctor urged the couple to have a 'temporary divorce' so that Rex could marry Kay and look after her for her remaining time. Rex said unhappily that he was not strong enough to do it and Lilli recalled how she persuaded him with the words 'you've got to consider it like a war mission'. According to her he only agreed if Lilli would remarry him afterwards, which she said she would, admitting in her book that she lied, because she was already planning to marry someone else. Rex and Lilli never did remarry.

Rex seems to have played the role of his life in his brief marriage to Kay. Insouciant sometimes to the point of callousness, he would make light of her severe bouts of sickness and never once hinted at the grim knowledge he carried. The playwright Terence Rattigan later paid tribute to Rex's 'great courage in never being able to let his concern show . . . Rex's great ability was to feign indifference: when Kay was ill, even desperately sick, he would still go off and play golf with me and be perfectly calm. I have never seen such fortitude.' Gradually the truth seeped out in show business circles. Noel Coward wrote bitchily in his diary for 1958: 'This is a truly horrible situation . . . The poor dear may have behaved badly in the first place when she went bald-headed after Rex, but having got her own way she is certainly paying a ghastly price for it.'

In the first week of September 1959, Kay's condition worsened rapidly while they were on holiday in Portofino, Rex's favourite resort, and she was rushed back to the London Clinic, carried on and off the Channel ferry and the Golden Arrow express to London. On arrival at the clinic, Kay managed to stand just long enough to tell waiting reporters: 'Don't think I'm coming here to die – I'm not.' A week later on Sunday, 6 September, she slipped into a final coma after whispering to Rex, 'I love you with all my heart.' She was buried quietly three days later, in Hampstead parish churchyard between the graves of two great acting legends, Herbert Beerbohm and George and Gerald du Maurier. Rex's behaviour was enigmatic to the end; after the funeral he told the impresario Binkie Beaumont that he wanted Lilli back – 'after all, she is my wife'.

James Sainsbury's name was not among the galaxy of stage and film stars, led by Sir Ralph Richardson, Sir Alec Guinness and Vivien Leigh, who turned out for Kay Kendall's memorial service later that month at St Martin-in-the-Fields on Trafalgar Square. In 1984, when he died after a long illness, aged seventy-five, newspapers carried the story of the £18m bequest in Kay's memory and dredged up what few details they could find on their brief romance. It was perhaps the most quixotic and certainly the saddest of all the many Sainsbury charitable gifts that were to benefit British public life.

CHAPTER 11:

SUPERMARKET WARS

BY THE EARLY 1960s, retailing in Britain, along with much else, was entering a new age. The poet Philip Larkin satirised the sense of a break with the past in his famous line 'Sexual intercourse began in 1963'. On Britain's high streets, newcomers included fashion boutiques (Mary Quant's Bazaar had opened in Chelsea's King's Road as early as 1955, but few people knew of it until the swinging sixties), betting shops (betting outside racecourses had just been legalised) and fast-food outlets. Self-service was spreading beyond food shops to petrol stations and restaurants. In 1962 *The Grocer* estimated that about a quarter of the food sold in Britain's 140,000 food shops came from self-service stores, though they were still largely confined to the south-east corner of England. Between 1960 and 1966 the number of supermarkets in Britain rose from 367 to 2,500, many of them located on edge-of-town or suburban sites to accommodate the fast-growing habit of shopping by car. By 1969 Sainsbury's had 100 self-service stores and these were outstripping the similar number of counter-service stores by leaps and bounds: the average weekly sales in a Sainsbury supermarket totalled £25,000, £10,000 above the group average.

Some years earlier, the chairman of Unilever had observed that the new retailing methods required a radical rethinking of all advertising and packaging: 'If your goods are to be sold by self-service,' he said in 1965, 'your package is fighting for you against every other package.' Sainsbury's were quick to realise this and set up their own design studio to create a recognisable, reassuring house style for everything, from packaging to store fascia to shopping bags. Alan Sainsbury told *Design* magazine in 1967: 'We think our design will have failed if our customers have to read the name over our entrance to know the name of the shop they are entering.' Despite having introduced the supermarket concept to Britain, Sainsbury's were wary for many years of using the term and took care to stamp the new stores with the familiar colour schemes and general appearance of the old ones.

The 1960s were notable for two principal developments in the Sainsbury empire. The first was the expansion by about 1,000 products of Sainsbury's own label range, described by John Sainsbury, Alan's eldest son, who was largely responsible for their development, as the firm's greatest postwar trading success. The durable slogan 'Good food costs less at Sainsbury's' had been introduced in 1959 and the ability to control the prices of the firm's own quality brands gave it a credibility that lasted well into the 1990s, by which time it was by no means as true a statement as it had been. Allied to the expansion of own brands was the introduction of wines and spirits in 1962, a move fiercely resisted at the time by Britain's off-licences and their trade association.

The other great issue was trading stamps, which first appeared among the smaller grocery chains in 1961 and became a competitive threat to the big groups when a chain called Fine Fare began to promote them. They were exchangeable for goods such as saucepan sets and televisions (if you had a wheelbarrowful of completed books) but not for cash. Tesco and other supermarket competitors joined the rush to offer stamps, but Alan Sainsbury was adamantly against the trend. He saw stamps as a costly tool that would push up prices to the shopper, arguing that an increase of 20 per cent in turnover would be needed to pay for the schemes, a level virtually impossible to sustain. Alan had been made a life peer in 1962 on the recommendation of Labour leader Hugh Gaitskell and had taken the title Baron Sainsbury of Drury Lane. He determined to use his platform in the House of Lords to fight the spread of stamps: rising food prices caused by the cost of stamps to the retailer, he argued, would hit the poorest section of society, and he tried in vain to get a bill on the statute book making it possible to exchange stamps for cash.

Both pro- and anti-stamp lobbies claimed victory as the guerrilla warfare raged on. The campaign undoubtedly helped Sainsbury to raise its profile of quality and value: in the very week that Fine Fare launched its stamps in late November 1963, Sainsbury's claimed the biggest single week's trading in its history. But a month earlier, Tesco's big Leicester store was reported to be under siege by housewives clamouring to get their hands on the stamps. In 1965 the battle reached the courts when both Sainsbury's and David Greig issued a writ for libel against Sperry and Hutchinson, one of the two big stamp companies (the other being Richard Tomkins' Green Shield Stamps).

Sperry and Hutchinson had sent a circular letter to retail grocers in the UK advocating the benefits of trading stamps and suggesting that experience showed they increased profits. In quoting the profit figures for non-stamp companies Sainsbury and Greig, S&H had mistakenly stated their increased net profit percentage at less than a quarter of the true figure, which of course bolstered the claim that stamps enhanced profits. S&H were forced to recognise the defamatory nature of their mistake and to pay damages to a charity. They also agreed to send out a new letter retracting the error and containing a full apology.

Yet trading stamps hung on tenaciously until 1977, when Tesco, after a bitter boardroom struggle, dropped them and invested instead in a discount campaign called Checkout, designed to show customers that it could offer quality products at affordable prices, and thus overcome its image as a downmarket trader. Tesco's chairman was still Jack Cohen, the East End trader who had co-founded the grocery company in 1932 with his friend T. E. Stockwell (hence the acronym derived from their names). Cohen liked to portray himself as the housewife's friend for his fight against resale price maintenance, the producers' mechanism for preventing discounting, but he was also a fervent champion of the stamps he had introduced in 1963.

In this he was at loggerheads with Ian MacLaurin, the public-school-educated professional manager who had risen up the business in eight years to join Jack and his sons-in-law on the board. MacLaurin realised by 1977 that the cost of stamps, £20m a year (£240m in today's values), was no longer justifying their use as a marketing tool and could be better invested in price-cutting. After furious argument around the boardroom table, it was put to the vote and MacLaurin won by a single proxy from an absent director who said he hated the 'sticky little things'. The Checkout campaign was a huge success, stung Sainsburys into its own 'Discount 78' promotion and began the repositioning of Tesco in the public's mind as a rival to Sainsbury's for quality and value.

In the 1960s Tesco was not yet a serious competitor: its shops were small, their windows cluttered with cheap-looking stamp promotions, and its own brands were far inferior to Sainsbury's. But there were straws in the wind elsewhere indicating that Sainsbury could not expect to have the supermarket field to itself for long. In 1965, a company called Asda was set up in Yorkshire by Noel Stockdale of Associated Dairies and Peter Asquith, a Pontefract butcher. The acronym, like Tesco, was formed out of the first letters of Asquith and Dairies. While Tesco lured the housewife with Green Shield stamps, Asda opted for straight discounting, and when Edward Heath's bill abolished resale price maintenance in 1965, it was well placed to benefit. Safeway, later to be a major competitor, was only just starting in the 1960s. A subsidiary of the US giant, it had one large supermarket in 1962, in Wimbledon on the south-west edge of London, selling everything from hosiery to catfood, but until it was acquired by the Argyll group in 1987, Safeway amounted to only a small chain located mainly in London and the south-east.

Alan Sainsbury retired as chairman and became life president in 1967, handing over briefly to his brother Robert while his eldest son 'Mr JD' prepared for the top job. JD, along with his brothers Simon and Timothy, represented a new strain of Sainsburys – public school and Oxford educated, with cultivated interests outside the business, in the arts, opera and politics. JD, born in 1927, attended Stowe (later to be the alma mater of a very different breed of businessman, the flamboyant Richard Branson), did his National Service in the élite Life Guards, part of the Household Cavalry that escorts the Queen, and took a Second in history at Worcester College, Oxford, where he flirted with the idea of teaching as a career but couldn't bear the risk that he might turn out 'a second-rate don'. He duly joined Sainsburys in 1950, did his stint at counter serving and was then put in charge of biscuit buying. Along with his uncle James, he developed the bacon business and introduced Canadian 'sweet-cure' to Britain. He joined the board at thirty-two, the sort of age by which family members were expected to have proved their directorial metal (those who failed were ruthlessly weeded out at an early stage by Alan and Robert). As a director, JD was given responsibility by his father for helping to develop the Sainsbury brands, which in the 1960s were the best in the business. By 1967, when Alan retired, he was vice-chairman.

JD was and remains an archetypal Sainsbury: perfectionist, obsessively hands-on, short-fused and driven by detail. 'Retail is detail' was the mantra he tediously recited for the rest of his career, as if he had coined the phrase. All matters for decision came to him after he became chairman in 1969, even items so trivial as the design of a promotion poster. Small wonder that by the time his cousin David inherited the chair in 1992, decision-making had become so centralised in the chairman's office that the senior management lacked all confidence in itself. Delegation was not a word in Mr JD's vocabulary: under Ian MacLaurin, on the other hand, Tesco was building a balanced and experienced team of equals. This basic difference between the two rivals would become a massive problem for Sainsbury in the mid-1990s.

JD's explosions of temper when something failed to meet his standards became as legendary as his grandfather's. Managers quailed when he made unannounced descents on their stores, sometimes by helicopter. A wilted lettuce leaf or a clumsily stacked tin would catch his eye at fifty paces and be enough for him to bawl out the manager in public. Sir Terence Conran, whose BhS store chain went into the Savacentre joint venture with Sainsburys in 1975 to create the UK's first hypermarket (Sainsbury bought out the BhS share in 1988), took a sophisticated view of JD's intimidating style. 'He's rather like an extremely good tutor at university,' he said. 'You've got to be on your toes and have a good answer for everything.' (Conran was always an admirer of the Sainsbury business philosophy: he said that when he started Habitat in the 1960s he tried 'to make it what Sainsbury's is to their customers. In other words, honest, decent and optimistic.') Lord Drogheda, who sat with Sainsbury on the board of the Royal Opera House and the *Economist*, was blunter but inclined to give JD the benefit of being a force for improvement. 'He's got a temper, there's no question about that,' he said. 'If he thinks somebody is being very stupid, he finds it hard to contain himself. I would say he was very much on the side of the angels on most issues.'

Like Bill Marriott of the eponymous hotel chain, JD habitually carried a small black notebook in which he would make notes incessantly. He personally tasted trays of new product samples three times a week in his gloomy office in Stamford Street, and he had an unfailing instinct for what customers expected from the store. When currency decimalisation loomed in 1971, and older members of the public feared it would put prices up, he ordered a million leaflets printed with the claim 'Sainsburys do guarantee to round prices down more than up.' He personified Sainsbury values, toughly enforced, and under his twenty-three-year chairmanship Sainsbury's annual profit figures rose as predictably as the sun.

Outside Stamford Street this intimidating man, who gave an impression of being much taller than he actually was, pursued cultural interests that would have been far beyond the horizons of his grandfather and great-grandfather. His passion for opera and particularly ballet was perhaps inherited from his mother, who had been a dancer with Dame Ninette de Valois, the pioneer of British ballet. It extended to his choice of wife, the former Sadler's Wells ballerina Anya Linden, whom he married in 1963. From the 1970s to the 1990s he would be involved in the fortunes of the Royal Opera House, Covent Garden, first as a director, then as chairman of the board, where he was known as both a bully and a charmer. With his younger brother Timothy educated at Eton and Oxford, and a rising Conservative MP from 1973 (for the then true-blue Sussex coastal town of Hove), the fourth generation of Sainsburys had definitively joined the Establishment and would soon harvest a clutch of peerages and knighthoods unrivalled by any other trading family.

By the time Sainsbury's celebrated its centenary in April 1969 – with a slice of birthday cake given away to every customer – the current ruling generation had good reason to be satisfied with its stewardship of the company, still privately owned. It was a good year for expansion, with twenty new branches opened, the largest annual number yet. The firm kept up with the infant technological revolution, installing an advanced ICL computer system. John Sainsbury, who became chairman in the centenary month, declared that computerisation would enable a large business like Sainsbury's to provide the 'quick and flexible response to consumer needs that is more often the characteristic of a really good small retailer such as we were 100 years ago'.

During the 1960s, sales had tripled and profits doubled in spite of the fact that only 20 per cent of the UK population lived within reach of a Sainsbury store. The company had managed its expansion with only modest borrowing, selling off some of its high street sites that had been prime locations when John Benjamin or his father bought them but were now too small to allow for conversion to supermarkets. Despite this comfortable financial underpinning, the family was by the early 1970s considering a major break with the past – by offering Sainsbury shares to the public. Concern over death duties was undoubtedly one prime reason for the move, but the owners also felt that the business was now of a scale and importance to benefit from a stock market listing.

In July 1973, 12.4 per cent of the company's equity was offered for sale, at that time the biggest flotation in the history of the London Stock Exchange. The company was valued at £117m, and one million shares were set aside for employees to purchase, leaving 85 per cent of the equity still in family hands. Within one minute of the share offer opening on 12 July, the list of applications was closed. Nearly £500m had been subscribed for the ten million shares, worth £14.5m at the offer price of £1.45. The allocations were weighted in favour of the small investor – the family clearly hoped that Sainsbury shoppers would buy into the firm – and a pension fund that tried to bid for the entire issue was quickly rebuffed.

The Sainsbury board now looked more appropriate to a public company, with six outside directors where there had been only two at the beginning of the 1960s. (Two more were appointed in the mid 1970s.) But family directors were still a powerful presence: the three brothers JD, Simon and Timothy, their cousin David and uncle James. Simon, forty-two, was vice-chairman and effectively the chief financial officer; Timothy, forty-one, was in charge of the property side. David, Sir Robert's son, had studied business management at Columbia Business School in New York, and was now finance director. The fourth generation was as remarkable as the Cadburys for its spread of management talent. As the *Observer* remarked at the time of the flotation: 'Most family businesses are happy to find one man in every generation to carry on the tradition. To have produced four able business managers in the most competitive sector of the retail trade seems to be just another part of the Sainsbury mystique.'

The Sainsbury flotation took place just before the oil crisis of autumn 1973, when the OPEC producers' cartel tripled oil prices, throwing all the western economies into turmoil. Sainsbury's shares suffered along with the rest of the market. The 1970s brought a host of other economic trials: a second oil crisis, sharply rising inflation, a round of bruising strikes, rising food prices (which happened to coincide with decimalisation, fuelling the common belief that any currency change is used by retailers as an excuse to lift prices), a payroll tax and Price Commission attacks on retail profits. Sainsbury countered these squeezes with improved productivity. Sales per employee rose by 25 per cent between 1969 and 1979. The number of branches shrank as the smaller shops were closed, but by this time sales at the group's 114 supermarkets were almost four times those of the remaining counter shops. In 1980 Sainsbury had 231 branches compared with 244 in 1969.

The move to modernise branches, however, ran up against growing resistance from local planners. In the early 1970s, the Sainsbury chairman observed with irritation, it was taking up to three years to get planning permission for a single new town-centre shop. At Tesco, Ian MacLaurin perceived that the solution lay in out-of-town sites, and led the move towards the much larger developments, set in ample car parks, that were to transform shopping habits yet again and, controversially, drain retail business away from the high streets. Sainsbury's, while following suit to edge-of-town sites, was not concerned to exceed or even match its competitors in store size. Only eight of its stores exceeded 25,000 square feet, much smaller than the average Asda. Nor did Sainsbury's attempt to expand its geographic base substantially from its south-eastern core. Where it was making steady impact on the market was in developing its own-brand range, sometimes aggressively at the expense of established brand leaders.

The Sainsbury style was always, and especially under the chairmanship of JD, to wield its clout unforgivingly on suppliers. Lord MacLaurin, the former Tesco chairman, recalls that suppliers were relieved to deal with Tesco after Sainsbury, where it was a matter of doing what you were told and at the price Sainsbury set, or else. There was little or no two-way dialogue between Sainsbury's formidable buyers and their suppliers, although many suppliers did stay with the company for decades; after all, it was the market leader. And when it came to promoting its own-brand margins, Sainsbury's could be lethal even against such a powerful supplier as Unilever. At one point it forced down the share of Unilever's Comfort brand fabric softener in Sainsbury stores to less than half over a year because Comfort's low pricing strategy was in turn forcing Sainsbury's own-brand softener to an unacceptably low margin.

The strategy worked, because by 1980 almost half Sainsbury's weekly sales were composed of own-brand products. Margaret Thatcher, the new prime minister, who liked to promote her image as a thrifty housewife who knew the price of apples, unlike most of her male predecessors, was famously photographed at Sainsbury's shiny new Cromwell Road supermarket in west London, with her trolley full of JS products. It was valuable publicity for both of them.

The first sign that Tesco was going to become a serious threat to Sainsbury's supremacy arrived in 1977, when Ian MacLaurin won his acrimonious boardroom battle against the founding Cohen family and the Cohens' beloved trading stamps were ditched to make way for an aggressive price-cutting strategy. After a few months, Sainsbury launched a counterattack in January 1978, cutting prices on 100 key products by up to 15 per cent. The era of price wars had arrived – soon it would spread to petrol between the big two – and Sainsbury, from its market strong-point, scored heavily, boosting its sales over the half-year by 25 per cent. Although forced into it, J. D. Sainsbury claimed that the group's 'Discount 78' marketing strategy was the most important since it established its own-brand range.

The 1980s were to be Sainsbury's glory decade – the peak, though no one yet suspected it, of the firm's market hegemony. The years passed in a steady progression of record profits and ever-rising market share, reflected in justifiably confident annual reports. Newspapers, usually starved in Britain of the opportunity to build up a business hero, loved to profile Sir John Sainsbury as a master of the retailing art under such headlines as 'The Checkout Champion of the World', 'Purveyors to the Nation' and 'How the High Street Fell to His Lordship' (JD had by 1989 joined his father as a life peer under the title Baron Sainsbury of Preston Candover, the Hampshire village where he had recently bought an estate from the flamboyant Peter Cadbury.)

By 1982, Sainsbury was the UK's biggest grocery retailer, toppling the venerable Co-op movement with 15.7 per cent of the packaged groceries market, at that time worth £24bn a year. This was a time when manufacturing Britain was mired deep in recession and former industrial giants such as ICI and Courtauld's were producing dismal figures. By contrast, food retailing had increased its sales fourteen times in thirty years: proof, if any were needed, that since everyone has to eat, food is a recession-proof business. Indeed, in 1980, as the ferocious monetary policies of the new Tory government put the squeeze on smokestack industries, Sainsbury boosted its annual profits over 1979 by 42 per cent. Sales had grown phenomenally in real terms: in 1979/80 turnover was more than £1250m, compared with £19m in 1950 (the equivalent in 1980 values of £100m). Eight years on, in 1988, Sainsbury's overtook Marks and Spencer as the UK's biggest retailer by sales, with a turnover of more than £5bn. Marks was still the only retailer to boast a Triple A credit rating from Standard and Poors, but Sainsbury was the world's highest rated food retailer with a Double A ranking. In the latter part of the 1980s the two companies were often spoken of in the same breath; both consistently successful on their own terms, both autocratically led, both proud of their long relationships with UK suppliers.

Sainsbury's was now so much the market leader that it could afford to buck trends that others followed, notably in its stand on irradiated food – the 1980s equivalent of the genetically modified food scare which was to sweep retailing in the late 1990s. Marks and Spencer, Asda, Tesco, Waitrose and Spar all declared themselves against the process, which was claimed to lengthen the shelf life of foodstuffs. Only Sainsbury's declared that it was satisfied to stock irradiated foods.

Food might be a surefire business in theory, but that did not mean every player could count on automatic success. Sir John Sainsbury liked to point out that his company was an exception to the rule in being both old-established and successful: most of the multiples whose names had been familiar to the high streets of his own youth had disappeared or been taken over. Newcomers, on the whole, had been more successful than those already in the field. Sainsbury's secret, said JD, was to combine the traditional with a responsiveness to change: to revere JJ's original emphasis on quality, service and attention to detail while cultivating innovation and embracing new methods such as self-service and computerisation.

'The greatest single reason for our success is that innovation has always gone into ensuring greater productivity,' JD said in 1980.

> If we had stood still in productivity terms in the past five years, instead of making £46m we should have made £25m. That's a hell of a difference ... Larger stores have in themselves an inbuilt productivity gain ... Welcome acceptance of change, in systems and equipment – that's what I think is really important.

By the mid-1980s, own-label goods accounted for two-thirds of all Sainsbury sales. It was said of the company that it had managed to 'transfer a company culture to own-label goods'. JD said the secret was that 'we have applied the principles to them [own-brand products] that we have always applied to perishable foods: that only the best should bear our label . . . [The customer] has to get from our label a product that is as good as the best leading brand on the market, but at a lower price.'

The Sainsbury chairman also trumpeted the virtues of continuing to act like a small family business in the supermarket age. 'We never allow ourselves to forget the virtues of the small business. It's very hard to be a successful large-scale retailer – you perhaps become less enterprising, more committee-bound, more bureaucratic. You are slower to change and find it harder to make decisions.' (Ironically, it was just this tendency to bureaucracy and slowness to appreciate competition-led change, such as loyalty cards, for which Sainsbury's was to be so savagely criticised in the mid-1990s.)

JD made the comment about acting like a small business just as Sainsbury made the leap from supermarket to hypermarket, selling a vast range of non-food products, by joining Terence Conran's BhS to create the Savacentres. He justified the move by saying that Savacentres gave the consumer a complete range of his or her needs at the lowest prices. From the business point of view, 'the mix of goods helps each other in terms of the profit margin, the sheer scale is economical and we avoid depot costs . . . food goes straight there from the manufacturer or supplier [and] you cut out the expensive distribution network'.

In the same interview JD revealed his management methods:

> I know at about 10 a.m. on a Monday our total trade the previous week at all our branches. A computer print-out shows the percentage increase on the week before that, on the same week the previous year, and categorises the different types of branches. The print-out shows the best and the worst, so we can quickly see how branches have gone up or down. We would expect to know if a competitor has opened or there has been some other local change . . .

Sainsbury's last counter-service shop closed at the end of 1982; a branch in suburban Peckham, south London, that had opened in 1931 and still had the ornamental panel at the back of the shop displaying the company name in gilt. The group was now all self-service, and sales galloped ahead at a rate to strike despondency into the competition. In 1983 it made its first move abroad, buying a 21-per-cent stake in Shaw's, a New England chain of groceries: this would become a controlling share before the end of the decade.

By the mid-1980s British retailing was enjoying an unparalleled boom. Consumer credit in 1986 had doubled over the previous five years (from £13bn to £28bn) and mortgage borrowing, heading for a mighty fall into negative equity, was up from £62bn to £136bn over the same period. People were living better, entertaining at home more and becoming more knowledgeable about wine, a trend for which the Sainsburys could take substantial credit. By the middle of the decade, it was said, every seventh bottle of wine purchased in Britain came from a Sainsbury store. Organic foods were on sale at Sainsbury and its rival stores by 1987 – Safeway was stocking them as early as 1982 – and the trade was reported even then to be expanding. Car ownership was up, encouraging more people to shop further afield and to buy more at one time; so was that of fridges and freezers, enabling households to buy in bulk for storage. Sainsbury benefited more than any other group in its market from this rip-roaring spending boom. The stock market crash of October 1987 barely dented its ability to deliver double-digit profit and sales growth year on year.

Financial commentators marvelled uncritically at the Sainsbury juggernaut. 'Sales up, volume up, margins up, profits up, earnings up, dividends up, market share up: the Sainsbury growth machine rolls on relentlessly,' gasped the normally sober-sided *Investor's Chronicle* in May 1984. Eleven years after its partial flotation, the grocery chain was now bigger in market capitalisation at £2bn than Barclays Bank or Unilever. In June 1985 the financial press recorded that for the sixth successive year Sainsbury had increased its pre-tax profits by more than 20 per cent, and it continued to do so for several more years. Over the previous decade it had raised profits from £15.4m to £168.5m, a compound annual increase of 30.4 per cent. Margins went over 5 per cent for the first time, without putting gross margins up. By 1985 Sainsbury's was Britain's eleventh largest company. At the end of the decade a report by the Economist Intelligence Unit on the retail trade said Sainsbury's had produced the most consistently good results of any major retailer over the preceding ten years. Its profits per square foot of selling space, at £60 per annum, were claimed to be 80 per cent higher than any of its major competitors.

> The secrets of its success seem to be a stable background, efficient management, close attention to detail, a strong retail identity and a rigorous approach to diversification. It has always preferred to grow organically rather than by acquisition, it always uses a joint venture when moving into a new area (geographically or product-wise) and it always has the same market positioning, of quality combined with price competitiveness.

The company's image in the public eye was good, too, although the massive philanthropy of the Sainsbury family, begun in the 1960s with the first of a labyrinth of trusts, was not widely known outside London arts circles until the building of the Sainsbury Wing of the National Gallery in the late 1980s. Although the 'green' revolution and concern for the environment were in their infancy in 1984, the firm won column inches for spending £5,000 on moving a section of Suffolk heathland from the edge of Ipswich to two sites further away to protect the natural habitat of a rare blue and silver butterfly which was otherwise about to be engulfed under another Sainsbury superstore. Not all the press coverage of Sainsbury's expansion was as positive: its store at Warrington, Cheshire, was described by one architectural critic as a 'horrible brick and metal lump, which stands right opposite one of the finest parish churches in England. For sheer ineptitude this has to be seen to be believed.'

The Sainsburys perhaps benefited in public esteem from the general warming towards business enterprise that accompanied the Thatcher years, but they had never been flash with their money. Alan Sainsbury once said that the Sainsburys didn't go in for racehorses or yachts. 'The more trappings, the less freedom,' said the old socialist in an interview with *Director* magazine. He also spoke about 'the guilt that comes with money' and gave it as his opinion that 'the very poor and the very rich are unhappy people'.

In 1985, a bumper year, as they all were in that shop-happy decade, JD and his cousin David, the firm's finance director (and the richest member of the family through inheriting one-half of the previous generation's shareholding) donated their entire after-tax haul of dividends to charity. (Two years later, however, that did not stop a so-called 'Robin Hood' blackmailer from attempting to force the firm to make cut-price goods available to the homeless, under threat of poisoning some Sainsbury products in the stores, The letter from the blackmailer referred to £21m in salaries and dividends paid to senior Sainsbury management in the previous two years.) In the 1980s the firm began its own programme of arts sponsorship, underwriting opera and ballet among other activities, but it has never made political donations – a canny decision, though perhaps a logical one for a board on which three family members supported three different political parties.

One issue over which the family did divide in the late 1980s and early 1990s was that of Sunday trading, which for decades had been one of the great anomalies in British life. A muddle of local by-laws had resulted in a farcical situation with some products deemed legal to be sold on Sunday, others (including, famously, Bibles and other books) illegal. As the new decade opened, permanent Sunday trading looked a certainty after Asda, Sainsbury and Tesco all announced they would open their major stores for seven days a week indefinitely – technically challenging the ambivalent law. Sainsbury's had once seemed the most reluctant to open on Sundays: now, suddenly, they were taking the lead. Only Marks and Spencer held out, saying in December 1991: 'It continues to be our firm belief that it is not in the interests of our customers, our staff or our shareholders for us to compromise our integrity by breaking the law.' The shopworkers' union USDAW remained solidly opposed to the liberalisation, and in summer 1991 local councils won back their power to stop Sunday trading. The tide, however, was running too strongly to be checked, and shops were finally given the legal right to trade on Sundays in 1994.

Lord Sainsbury was criticised over Sunday trading by some shareholders at his last AGM, and among his strongest critics was his brother Tim, a devout Anglican whose wife Susan was a born-again Christian. Tim, who had a record as an MP of trying to improve public morals – he sponsored a bill to clean up indecent displays in London's Soho – publicly stated that Sunday trading was 'fundamentally wrong'. He failed to move his brother, who saw the way the commercial wind was blowing and argued that the customer had shown a clear preference for the ability to shop on Sundays.

In September 1989 the *Economist* in conjunction with Loughborough University conducted a poll of nearly 1800 leading UK businessmen and financial analysts to discover Britain's most admired companies among the business community. Sainsbury emerged fourth, after Shell, Glaxo and Marks and Spencer, though in fact it had come top in all but two of the categories offered for ranking. It came second in quality of products or services and third in innovation. The business leaders ranked it first in quality of management, financial soundness, ability to attract, develop and retain top talent, value as long-term investment, quality of marketing and community/environmental responsibility.

Not everyone was so impressed by the Sainsbury management. In 1986 the new glossy magazine *Business* presciently observed that John Sainsbury's strength to the firm was also likely in time to turn into its greatest weakness. 'John Sainsbury knows more about his business than anyone else, and has succeeded in making himself irreplaceable,' the magazine commented. A retail analyst also spotted the Sainsbury Achilles heel about this time: 'There has always been a sort of arrogance about them that they knew exactly what they were doing and that it was up to the opposition to follow them.'

The opposition, however, was no longer content to do that.

Chapter 12:

Losing the Crown

David Sainsbury succeeded his cousin John as chairman and chief executive in May 1992. He was fifty-one and had been with the company for twenty-six years – seventeen of those as finance director. In an interview with *Director* magazine some months later, he ruminated that his own successor was likely to come from outside the family. Even if his own children or their cousins, then at university, chose to make a career in the firm, it would take years before they could prove their worth and it was now much more difficult, as he pointed out, in a more complex and professionally managed company, for family members to get on the board than in his young days. 'The next generation would have to work pretty hard to become chairman by the time I give up,' he chuckled, plainly thinking in terms of a long haul in Stamford Street.

Events would dramatically foreshorten those plans. Within seven years not only was David gone as the sixth and last family chairman, but the unthinkable had happened: Sainsbury had been toppled as market leader and was struggling in the powerful wake of Tesco; a new threat had appeared in the shape of the world's biggest discounter, Wal-Mart, taking over Asda, which was already nipping at Sainsbury's heels, and there were even mutterings that Sainsbury itself might fall to a predator and the family bail out of its vast shareholdings.

None of this was even remotely on the horizon as Lord Sainsbury of Preston Candover – 'Mr JD' – stepped down in May 1992, leaving the family business at the zenith of its power and glory. Its stock market value was £7.6bn and the Sainsbury family still owned 43 per cent of the equity. That week the family appeared at number 4 in the league table of Britain's richest compiled annually by *The Sunday Times*, with a fortune estimated from their shareholdings at £2.42bn. It would double that in the next few years. Compared to Tesco chief Ian MacLaurin, whose salary was over £1m a year, John Sainsbury drew a modest remuneration of only £221,000, but he had the weight of family billions behind him.

The firm's operating margins at 8 per cent were three or four times higher than the US/European supermarket average and – most satisfying of all to the departing chairman – the company had just outstripped Marks and Spencer as Britain's most profitable retailer. In his farewell speech to shareholders, JD said that when he became chairman in 1969, M&S profits were nine times those of Sainsbury's. 'It seemed impossible that we would one day beat them.'

Sales in 1969 had been £165.7m and profits £4.3m; sales in 1991/92 were £9.2bn and profits £628m. In the last year of JD's chairmanship sales were up £1bn, a 12.2 per cent increase, and pretax profits up by 21.2 per cent despite a biting recession that had other high street traders shivering and was widely described as the worst since the Second World War. (JD's explanation was that people traded up to better food in recessionary times because they could not afford to eat out.)

Under JD the business had grown at a phenomenal 23 per cent a year, and 1991/92 was the thirteenth year in succession that Sainsbury shareholders had received an increase of 20 per cent or more in their dividends. Over that period profits had risen nineteen-fold in real terms compared with an eight-fold increase in sales, yet Sainsbury still claimed that its prices were 2 per cent lower on average than its major competitors. Commentators were prompted to make flattering assessments of Sainsbury's national importance: over the past two decades the company was said to have had more cultural impact on

British life than any other institution. Admittedly those decades coincided with an explosion of foreign travel and a revolution in the appreciation of food and wine, but it was still a remarkable tribute.

The Marquess of Queensberry, sixty-year-old descendant of the man who ruined Oscar Wilde, recalled how, thirty years earlier, if you wanted to buy garlic you had to go to 'some little shop in Soho', while in Stoke-on-Trent in the 1950s (an area he knew well as a professional potter), 'olive oil was only sold for medicinal purposes'. A writer in the London *Evening Standard* eulogised Sainsbury's stores as 'a perpetual harvest festival'. Picking up on John Sainsbury's theory that people wanted good food as treats in hard times, she added that the firm provided 'small, affordable luxuries that perked the spirits up when one could not afford holidays or mortgage repayments'. Quietly, as the trade acknowledged, Sainsbury's had pushed food retailing on to a new aspirational level. As one advertising executive commented: 'Normally you find out what people want, then supply it. What Sainsbury did was to anticipate what people wanted. Everybody is going upmarket.'

The year 1992 was a personal *annus mirabilis* for John Sainsbury in more ways than leaving the business at the peak of its performance. To add to his earlier knighthood and peerage, the Queen made him a Knight of the Garter, an unprecedented honour for a modern businessman, though financiers and bankers had been given the Garter in years past. The Garter is England's oldest order of chivalry, dating back to the days of King John, and its modern membership is restricted to twenty-five living knights, including the Prince of Wales. Recipients have traditionally been eminent diplomats, statesmen, ex-prime ministers, distinguished military commanders. Since it is in the personal gift of the Queen, not a recommendation by the prime minister of the day, no citation is ever published for the Garter, but it is reasonable to assume that the honour was in some way connected with Sainsbury's generosity in leading the family's funding of a new wing for the National Gallery in 1991.

'Mr JD' was clearly going to be a daunting act to follow both within the company and under the basilisk glare of the City, but there was a general goodwill towards David and an expressed feeling that the time was ripe for a change of emphasis. With his interest in all things scientific, it was felt that he was probably the right man to lead the company into a more science-based era of retailing. Electronics, after all, now governed the business and the day of instinctive, seat-of-the-pants retailers like the earlier Sainsburys and Tesco's founder Jack Cohen was receding into history.

David was indeed a very different animal from his cousin. Where John barked at his managers and suppliers, David spoke softly and invited others' opinions. The two had never got on particularly well. When JD got his peerage, someone asked David whether he thought his cousin would be attending the House of Lords much. 'I don't think so,' was his amused answer. 'He doesn't really believe in the right of reply.' David's style was always too unassuming to intimidate Sainsbury store managers in the JD fashion. He was educated at Eton (a fact he chooses to omit from his *Who's Who* entry) and King's College, Cambridge, where he switched from history to psychology, later confessing that he might have gone into academic research had he got a First: he has been known to joke that he only has a '2:1 brain'.

After university he broke the family mould by taking an MBA – Master of Business Administration – degree at Columbia University, New York, specialising in retailing. The training gave him an analytical rigour to balance his cultivated upbringing as the son of one of Britain's great art patrons, Sir Robert Sainsbury. Henry Moore was his godfather and he grew up in a house stuffed with avant-garde works of art. No Sainsbury had previously enjoyed such a cultured early background, and it would be reflected in David's restless intellectual curiosity and passionate belief that opportunities for a fuller life through education and training could be improved by a radically different approach to British politics. Despite – or perhaps because of – his youthful steeping in the arts, his own massive philanthropy was to be directed away from that area, focusing on science, education, business and politics.

David dutifully joined the family business in 1966 and became finance director at what he called 'an absurdly young age', in time to help pilot the firm through its flotation in 1973. That was also the year he got married, again in typically low-key fashion at St Pancras Register

Office, to Susie Reid, an editor of children's books. They set up home in Notting Hill Gate, many years before that once charmingly shabby quarter of west London became a fashionable and overvalued stretch of real estate, and raised a family of three daughters there and in a converted farmhouse in Berkshire, not far from cousin Tim. A professor at London Business School, to which David Sainsbury contributed a research centre for business strategy in the hope that LBS might become the west's second most important centre of business studies after Harvard, said of him: 'He is the most thoughtful and self-effacing businessman I have ever met. He has a genuine intellectual interest in business studies.'

Although David told *Director* magazine in 1992 that 'it was always my ambition to be chairman', his heart was never wholly in the business of shifting food off shelves, and he always looked ill at ease posing at a meat counter or checkout for press photographers. As time went on he seemed to be back-tracking on that earlier declared ambition, saying: 'If someone said I could either be a Nobel prizewinner in plant genetics or a successful chairman of Sainsbury's, I'd find it a difficult choice.' (An ironic observation, given his controversial later association, while minister for science during the row over genetically modified crops, with a biotechnology company doing work in precisely that area. Under his successor, Sainsbury's became the first supermarket group in 1999 to state that it would ensure as far as possible that all its own-brand products were GM-free.)

David was, however, much more interested in developing Sainsbury's human assets than his predecessors, and it was his bad luck not to have been given the breathing space to do so as the supermarket wars went ballistic. In his interview with *Director*, he became noticeably animated when talking about the need to release employees' untapped talents through better education and training. 'You've only got to look at the marvellous things people do as hobbies to see there's a lot of latent talent that people could use in the business,' he enthused.

David Sainsbury's political sympathies were leftish, in another contrast with cousin John, although Sainsbury's the firm had always scrupulously avoided political donations. It was the worst-kept secret in

British politics that David had bankrolled (to the tune of nearly £1m) the fledgling Social Democratic Party, created by four breakaway Labour MPs in 1981 who sought, ahead of their time, to jettison old ideological baggage and seek a new coalition of the left that would not be tied to organised labour. David, who had earlier contributed to the old Fabian Society, was involved with the SDP as much more than a banker, acting as a trustee of the party and contributing to policy. When the great split came in 1987, with Dr David Owen, one of the four founders, condemning the proposed merger with the Liberal party, David Sainsbury backed Owen all the way in standing alone, until the rump of the SDP died a natural death in 1990.

David is by far the richest of all the Sainsburys, his personal shareholding at the high point of the company's share price in the early 1990s being worth well over £2bn – in 1999 it was about half that. In 1966, aged twenty-five, he received through shrewd family financial planning all of Sir Robert's own inherited stake in the firm, then worth some £12m. Robert and Alan had divided their father's share between them in 1938, but Alan's sons John, Tim and Simon had to split their inheritance three ways. David has also been the greatest in a family of public benefactors, funnelling hundreds of millions of his own share dividends into a myriad causes, mainly connected with science, research, training and mental health.

Like other members of the family, he operated a web of charitable trusts, veiled in secrecy. He called his main vehicle of financial redistribution the Gatsby Charitable Foundation, a wry literary conceit. In Scott Fitzgerald's *The Great Gatsby*, David's favourite novel, Jay Gatsby is a sad fraud, a former petty criminal trying to invent a privileged background for himself and to buy friendship and love. The Gatsby Foundation spends about a third of David's dividend income in a year and in the mid-1990s was capitalised at nearly £500m. (Today all the Sainsbury trusts between them are estimated by the *Sunday Times* to have assets of £2.3bn, disbursing around £41m a year in donations.)

Without the Gatsby largesse in particular, quietly distributed and guarded from publicity, British life in dozens of ways would be much the poorer. Among its beneficiaries have been the School of Tropical

Medicine in Liverpool, the London Business School, universities up and down the land, work on cognitive neuroscience (David is fascinated by the mechanics of thinking), tiny theatre companies like the Chicken Shed, schools, museums, local festivals, mental health charities, children's welfare, work for the disabled and training young engineers in general management.

One particular interest was to return to haunt him when scare stories over genetically modified foods blew up in 1999, by which time he was minister for science in the Blair government. David Sainsbury has taken a special interest in plant science from the time in the 1980s when genetic modification was viewed as a beneficial means of plants controlling their own diseases, thereby cutting use of chemical toxins. His biggest single philanthropic investment through the Gatsby Foundation is the Sainsbury Laboratory for Plant Science at the John Innes Centre in Norwich, which specialises in research on molecular plant pathology and genetic modification to resist diseases. The laboratory has been funded by more than £20m of David Sainsbury's money over two five-year cycles. He also has an interest in a company called Diatech that backs fledgling biotechnology companies.

In 1992 David took over a business at the peak of its success and wealth, but unknown to him and all the massed ranks of City analysts, rot had already begun to eat away at its core. Or to take a more precise metaphor, the tiny landslips well below a mountain's surface snow that eventually turn into a lethal avalanche were beginning to shift well before David took over. In many ways Sainsbury's was a classic example of the principle, long advocated by the Californian management guru Richard Pascale, that every successful company carries within it the seeds of its own failure if it will not nurture dissension, creative tension and the challenging of hitherto successful ways of doing things.

An unbroken run of twenty-three years' growth under the same chairman would have been enough in any previous era to encourage a belief that there was no need to change the way the company was run. But the 1990s were not the same as the 1980s or the 1970s. For a company which regularly declared (as it continued to do under David Sainsbury) its 'passion to innovate', there had been precious little evidence of new thinking in the boardroom. Meanwhile the competition was charging ahead, innovating from the top down. In 1993, four years ahead of the event, Tesco announced that Ian MacLaurin would retire the minute he hit his sixtieth birthday in 1997, and would be succeeded by Terry Leahy. A tough, ambitious meritocrat not yet in his forties, Leahy was known as 'a hard man with the common touch' who ate, slept, drank and breathed retailing. He had also, with MacLaurin's backing, built a strong management team. David Sainsbury would face a formidable opponent.

The culture at Tesco's drab headquarters in Cheshunt, Buckinghamshire, reflected MacLaurin's ambition to achieve in ten years what had taken Sainsbury more than a century. MacLaurin, a noted sports star in his years at Malvern public school, began his days at 5.45 a.m. running with his dogs through the lanes near his Hertfordshire home. Tesco meetings often started at 6.30 a.m., with the chairman freshly energised by his run. The company was aggressively expanding, drawing on its accumulated land bank to open one giant superstore after another, up to 50,000 square feet in size. In the early 1990s it anticipated by nearly a decade the public's concern over chemical treatment of foodstuffs by announcing itself as 'the greener grocer', advertising a ban on suspicious-sounding substances like chlorofluorocarbons and promising its customers that by buying at Tesco 'you'll be shopping for your great-grandchildren'. Sainsbury's was caught on the back foot and reacted in tit-for-tat fashion by claiming to be 'the greenest grocer'. (In fact it was another supermarket grocer altogether, Safeway, which had introduced organic produce as early as 1982, too soon to catch the tide of fashion.)

There had been signs here and there during the last two years of John Sainsbury's rule that the triumphant market leader might be growing complacent and slow to react to new forces. As early as November 1990 analysts were predicting that Tesco would pull ahead sooner rather than later, powered by its expansion programme and new 'green, caring and quality' image. Both Sainsbury and Tesco were also having to tap the stock market with rights issues to pay for their store-building race and there were forecasts that these cost pressures would squeeze margins and that the fat years of food retailing might be about to come to an end.

David Sainsbury himself warned in late 1993 that growth in the industry would slow down in the 1990s and in January 1994 Sainsbury's issued its first profits warning, an event that sent a minor shock-wave through its share price. Then the Conservative government, belatedly waking up to public concern about England's green acres being covered with hypermarkets and car parks, and city centres being denuded of small traders, clamped down on out-of-town retail developments. In 1994, Sainsbury won only one of its nine planning appeals, Tesco one out of ten and Safeway one out of six: in previous years, all might have confidently expected to win at least half.

Tesco, sharp on the draw as ever, had already hedged its bets in 1992 on the future of giant supermarkets by opening its first Metro, a smallish city-centre food store, located in the former Moss Bros. menswear store in London's Covent Garden. Sainsbury's followed suit in 1994 in a pattern that was to become familiar; reacting to Tesco innovations rather than taking the lead. The year 1994 was a bad one for the new chairman of Sainsburys: not only were profits down for the first time in a generation, but he was outbid by MacLaurin for the Scottish grocery chain William Low, known as the Sainsbury's of Scotland.

The Sainsbury board had been stalking Low for a year but was thought to be wanting to 'cherry-pick' instead of taking on all its stores. The bidding war was portrayed in the popular press as a 'shootout' between David Sainsbury and Ian MacLaurin, two very different retail bosses who both hated to lose. The following year Sainsbury went on the acquisition trail in a different direction, expanding its DIY operations by adding Texas Homecare to its successful Homebase stores. These were widely admired in the industry for applying the efficient stock control and quality methods of Sainsbury's food business to the less organised world of DIY products, and succeeding so well that Homebase could get away with premium pricing.

A more damaging loss of face occurred early in 1995 when Tesco came out with an entirely new innovation – the loyalty card. David Sainsbury rashly issued a press release dismissing the scheme as little more than 'electronic Green Shield Stamps' – the issue over which his father and uncle had successfully faced down Tesco in the 1970s. 'Sainsbury may rue those words,' said the *Financial Times* presciently, noting that five million Tesco customers had already signed up to Clubcard, as the new scheme was known. Clubcard furnished the group with an unrivalled database of information about its customers as well as the promise of rapid new trading growth. Indeed, within four months Sainsbury's had caved in and launched its own loyalty card. David Sainsbury's dismissive gibe was one he later admitted regretting.

This, in retrospect, was the crack in the mountainside that started the avalanche. Sainsbury had its successes to come – its own-brand Classic Cola outsold Coca Cola in its stores although it had a spat with the US drinks giant over look-alike cans – but by the end of 1995 sales volume, margins and profits were all on the slide. 'Britain's favourite grocer is in crisis,' proclaimed the *Observer* in January 1996, in an article that for the first time suggested David Sainsbury was himself part of the problem. The media blowtorch was now turned on the chairman's office in Blackfriars: David commented mildly in public that he thought some of the comments 'OTT' (over the top), but privately he was smarting. It was a typical example of the British press's fondness for personalising business triumphs and disasters, and a dramatic reversal of the fulsome 1980s profiles that had cast John Sainsbury as some kind of infallible high priest of retailing. (One business competitor actually described Sainsbury's supremacy at that time as 'papal'.)

From now on, Sainsbury's could do nothing right in the eyes of the business-page editors, and, indeed, its attempted internal reforms often seemed confused. The board appointed Dino Adriano (an accountant, like so many senior Sainsbury managers, with thirty-two years in the business under his belt) as chief executive in 1996, but David Sainsbury retained the title of chief executive with strategic responsibilities as well as the group chairmanship. At one point, indeed, there appeared to be three chief executives, because Tom Vyner, a trusted lieutenant of JD's, was joint chief executive for a while with Adriano.

May 1996 was a low-water mark. Sainsbury's posted its first actual fall in profits for twenty-two years – down £100m to £712m – and analysts blamed the misjudgment over loyalty cards as the main reason. Sainsbury's itself had calculated that it needed to increase sales by

£400m a year to cover the costs of its belated card. *The Times* cited 'arrogance and complacency' as the causes of Sainsbury's fall, and David's role as both chairman and chief executive began to come under close scrutiny. The Cadbury Report on how public companies should be governed had recommended that these functions be separated, and fewer chairmen now combined the two. Beyond that, Sainsbury's was now perceived as hobbled by a fatal slowness to adapt to change – that, too, was a legacy of the loyalty card fiasco. One commentator compared the stores group to the Civil Service for its inward-looking, tradition-bound culture. 'They have never had any new people coming from the outside into the top jobs, so they never had any new ideas.'

Tesco meanwhile was full of new ideas. In the summer of 1996 it boldly broke into the financial services market, leading to an explosion of brand-stretching as other supermarkets along with Richard Branson's airlines-to-entertainment Virgin group plunged into competition with banks, building societies and pension providers, offering banking services, mortgages and pensions. By October David Sainsbury was admitting to his City critics that 'we have allowed ourselves to be deflected from [our] basic strategy of delivering quality and choice backed up by value for money'. Sainsbury's advertising had reflected this uncertainty, swinging between emphasis on quality and emphasis on price value and adding to a sense that the company was performing continual U-turns.

Yet this was still a company with vast funds of expertise and goodwill – and it still had the highest margins in the trade. It was quick to react to threats, getting swiftly into banking services, but the trouble was that it seemed always to be reacting, not leading. Nevertheless, critics retained some sympathy for David's difficult task in managing the transition from old to new-style management. 'They are moving from a benevolent dictatorship to a democracy,' said one commentator. 'That tends not to go too smoothly.'

One problem was that, because of its tradition of a hands-on family boss, Sainsbury's had never had a strong and visible number two, as Tesco had in Terry Leahy, MacLaurin's designated successor, and Asda's charismatic Archie Norman had in Allan Leighton. An attempt to strengthen the top management team by appointing a streetwise marketing director from Liverpool, Kevin McCarten, was seen by the pundits as the best hope for Sainsbury's revival, but he was not felt to have the clout in the boardroom that Leahy and Leighton enjoyed.

By February 1997, with the third profits fall in four years, David Sainsbury felt himself to be 'in the firing line', as he publicly admitted. Among the angriest of his shareholders were his own family members, who saw £527m wiped off their holdings in just over a week. Industry watchers began to predict blood in the boardroom and to ask the hitherto unthinkable: could a Sainsbury be ousted as chairman of J. Sainsbury? David sounded plaintive and defensive as he said: 'I have made tough decisions on the structure of the group. I have a clear strategy in place. I am determined that a turnround will happen.' But he added with his customary honesty: 'If we don't produce results in the next year, then one's credibility will be very seriously under pressure.'

There had never been any love lost between David and his formidable cousin John. Now, as the management of Sainsbury's was being roundly criticised on all sides, there was even less. John, his father Alan – now in his late nineties but still sharp as a tack – and his uncle Sir Robert, also in his nineties, were all keeping a stern eye on David. Caught between his famously short-tempered family and the strictures of City editors, he must have gone through a bitter time in the early months of 1997. The one public criticism that would have infuriated JD most – he who continually chanted the mantra 'retail is detail' – was the comment from one analyst that Sainsbury had lost its mastery of 'the basic details of retailing'. Even the hitherto successful foray into US supermarkets with a majority holding in Shaw's of New England was running aground.

But at least the political horizon was brightening for a man who had long since transferred his allegiance and deep pockets from the Social Democratic Party, which mutated into the Liberal Democrats, to Tony Blair's New Labour. For months before the 1997 election it was known that David Sainsbury was backing Blair, the young and charismatic successor to John Smith and Neil Kinnock, who had succeeded with all the arts of spin-doctoring and focus groups in making the Labour party look electable for the first time in twenty-three years. It was highly likely that should Labour succeed in replacing the burned-out Conservative government, Sainsbury would be offered a place in the new administration, probably as a working Labour peer.

Blair's remodelled party, full of youthful and unfamiliar faces – some of whom, like the candidate who toppled defence secretary Michael Portillo in his suburban seat, looked barely old enough to vote – duly swept to power on 1 May 1997 in a landslide that dwarfed Clement Attlee's postwar triumph over Winston Churchill. David Sainsbury, for so long an investor in political dreams that never materialised, would soon have the opportunity to do more in politics than write cheques. It was a prospect that looked increasingly attractive set against the stony road he was treading as Sainsbury's chairman.

Just before Christmas 1997, David discussed his future with his cousins John, Tim (who had sold £4.53m worth of his shares that summer, still leaving him with nearly 4 per cent of the company) and Simon. Five months later, in May 1998, David announced his resignation as chairman of Sainsbury's, and in July that year stepped down in favour of the first non-family chairman, Sir George Bull, an industrialist with a long track record in the drinks and food business. Observers said he seemed unable to hide his relief at vacating the chair after six tormenting years. As expected, he was made a Labour working peer as Lord Sainsbury of Turville, the name of the Buckinghamshire village where he maintained a country house, and was given the portfolio of his dreams, minister for science. He had once, friends said, nurtured hopes of becoming the SDP's first secretary of state for trade and industry; now at last he was a minister in that department. After 129 years the company had finally passed out of the family's executive hands: the only Sainsbury remaining on the board was the former MP and Conservative minister Sir Timothy, and that only in a non-executive capacity. The family, however, still held roughly 35 per cent of the equity, David's stake alone hovering between 17 and 18 per cent.

His resignation was greeted by a rise of 22½ p in the share price, a mortifying comment by the market, although it added some £50m to his personal fortune. A confluence of factors had caused the market value of the firm virtually to halve during the period of his chairmanship, from £10bn to a low of £5.7bn in 1997. But one of those factors, all agreed, was the change of management style. David's very niceness – and not even his fiercest competitors fail to express their personal liking when speaking of him – was destined to work against him, partly because John Sainsbury had run such a tight ship, with all the halyards in his hands, and managers had been 'used to being barked at', as one competitor put it. 'Then the extremely nice David Sainsbury took over with this loose management style and everything ground to a halt.' A former colleague described Sainsbury's when David took over as being 'a bit like eastern Europe before Gorbachev, held together by the force of one man, and once he left it all collapsed'.

Ian MacLaurin, who was to prove Sainsbury's nemesis during his twelve years as head of Tesco, was even more outspoken when asked in mid-1999 for his view on the Sainsbury decline.

> When you have the sort of dominant, autocratic leader that John Sainsbury was, you find that the team underneath are not strategic thinkers, they are almost yes-men. I think David is much more of a team player but he inherited a team that was probably good enough for the Third Division but not good enough for the Premier Division. So he struggled with his management style and we could see the thing starting to fall away. I think they probably lost touch with their customers and got a bit arrogant.
>
> David will go down almost as a Gerald Ratner* for saying Tesco's loyalty cards were nothing more than electronic green shield stamps and within months he was launching his own. That sort of thing lives to haunt you.

MacLaurin thinks the root of the problem is that the family succession went one generation too far.

---

*Ratner was the chairman of a successful family jewellers who joked to a business conference in 1991 that one of his firm's products was 'crap' and that its gold earrings wouldn't last as long as a Marks and Spencer prawn sandwich. He lost his job and control of the firm, which has since been renamed, and the costly gaffe is remembered every time his name is mentioned.

It goes back to the question of whether it is right that a member of the family should automatically inherit the chairmanship of anything. Sainsbury's lost the opportunity of a very, very good chief executive in Peter Davis, whom I've known for years. Peter and I were promoted in our respective companies at roughly the same time, but Peter said to me: 'The difference between your appointment, Ian, and mine is that you will become the next chairman of Tesco but I will never become chairman of Sainsbury's.'

(Davis, who had been Sainsbury's deputy managing director and marketing chief, responsible for the highly successful Discount 78 campaign, made no secret of his disappointment at the glass ceiling he saw overhead and resigned in 1986, first to run the Reed publishing group and later to chair the Prudential insurance giant.)

MacLaurin, now Lord MacLaurin and a Conservative working peer since his retirement from Tesco, added: 'I will go so far as to say that if Peter Davis had become chairman of Sainsbury's, they would not be in the position they are in today. It would have made our job of overtaking them in brand leadership very much more difficult.'

(As this book went to press, Sainsbury's announced that Davis, now Sir Peter, was to rejoin the firm as chief executive, replacing Dino Adriano. Although he was wooed with a pay and bonuses package approaching £1m, Davis accepted the job only after being assured of the Sainsbury family's full support. The firm's share price immediately rose by five per cent.)

Sainsbury's market leadership, once lost, was never going to be easy to regain. At one stage in the summer of 1999 it was being closely chased by Asda, newly merged with America's Wal-Mart, whose annual sales of $138bn dwarfed those of Britain's three supermarket leaders put together. Sainsbury's new chief executive, Dino Adriano, admitted 'big mistakes' that had cost it sales to Tesco. Meanwhile Wal-Mart's threatened entry to the UK, operating out of Asda's biggest sites, brought the prospect of a price war fiercer than anything the British multiples had known among themselves. Under the approving gaze of the Labour government, which had been mounting a sporadic campaign against Britain's high retail prices – from cars to designer clothes to cereals, most things cost more on the British high street than in continental Europe or the US – it seemed that Wal-Mart might even gain permission for big greenfield sites that had been denied the domestic supermarkets in the name of protecting the environment. With Hillary Clinton, wife of the US president, on its board, Wal-Mart had international clout that might be turned to Asda's advantage.

All the multiples were reviewing their sales strategies under the Wal-Mart threat. Faced with such a mammoth discounter, it was never likely that any of them could win a price war, although no one yet knew how far Wal-Mart would go in this direction: it too might want to benefit from the fatter margins in the UK. Sainsbury's, in particular, looked likely to revert to the sales pitch that had served it so well in the past – quality, including own-brand quality, and value for money. It was also going back to its local neighbourhood roots. In the spring of 1999 it announced plans for a tennis-court-sized store on a prime Mayfair site near the Ritz Hotel, cocking a belated snook at the Tesco Metros, and later it declared it would open 1,000 similar local stores across the country over three years, mostly in the south-east. Adriano took an axe to overheads, chopping out managers to the tune of £30m and putting more staff on the shop floor. Mindful of the group's reputation for starchiness, he and the new marketing director Kevin McCarten launched a drive to reinvent Sainsbury as more customer-friendly, shamelessly copying Asda in calling staff 'colleagues', dressing them in new orange and blue uniforms with baseball caps and encouraging a more helpful style of customer service.

Meanwhile, David's trial by media was not yet over. On becoming a government minister all his shares in the family firm and other companies had been placed in the customary blind trust (controlled as trustee by a Sainsbury family lawyer, Judith Portrait, a specialist in charity law), but his interests in plant biotechnology made him a political target for those who opposed genetically modified crops and the government's approval of field trials. He responded by stating that he had no connection with government policy on that issue and, indeed, left the room whenever the subject was being discussed – a somewhat farcical picture worthy of the satirical TV series *Yes, Minister.*

David also suffered criticism from the disclosure that some of his dividend income derived – quite legitimately – from offshore trusts. Although UK tax would have to be paid on any such proceeds, the very notion of offshore tax havens had gone sour on the Labour government when the Byzantine financial arrangements of its former Treasury minister, Geoffrey Robinson, became common knowledge in 1998. A third campaign was launched against him when the Labour party published its list of donors and there was Sainsbury, the science minister, top of the heap with a donation of £2m, 10 per cent of the total. Perhaps it is easier for a camel to pass through the eye of a needle than for a rich man to enter government in Britain.

As the supermarket business struggled to regain ground, the younger Sainsburys showed little apparent interest in entering the business. Indeed, there was little incentive for them to do so: even when a family member had been in charge with other family members on the board, there had been ruthless culling of Sainsbury young who failed to measure up. Instead, charities, the arts and social policy – all subjects of Sainsbury financial largesse – offered more attractive career choices. One of John's sons, Julian, is a sculptor with several shows to his name. Of Tim's four children, Alexander worked briefly as a graduate trainee at Sainsbury's but left after six months to work for one of the family charities. His elder brother James, once a student hellraiser at Oxford, became a social policy researcher at Demos, the fashionably Blairite think-tank which provided many foundation stones for New Labour's election platform. One sister, Jessica, was working in Sainsbury's in early 1999 as a technical consultant, while the other, Camilla, is a counsellor married to a Conservative MP, Shaun Woodward, who dramatically defected to New Labour in late 1999. In the summer of 1999 the last Sainsbury to serve on the board, Sir Timothy, announced he was giving up his non-executive directorship.

In time it may well be that the Sainsbury name, like that of Getty and Carnegie before them, will end up better known for philanthropy than for the industries that made their billions. Since the 1960s the Sainsburys have truly earned the title of a modern Medici family, pouring money into opera, ballet, art galleries, museums and universities; all this enrichment of the nation's cultural life coming on top of scores of lesser-known beneficiaries in education, children's welfare, help for the disabled, scientific research, mental health, aid for Third World refugees, even legal advice for poor people contesting land cases in the Western Cape of South Africa (one of David's Gatsby Foundation offshoots).

It was David Sainsbury's father, Sir Robert, who began the family's philanthropic activities in the mid-1960s. He had been collecting modern art since he was at university. He bought Epstein's work in the 1920s when the sculptor was at his most controversial, and later on set aside £1,000 a year for works of art. Around 1965 he was ruminating to David about bequeathing his collection to the University of East Anglia in Norwich, an institution he chose partly because he admired its arts and music courses, but partly also because it was something of a Cinderella when it came to endowments. He also wanted the collection housed in a state-of-the-art gallery, and the Norwich university with its stark 1960s concrete architecture offered a promising setting.

Sir Robert told David that he would be eventually responsible for organising the bequest, to which David more or less replied, why not do it now, and his father agreed. The pair set about choosing an architect in typically pragmatic Sainsbury fashion, by driving around Britain and looking at the latest public buildings. They found the style they wanted in Sir Norman Foster's high-tech terminal for the Fred Olsen shipping line in London's Docklands, and in 1973 Sir Robert's collection of some 400 works by artists including Picasso, Bacon, Modigliani, Degas and Moore was handed over to the new gallery, known as the Sainsbury Centre for Visual Arts, along with an endowment of £3m. Sir Robert kept almost nothing for his own modest home in south-east suburban London.

Across the family, a number of trusts were set up in the 1960s, each with its own portfolio of good causes. JD and his wife, the former ballerina Anya Linden, combined their names to form the Linbury Trust, which has contributed to the Royal Opera House development programme and backed a number of ballet productions. Tim Sainsbury and his wife Susan, a born-again Christian, funded the Jerusalem Trust, which supports Christian relief organisations and helped to buy the Madonna by Elisabeth Frink for Salisbury Cathedral and a Chagall window for Chichester Cathedral. They also established the Headley Trust, which helps arts and environmental charities at home and overseas, along with medical causes, developing countries, health, social welfare and education; its beneficiaries are as diverse as the Woodland Trust, an environmental charity, and the art deco De La Warr Pavilion in Bexhill on the Sussex coast.

Simon Sainsbury's biggest benefactions have been to the National Trust, and another Sainsbury trust, the Monument, whose trustees are three non-family members, contributes to a range of health, welfare, environmental and social causes including AIDS research and treatment. Lady Lisa Sainsbury, Sir Robert's wife, supports her own range of charities, particularly in caring for the terminally ill, while during the Vietnam War Alan Sainsbury's wife ran a scheme for bringing maimed Vietnamese children to Britain for treatment, which she operated from a bedroom in their family flat near London's Marble Arch.

All this activity, apart from the Norwich gallery, was low-key and virtually unknown to the public until 1985 when the three brothers John, Tim and Simon emerged as saviours of the long-troubled project to build an extension to London's National Gallery in Trafalgar Square. The new wing, which was needed to ease pressure on the overcrowded nineteenth-century building, where glorious paintings stood stacked in basements for lack of exhibition space, had been planned since the late 1930s. At that time the Turkish-born oil magnate Calouste Gulbenkian offered to buy out Hamptons, an old-fashioned furniture store that stood to the west of the National Gallery, build the extension and donate his own impressive art collection to it.

Gulbenkian hired a distinguished American architect, William Delano, to produce a classical design in keeping with William Wilkins' 1833 main building, and all was set to go ahead when the Second World War broke out. Some blinkered functionary in the Foreign Office then decided to designate Gulbenkian an enemy alien, despite the fact that he had been a naturalised British subject since 1902. Gulbenkian, under-standably outraged, switched to Persian citizenship and his great philanthropic gesture to Britain was lost through a piece of bureaucratic bungling.

Fate and the Luftwaffe then intervened. Hamptons was bombed to ruins in the Blitz that devastated large tracts of central and east London in late 1940. It remained a bomb site long after the war and was finally acquired by the National Gallery in 1958. Still nothing happened, and the site became a car park while the gallery trustees went on hoping for the government to assume the Gulbenkian mantle which its wartime predecessor had so carelessly thrown away. By the time Margaret Thatcher's market-oriented government was in power in the 1980s it was clear that the arts were going to have to fend much more for themselves, and the trustees concluded that they would have to involve a commercial developer in constructing the building.

A long and farcical saga ensued in which one design after another, each more blatantly modernistic and at odds with the existing building, was presented to the developers, Trafalgar House. They, in turn, found themselves caught up in a tangle of conflicting arts advisers and were completely out of their depth. This was the era in which avant-garde architects were at their most arrogant: the tone was summed up in a comment by Owen Luder, president of the Royal Institute of British Architects (RIBA), on a stark space-age design with a tower that had been submitted by the Richard Rogers partnership. Luder said approvingly: 'It is the work of a man who has said, "That is what I think the answer is and sod you."'

The entry that might well have won by default, had it not been for a famous public intervention by Prince Charles, was a more conventional but still uncompromisingly modern building, also with a futuristic tower topped with masts. It was designed by the partnership of Ahrends, Burton and Koralek, and after numerous modifications had succeeded in gathering the least number of objections from the judges. A public inquiry was announced as a final test. A few weeks before it was due to report, the Prince of Wales was invited to speak at a dinner to mark the 150th anniversary of the RIBA. With the ABK architect sitting in front of him, Prince Charles proceeded to lambast modern architecture, singling out the National Gallery design as 'a monstrous carbuncle on the face of a much-loved and elegant friend'. Not surprisingly, the government minister ultimately responsible for the decision, who had half-heartedly decided to endorse the ABK design, dropped it like a hot potato.

At this point, Sir John Sainsbury, a trustee of the National Gallery who had already brought some commercial discipline to parts of the institution such as its shop, unexpectedly stepped forward and offered to cut the whole Gordian knot by underwriting the wing with his brothers Tim and Simon. At that time the likely cost was put at £18m to £25m, but by the time the Queen opened it in 1991, it had soared to nearer £40m. Like Gulbenkian in 1938, the Sainsburys chose an American architect, Robert Venturi of Philadelphia, who ran a practice with his wife, Denise Scott Brown. The eventual design, a post-modern mix of classical pastiche facing the square and glass walling elsewhere, was predictably spurned by a number of critics who found it dull, unadventurous, the worst of both worlds.

A certain snobbery was also evident about where the money had come from. Brian Sewell, the acerbic art critic of the London *Evening Standard*, commented that the first thing you saw on entering was the shop, 'but perhaps that's the influence of the Sainsburys'. The public, however, liked the way it conformed to its familiar environment on the square, the interior design was widely praised, and it became the home of the National's unique collection of Early Renaissance pictures, the finest in the world. Prince Charles wrote to the Sainsburys that it was 'a building of which London can be proud'.

Tim Sainsbury, given his head, might well have voted for something more avant-garde. Outwardly as conservative in manner as in his politics, he startled his country neighbours in the wealthy triangle where Berkshire meets Buckinghamshire and Hampshire when he commissioned Denys Lasdun, architect of the brutal concrete National Theatre on London's South Bank, to design him a country house. The manicured villages in this idyllic patch of England boast many seriously rich scions of industry – a Cunard Line heiress and a Colman's mustard heir among them, as well as the composer Andrew Lloyd Webber – living in Georgian, Queen Anne or Lutyens-type manors. Tim Sainsbury's new home, by contrast, was said to resemble the National Theatre spread out a bit. Unfazed, Tim remarked: 'An age that lacks confidence in its own art lacks confidence in everything.'

The Sainsburys are reckoned to give away more than £41m a year between them, making them Britain's second most philanthropic family after the oil expatriate Gettys. On a lower, more personal level, individual Sainsburys have always liked investing in small entrepreneurial businesses – a share in a furniture store here, a biotech company there. Tim was a founder of the upmarket travel firm Serenissima, named after the gracious old synonym for Venice. One of David Sainsbury's earliest business investments in the 1960s was to help the London fashion designer Michael Fish, best known for the 'kipper' tie, open his own shop at the age of twenty-six. Corporately, the firm of J. Sainsbury comes in much lower down the charitable league than its founding family, but it has benefited Britain's National Youth Theatre among many arts ventures and sponsorships.

The family's Medici parallels have extended beyond bags of gold to active involvement in managing the heights of British culture. Sir John Sainsbury (Lord Sainsbury of Preston Candover) served for years on the board of the Royal Opera House and in 1987 took over the thankless task of chairing the chronically indigent organisation, into which millions in government subsidy poured annually without making a dent in its huge debts. When JD became chairman, one nervous middle manager at Covent Garden was reported as saying: 'He's going through this place like a knife through butter. He's going to run the whole thing like a grocery store.' Unfortunately for the taxpayer, the grocery king was not able to do so. In 1991, he retired a year early, saying he could not devote enough time to the financial crisis of the ROH. Despite Sir John's famously bullying charm and skill at attracting business sponsorship, the opera house still had a deficit of nearly £5m and the Arts Council balked at bailing it out further.

Like most seriously rich people, the Sainsburys are an obsessively private family. They like as little as possible to be written about them;

indeed, Tim Sainsbury once confided to a respected business historian who was researching into the family history that he thought there should be a law protecting people who did not want books written about them. After initially agreeing in writing to co-operate on an earlier version of this book, Lord Sainsbury of Preston Candover withdrew the promise of co-operation without explanation. It was all done at arm's-length and verbally, via a Sainsbury press officer.

The usual reason advanced for wanting to keep publicity at bay is security, and members of the Sainsbury family did figure on several IRA hit lists around 1990. Twenty years earlier, they were also involved, indirectly, in a terrorist attack when another store magnate, Joseph Edward (Teddy) Sieff, president of Marks and Spencer, was shot in the face in his St John's Wood home by Carlos, the Venezuelan-born terrorist known as the Jackal. Carlos was acting as hitman for the Popular Front for the Liberation of Palestine as part of a campaign against prominent British Jews. The names of Sainsburys together with Sieffs and an assortment of other notables – including, oddly, the playwright John Osborne – were found on a list in a black holdall belonging to Carlos, which also contained gelignite and automatic weapons.

Security aside, there may be other reasons to do with family dysfunction that make the Sainsburys sensitive about themselves. The cousins David and John are known to have a cool relationship. A van den Bergh cousin says there is no love lost between the two families, and that the Sainsburys have always wanted to climb the British social tree – if that is so, they have been spectacularly successful.

In terms of their business, however, they have no reason to be reticent, even if John James left a moral question mark over his grandmother's death in the workhouse. They have amassed (and latterly given away) an immense fortune through five generations of hard work and dedication to a genuinely original business idea in Victorian London – fresh, affordable food for the masses in hygienic, well-managed shops. If they were hard taskmasters in earlier generations, they did not cut corners, mistreat their employees or become tax exiles in Belize. In recent years, J. Sainsbury has regularly featured among the

companies in Britain deemed most ethical and desirable to work for –
along, as it happens, with the two other family-founded businesses in
this book, Cadbury Schweppes and John Lewis Partnership, both of
whose philanthropic tendencies differed from the Sainsburys by being
exercised chiefly on their own employees.

One can never imagine the hard-nosed Sainsburys setting up a
Bournville experiment in company welfare or handing over their
shareholdings to the people who worked for them. But like the
Cadburys and the Lewises, they did succeed in creating an organisation
that for nearly 130 years believed itself to be the best, and to which
people were proud to belong. Whatever happens to it in the next few
years, whether it recovers its confidence and flair under Sir Peter Davis,
its former marketing dynamo, or flounders further behind its competitors and is sold off, it starts with one of the most powerful retailing
brands in Britain and a justified reputation as a pioneer of quality food.
It needs to be 'true to its brand', said one leading competitor, and not
try to match every promotion or price war among its rivals. But the
odds, as Europe's supermarkets began to consolidate into bigger groups,
were still on some alliance that would change the company as
fundamentally as Cadbury changed in 1969.

When family companies are consistently well run for generations,
they build a culture that outlives the family. The present-day Cadbury
Schweppes still benefits from that; so does the John Lewis Partnership,
now going through a supreme test of its culture. David Sainsbury was
one of many family chairmen to identify the key advantages of a family
firm as being able to take a long-term strategic view and having a
personal commitment to the business. In the end, as he once said, 'it's
never quite as personal as when your name is over the door'.

SELECT BIBLIOGRAPHY

PART ONE: THE CADBURYS

Experiments in Industrial Organization, by Edward Cadbury (London, Longmans Green and Co., 1912)

The Life of George Cadbury, by A. G. Gardiner (London, Cassell, 1923)

The Firm of Cadbury 1831–1931, by Iolo A. Williams (London, Constable and Co., 1931)

Industrial Record 1919–1939, (Bournville, Cadbury Brothers, nd)

Geraldine S. Cadbury, a biography, by Janet Whitney (London, George G. Harrap and Co., 1948)

Elizabeth Cadbury 1858–1951, a biography, by Richenda Scott (London, Harrap, 1955)

Social Mix: The Bournville Experience, by Wendy Sarkissian and Warwick Heine (Bournville Village Trust and South Australian Housing Trust, 1978)

The Cadbury Family, by John F. Crosfield (Cambridge, privately printed for the family by Cambridge University Press, 2 volumes, 1985)

The Chocolate Conscience, by Gillian Wagner (London, Chatto and Windus, 1987)

The Quakers: Money and Morals, by James Walvin (London, John Murray, 1997)

The Chocolate Wars: Inside the Secret Worlds of Mars and Hershey, by Joel Glenn Brenner (London, HarperCollins, 1999)

Files of the Bournville Works Magazine

Files of *The Times*

PART TWO: THE LEWISES

The Universal Provider: A Study of William Whiteley and the Rise of the London Department Store, by Richard Lambert (London, Harrap, 1938)

Partnership for All, by John Spedan Lewis (London, Kerr-Cross Publishing, 1948)

Fairer Shares, by John Spedan Lewis (London, Staples Press, 1954)

Retail Trading in Britain 1850–1950, by J. B. Jefferys (Cambridge, CUP, 1954)

Selfridge, by Reginald Pound (Heinemann, 1960)

Retailing in England in the Industrial Revolution, by D. Alexander (Athlone Press, 1970)

A History of Regent Street, by Hermione Hobhouse (London, Macdonald and Jane's, 1975)

John Spedan Lewis 1885–1963 (London, the John Lewis Partnership, 1985)

A Shepton Mallet Camera, Vol. IV, by Fred Davis (Shepton Mallet Amenity Trust Ltd., 1996)

Files of *The Gazette* (the John Lewis Partnership house journal)

PART THREE: THE SAINSBURYS

Retail Trading in Britain 1850–1950, by J. B. Jefferys (Cambridge, CUP, 1954)

The History of Unilever, by Charles Wilson (London, Cassell, 1954)

Retailing Revolution, by P. Mathias (London, Longmans, 1967)

JS: The Story of Sainsburys (J. Sainsbury, 1969)

Retailing in England in the Industrial Revolution, by D. Alexander (Athlone Press, 1970)

The Service Industries, by Derek F. Channon (London, Macmillan, 1978)

Making Provision: a Centenary History of the Provision Trade, by Hugh Barty-King (London, Quiller Press, 1986)

The Best Butter in the World: a History of Sainsburys, by Bridget Williams (London, Ebury Press, 1994)

The Grocers, by Andrew Seth and Geoffrey Randall (London, Kogan Page, 1999)

Tiger by the Tail, by Ian MacLaurin (London, Macmillan, 1999)

INDEX